Unspeak

Unspeak

How Words Become Weapons,
How Weapons Become a Message, and
How That Message Becomes Reality

STEVEN POOLE

GROVE PRESS
New York

First published in Great Britain in 2006 by Little, Brown,
an imprint of Time Warner Book Group UK, London

Printed in the United States of America

FIRST AMERICAN PAPERBACK EDITION

The publishers are grateful for permission to reproduce extracts
from the following: *Politics in the English Language* by George Orwell
(Copyright © George Orwell, 1946) by permission of Bill Hamilton as the
Literary Executor of the Estate of the Late Sonia Brownell Orwell and Secker &
Warburg Ltd; *The Analects* by Confucius, translated with an introduction by D.C.
Lau (Penguin Classics, 1979). Copyright © D.C. Lau, 1979; 'State to High Court:
Fence Route Determined Not Only By Security Considerations', by Yuval Yoaz,
that appeared in Haaretz. Copyright © Haaretz, 2005; 'Without a Doubt' by Ron
Suskind, article in the *New York Times,* 2004, courtesy The Wylie Agency; *The
Language of the Third Reich* by Victor Klemperer, translated by Martin Brady,
2000, courtesy Continuum Publishing. Every effort has been made to trace
copyright holders in all copyright material in this book. The publisher regrets
any oversight and will be pleased to rectify any omission in future editions.

Library of Congress Cataloging-in-Publication Data

Poole, Steven, 1972–
    Unspeak : how words become weapons, how weapons become a
message, and how that message becomes reality / Steven Poole.
        p. cm.
    Includes bibliographical references and index.
    ISBN-13: 978-0-8021-4305-1
    ISBN-10: 0-8021-4305-9
    1. Language and languages—Political aspects. I. Title.
P119.3.P658 2006
306.44—dc22   2006040054

Grove Press
an imprint of Grove/Atlantic, Inc.
841 Broadway
New York, NY 10003

Distributed by Publishers Group West

www.groveatlantic.com

07 08 09 10 11 12   10 9 8 7 6 5 4 3 2 1

Contents

1

Introduction

A long time ago in China, a philosopher was asked the first thing he would do if he became ruler. The philosopher thought for a while, and then said: well, if something had to be put first, I would rectify the names for things. His companion was baffled: what did this have to do with good government? The philosopher lamented his companion's foolishness, and explained. When the names for things are incorrect, speech does not sound reasonable; when speech does not sound reasonable, things are not done properly; when things are not done properly, the structure of society is harmed; when the structure of society is harmed, punishments do not fit the crimes; and when punishments do not fit the crimes, the people don't know what to do. 'The thing about the gentleman,' he warned, 'is that he is anything but casual where speech is concerned.'[1] The philosopher's name was Confucius, and he was referring to a phenomenon that is all around us today. He was talking about Unspeak.

Let's see how it works. What do the phrases 'pro-choice', 'tax relief', and 'Friends of the Earth' have in common? They are all names that also contain political arguments, in a way that alternative names – say, 'opposed to the criminalisation of abortion', 'tax reduction', or 'a group of environmental campaigners' – do not.

Campaigners against abortion had from the early 1970s described their position as defending a 'right to life'. The opposing camp, previously known as 'pro-abortionists', then renamed their position 'pro-choice', rhetorically softening what they favoured. Defending a woman's 'right to choose' whether to have a baby or not, the slogan 'pro-choice' appealed to an apparently inviolable concept of individual responsibility. It sought to cast adversaries as 'anti-choice': as interfering, patriarchal dictators. However, the phrase also carried unfortunate associations with the consumerist ideal of 'choice', as though choosing cereals in a supermarket were an appropriate model for ethics. Indeed, anti-abortionists quickly trumped that linguistic strategy by beginning to call themselves 'pro-life', a term first recorded in 1976.[2] The phrase 'pro-life' appeals to a sacred concept of 'life', and casts one's opponents – those who think abortion should be legally available – necessarily as anti-life, in fact pro-death. In a conceptual battle of two moral ideals, 'life' easily wins out over 'choice'.

To talk of 'tax relief', meanwhile, is already to take a position on socially desirable levels of taxation. One is *relieved* of a load, or a pain, or an illness. In 2004, the White House website advertised the Working Families Tax Relief Act with a peculiar little animation, in which white bars zoomed out across the screen, accompanied by a whooshing metallic sound effect. 'Tax relief' was thus pictured dynamically as like being released from prison. So, even before you start having a debate about tax levels, the phrase 'tax relief' already contains an argument that tax should be minimised whenever possible. 'Tax relief' goes hand in hand with a similar name for what it seeks to reduce: the 'tax burden', which describes something while already arguing that it should be as low as possible. After all, no one likes a burden.

'Friends of the Earth' is a network of environmental groups in seventy countries. The name efficiently consigns anyone who disagrees with their specific policies to the category of 'Enemy of the Earth'. An enemy of the earth must be a very nasty sort of person indeed, a sci-fi villain like Ming the Merciless. Moreover, the claim that the Earth is the sort of thing you can be 'friends' with smuggles in a further holistic concept of the entire planet as a living organism: a Gaia theory, which carries a large implicit cargo of policy implications.

Each of these terms, then – 'pro-life', 'tax relief', 'Friends of the Earth' – is a name for something, but not a neutral name. It is a name that smuggles in a political opinion. And this is done in a remarkably efficient way: a whole partisan argument is packed into a sound bite. These precision-engineered packages of language are launched by politicians and campaigners, and targeted at newspaper headlines and snazzy television graphics, where they land and dispense their payload of persuasion into the public consciousness.

Words and phrases that function in this special way go by many names. Some writers call them 'evaluative-descriptive terms'.[3] Others talk of 'terministic screens',[4] or discuss the way debates are 'framed'.[5] I will call them Unspeak.

Double or nothing

Why the name Unspeak? It is an attempt to capture the Janus-like nature of such language. On the one hand, a phrase like 'pro-life' carries with it a whole *unspoken* argument – that a foetus should be considered a person; that 'life' must be preserved in all situations – that it does not set out explicitly. It represents an attempt to say something without saying it, without getting into an argument and so having to justify itself. At the same time, it tries to *unspeak* – in the sense of erasing, or silencing – any possible opposing point of view, by laying a claim right at the start to only one way of looking at a problem: in terms of 'life' rather than 'choice', or in terms of tax as something to be 'relieved' rather than, say, a way of 'contributing' to society. Now, all language does both of these things to some extent. Every word arrives at the ear cloaked in a mist of associations and implications; and every choice of a particular word represents a decision not to use another one. But Unspeak deliberately amplifies and exploits these properties of language for political motives.

The word Unspeak also inevitably recalls the vocabulary of George Orwell's novel *Nineteen Eighty-Four*, specifically the Newspeak of his totalitarian society. But Newspeak was a cruder tool of manipulation. By erasing words from the lexicon, Newspeak made old, troublesome concepts literally unthinkable. Its B Vocabulary, meanwhile, consisted of 'words which had been deliberately constructed for political purposes' – often crude euphemisms, such as 'joycamp' for 'forced-labour camp'.[6] (In fact, the existing phrase 'concentration camp' already did the same thing somewhat more subtly: people in 'concentration camps', after all, did not sit around in tents playing chess or writing poetry. That phrase originated as a British euphemism for its own practices in South Africa. Language that was originally used by the perpetrators of violence in order to justify it became the normal term: a pattern that we will see repeated in Chapter Four.) But Unspeak does not need to burn dictionaries or invent totally new words to accomplish a similar task. As an Unspeak phrase becomes a widely used term of public debate, it tends to saturate the mind with one viewpoint and to make an opposing view ever more difficult to enunciate.

Another term often used to describe political language is 'doublespeak', a word not coined by Orwell himself but clearly modelled on his concepts of Newspeak and Doublethink (in *Nineteen Eighty-Four*, the ability to believe two opposing ideas simultaneously). Introduced in the 1950s, 'doublespeak' (or 'double-talk') is generally used to describe the phenomenon of saying one thing while meaning another. Ironically for a term that is often used by critics of euphemism, 'doublespeak' itself is really a euphemism for lying. But Unspeak does not say one thing while meaning another. It says one thing while *really meaning that thing*, in a more intensely loaded and revealing way than a casual glance might acknowledge.

Indeed, this book is intended as a corrective to the common idea that politicians do nothing but spout hot air: that their speech, when it is not frankly misleading, is just empty and meaningless. In an excellent anatomy of the logical fallacies in the rhetoric of Tony Blair, for example, philosopher Jamie Whyte nevertheless claimed: 'Most politicians waste our time with platitudinous, visionary waffle.'[7] The most celebrated statement of such an opinion, meanwhile, was written by George Orwell himself, in his essay 'Politics and the English Language', published in 1946:

> In our time, political speech and writing are largely the defence of the indefensible. Things like the continuance of British rule in India, the Russian purges and deportations, the dropping of the atom bombs on Japan, can indeed be defended, but only by arguments which are too brutal for most people to face, and which do not square with the professed aims of political parties. Thus political language has to consist largely of euphemism, question-begging and sheer cloudy vagueness. [. . .] The great enemy of clear language is insincerity. When there is a gap between one's real and one's declared aims, one turns as it were instinctively to long words and exhausted idioms, like a cuttlefish squirting out ink. [. . .] Political language – and with variations this is true of all political parties, from Conservatives to Anarchists – is designed to make lies sound truthful and murder respectable, and to give an appearance of solidity to pure wind.[8]

'Cloudy vagueness?' 'Pure wind?' On the contrary, we can often learn a great deal about what politicians' 'real aims' are from taking seriously, and closely studying, their 'declared aims'. Take the time to unravel the assumptions packed up in a piece of Unspeak, and you will be better able to attack that chain of reasoning at its base. Forewarned is forearmed. Even the most brutal kind of euphemism teaches us valuable things about the mindset of the people who employ it – as we shall see, for example, when looking at the abominable case of 'ethnic cleansing' in Chapter Four. (In the above passage, even

Orwell himself unthinkingly adopts the Soviet euphemism for mass murder – referring to 'the Russian purges' – without considering what it implies.) The truth is that propagandistic speech can never be totally efficient. Language will not serve just one master. In sealing up their worldviews in little shells of Unspeak, politicians cannot help but reveal a lot about what they really mean, to anyone who listens closely enough.

Orwell's essay, much-quoted as it is, evinces a kind of defeatist attitude: it boils down to saying that politicians are simply not worth listening to. A more valuable approach was demonstrated by Victor Klemperer, a Jewish writer who narrowly escaped death in Nazi Germany. Klemperer survived because he was married to a non-Jewish woman and so was able to hand down to posterity a masterful analysis of propaganda: his diary of the changing German language under Nazi rule, *The Language of the Third Reich*, first published in 1957. In his introduction, Klemperer emphasises the point that propagandistic speech can never completely hide what it is up to:

> People are forever quoting Talleyrand's remark that language is only there in order to hide the thoughts of the diplomat (or for that matter of any other shrewd and dubious person). But in fact the very opposite is true. Whatever it is that people are determined to hide, be it only from others, or from themselves, even things they carry around unconsciously – language reveals all. That is no doubt the meaning of the aphorism *Le style c'est l'homme*; what a man says may be a pack of lies – but his true self is laid bare for all to see in the style of his utterances.[9]

Klemperer goes on to demonstrate the truth of this by building up a portrait of the worldview of Hitler and Goebbels through detailed analysis of their attempts to twist the language to their own purposes: from the adoption of 'fanatical' as a term of praise, and a crazed insistence that the most trivial event is 'historical', to the dehumanisation of human beings through mechanical or financial metaphors (which continues, as we shall see, in contemporary English). So, too, this book will contend that we may better understand the motivations of politicians, as well as the substance of political arguments, by paying close attention to terms of Unspeak such as 'anti-social behaviour', 'tragedy', and even 'war on terror', rather than sniffily dismissing them as 'pure wind'.

Bite-sized chunks

Unspeak will only reveal its rationale, however, if it is challenged. If it is allowed to pass unexamined into the wider language of public debate, it has already won an important propaganda battle. One must avoid the simple notion that such loaded use of political language just accomplishes a kind of 'brainwashing'. No one will be taken in by a term of Unspeak who has the time to investigate the facts and think about it seriously. But a lot of people do not have the time; or they assume, not without reason, that journalists – the people whose full-time job it is to think about the way issues are reported – will do this sifting and analysis for them. The journalists, however, too often let them down. Instead, the media are directly culpable in the prevalence of Unspeak today.

For example: when newspapers and TV stations adopted the phrase 'Coalition of the Willing', or even just the shorthand 'coalition', to describe the March 2003 invasion of Iraq conducted by overwhelmingly US and British forces, they quietly endorsed the idea that this was a far-reaching alliance which only a few obstreperous or sulky nations opposed. In fact the countries that opposed the war, such as Germany and France, did not lack conviction; it was just that they were *willing* to do something else, for instance to allow weapons inspections to continue. The term 'coalition' also helpfully called to mind the far wider and more robust UN-authorised coalition that had gone to war against Saddam Hussein in 1991. Meanwhile, when the Fox News Channel introduced every report from that war under a graphic banner reading 'WAR ON TERROR', it perpetuated the claim that Iraq was relevant to the battle against Al Qaeda, as well as endorsing all that phrase's other curious implications, which are examined in more detail in Chapter Six.

Politicians have noticed that television, and increasingly newspapers, have an inbuilt structural bias towards the snappy phrase, the soundbite. And so they offer such phrases, deliberately engineered to smuggle in their preferred point of view, to the media, which gratefully lap them up. As Stephen Whittle, head of editorial policy at BBC News, observes:

> Politicians have worked out, here, there and everywhere, no matter where they are, that because of the nature of the medium, the message has to be in bite-sized chunks. And therefore they concentrate very hard on bite-sized chunks which are a mixture of politics and PR and advertising copy. So it's inevitable, I think, that, from time to time, a phrase will really start to resonate, because a load of people have worked on the phrase, and it's about selling an idea, selling a proposition, and I think unfortunately the fact is that, with both television and radio, they're both media which are prone to be used in that way. You see this in newspapers increasingly as well. Soundbite thoughts become part of the fabric there, especially in terms of the tabloidisation of formats.[10]

It is important to point out the ways in which politicians attempt to cloak dubious policy in the language of virtue, to challenge the Unspeak at its source; but it also needs to be shown how the media, and even ostensibly scholarly writers, are complicit in allowing such attempts to succeed. Writing of the misleading language in which the 2003 war in Iraq was reported, journalist Robert Fisk expressed dismay at the way in which '[W]e journalists go on insulting [. . .] readers and viewers by thinking we can con them.'[11] He thought that readers were not so easily 'conned'; if some people, on the other hand, did view events through the Unspeak lenses held in front of their eyes by the media, the media themselves were largely to blame. If such propaganda were not enabled and spread by TV, radio, and newspapers, if politicians found their little bubbles of Unspeak bursting and popping into silence as soon as they left their mouths, the world might – you never know – be made just a slightly more comprehensible place.

Public diplomacy

Naturally, politicians are loath to admit that they are in the propaganda business. Donald Rumsfeld, who spins and dances through the pages of this book like the hyperactive photojournalist in *Apocalypse Now* – the Dennis Hopper, if you will, to Dick Cheney's Marlon Brando – claimed that it never happened. 'We have an aversion in our country,' he claimed primly, to 'having propagandising take place by public officials in government.'[12] Of course, propagandising did take place; it just wasn't called that. Sometimes it was called, instead, 'public diplomacy'.

You see how this phrase itself is already surrounded by a little glow of Unspeak. 'Diplomacy' implies back-and-forth discussion about terms that everyone eventually agrees on: it implies a civilised, two-way conversation. The phrase 'public diplomacy' borrows that implication of peaceful negotiation, but applies it instead to the government unilaterally choosing its own form of language and trying to make it stick in people's minds by sheer force of repetition. George W. Bush made clear the real meaning of 'public diplomacy' when he said: 'Our public diplomacy efforts aren't . . . aren't very robust, and aren't very good, compared to the public diplomacy efforts of those who would like to spread hatred and . . . and vilify the United States.'[13] How odd that Bush should speak in terms of Al Qaeda practising 'public diplomacy'. Of course, if he said out loud that Osama bin Laden indulged in 'propaganda', he could not make the comparison he wants to, because he would have to acknowledge that the US does 'propaganda' too.

Rumsfeld himself had put it this way: 'I [. . .] think the United States is notably unskilful in our communications and our public diplomacy. I think that we need to do a better job. What that will accomplish, I don't know.'[14] Not for the last time, Rumsfeld shows himself a virtuoso of the switchback and the mystical non sequitur. First he claims that the US doesn't do a good job with its 'communications' and its 'public diplomacy' – in other words, with its propaganda. But then he says he has no idea why it would be good to do a better job. Bush, though, had an idea: 'I made some very difficult decisions that made public diplomacy hard in the Muslim world,' he said ruefully. 'One was, obviously, attacking Iraq.'[15] That must indeed have been disappointing.

Denying the existence of 'propaganda', while thinking simultaneously that the US should do a better job of it, if not confessing to know why, Rumsfeld had in 2002 set up a department in the Pentagon called the Office of Strategic Influence, which was 'developing plans to provide news items, possibly even false ones, to foreign media organizations'.[16] There was something of a public outcry when news leaked out about this propaganda machine, so it was formally disbanded, only months after its inception. But Rumsfeld later said of it: 'You can have the name, but I'm going to keep doing every single thing that needs to be done, and I have.'[17] Impressive flexibility. He was not wedded to any particular name: call it 'public diplomacy' or 'strategic influence', there would always be another term of Unspeak to describe the machinations of Unspeak itself.

The rectification of names

Let us not fall into the trap, however, of imagining that Unspeak is unprecedented, that there existed a historical golden age when politicians spoke nothing but the unvarnished, uninflected truth.

British journalist Peter Oborne, for example, published in 2004 a book called *The Rise of Political Lying*,[18] which ably analysed the misleading rhetoric of Tony Blair's government, but did not convincingly show that 'political lying' had substantially increased. The very title of a satirical pamphlet, first published in 1712 and known as *The Art of Political Lying* (under the nom de plume Martin Scriblerus, usually attributed to John Arbuthnot), suggests otherwise. The pamphlet took the form of an extended advertisement for a fictional forthcoming book about political lying. 'He shews,' wrote Arbuthnot, speaking of the imaginary writer, 'that the People [. . .] have no Right at all to *Political* Truth: That the People may as well all pretend to be Lords of Manors, and possess great Estates, as to have truth told them in Matters of Government.'[19] Indeed, the book would go on to prove, it was promised, that 'Abundance of *Political Lying* is a sure Sign of true *English* Liberty.'[20]

Lying, of course, is older than that; and so is Unspeak itself. Consider the parable about Confucius with which we began. Unspeak consists in giving argumentative *names* to things. What Confucius calls 'the rectification of names' might then be, depending on your point of view, either the restoration of more neutral language, or its replacement with Unspeak. (Mao's 'great rectification' of China in the twentieth century, for one, depended heavily on Unspeak rhetoric.) Indeed, naming things has long been thought of as a special, even magical ability. Sociologist Pierre Bourdieu informs us that for this reason, the poets of traditional tribes in the Kabilya region of Algeria were accorded 'major political functions, those of the war-lord or ambassador'.[21] But sometimes the names given by war-lords and ambassadors need to be contested.

The necessity to challenge names also exercised the minds of the great Roman orators. In a guide for students of the art, Cicero advised:

> [I]t will be desirable to invalidate the definition of the adversaries; but that will be invalidated if it be proved to be false.

This proof must be deduced from the belief of men concerning it, when we consider in what manner and under what circumstances men are accustomed to use that expression in their ordinary writing or talking.[22]

Insofar as this book has a method, that is it.

As Confucius and Cicero show, Unspeak has probably been with us for as long as there has been politics. '[I]t is a common topic,' noted Cicero, 'to dwell on the wickedness of that man who endeavours to wrest to his own purposes not only the effect of things, but also the meaning of words, in order both to do as he pleases, and to call what he does by whatever name he likes.'[23] On the other hand, Unspeak has become a more efficient means of global propaganda in parallel with the spread of mass media. And the ever-more-confining structure of television and radio newsbites, in particular, makes Unspeak the ideal vehicle for the dissemination of propaganda, because it packs the maximum amount of persuasion into the smallest space. Sometimes, moreover, real historical increases in the prevalence of Unspeak can be traced: for example, with the birth in English of 'ethnic cleansing', in Chapter Four; or in the relatively recent use of public names for military operations, discussed in Chapter Five.

Once wars, in particular, became media events, Unspeak became the norm rather than the exception of political discourse. Names became weapons. Weapons were given persuasive names. Distinctions were deliberately blurred. Realities were denied. Punishments, as Confucius predicted, did not fit the crimes. Language created a permanent culture of war.

Before the book's attempt to justify such statements begins, the reader may wish to leap in, with an apposite question: 'Who are you to write such a book?' That is easy to answer in the negative. I am not a linguist; nor am I a political reporter. I claim no authority or expertise beyond a habit of close reading, practised in literary journalism. If the book has some interest, however, it may be simply that it demonstrates that you don't have to be a specialist to resist the tide of Unspeak: you just have to pay attention. Naturally, in such a book, it is impossible that I will not myself have committed various acts of Unspeak. I leave it as an exercise for the interested reader to identify them.

'You've got to be mindful of the consequences of the words,' said George W. Bush.[24] Let us follow his advice.

2

Community

Anti-social

In 2003, an eighty-seven-year-old man from Merseyside, England, was ordered by a court not to make 'sarcastic remarks' to his neighbours.[1] The following year, two teenage brothers were forbidden from uttering the word 'grass'.[2] Then a twenty-seven-year-old Scottish woman was threatened with jail if she was seen by neighbours at her window 'wearing only her undergarments'.[3] What did these prohibitions have in common? They were all examples of a new legal device that sought to repress 'anti-social behaviour'.

Anti-Social Behaviour Orders, which rapidly became known as Asbos, were introduced by Britain's Labour government in the 1998 Crime and Disorder Act. If a person was found by a court to have engaged in 'anti-social behaviour', she could be served with an Asbo prohibiting her for a period of at least two years from engaging in a wide range of activities, not limited to those already indulged in. Subsequently, if she was found to have broken the order, she would face a prison term of up to five years.

In threatening recidivists with a big penal stick, the Asbo was in one way related to the 'three strikes and you're out' legislation enacted in many states of the US since the late 1980s. California has among the harshest such laws: in 2003, the Supreme Court upheld a man's sentence of fifty years to life after his 'third strike' offence, in which he shoplifted some video-tapes.[4] But though Asbos threatened much shorter sentences, they were in a sense more radical. The actions they prohibited were not crimes in the first place – otherwise they could have been dealt with in the normal fashion by the criminal law. And yet, if you were found to have committed a forbidden act under an Asbo – an act which was not in itself a crime, such as drawing the curtains while not fully dressed – you would nonetheless become a criminal, by virtue of having breached the Asbo. The government itself seemed confused about this issue, since 'Anti-Social Behaviour' was listed as one of many 'Crime Types' on the Home Office website, even though 'anti-social behaviour' was not itself a crime.

Since people were going to be threatened with long periods of incarceration as a result of committing acts that were not crimes in themselves, it was presumably of the utmost importance to be quite definite about what 'anti-social behaviour' really was. In fact, the government chose the opposite route. Alun Michael, Minister of State at the Home Office, was responsible for steering the legislation through scrutiny by the House of Commons. During questioning by a Commons committee, Michael steadfastly refused to define 'anti-social behaviour'. He rejected proposed amendments that would 'specify the behaviour, or [. . .] define it as serious, [or] specify that a threshold should be defined'.[5] As eventually passed, the Crime and Disorder Act defined 'anti-social behaviour' only in this way: as behaviour by an individual 'that caused or was likely to cause harassment, alarm or distress to one or more persons not of the same household as himself'.[6]

Such vagueness of language was not in itself new. The Public Order Act of 1986 considered a person guilty of 'Harassment, alarm or distress' if he used 'threatening, abusive or insulting words or behaviour, or disorderly behaviour', or displayed 'any writing, sign or other visible representation which is threatening, abusive or insulting', 'within the hearing or sight of a person likely to be caused harassment, alarm or distress

thereby'.[7] But the maximum penalty for such an offence under
the POA was merely a fine. The Asbo legislation enabled behaviour that might not even constitute an offence under the earlier
law to be banned by a court, and if that ban was broken, the
subject could spend five years locked up. Moreover, the decision as to whether the subject had been 'anti-social' in the first
place, and so the subsequent imposition of an Asbo, depended
only on the civil standard of proof (the 'balance of probabili-
ties'), rather than the criminal standard ('beyond a reasonable
doubt'). Given that the stakes were so much higher, and the
burden of proof so much lower than in normal criminal procedures, the continuing woolliness of definition for Asbos was a
much more serious problem.

What particular level of 'harassment, alarm or distress' in
the beholder's mind, for example, should trigger the label of
'anti-social behaviour'? The notion that one should be able to go
about one's daily life blissfully cocooned from *any* possible
'harassment, alarm or distress' is evidently silly. You might feel
harassed by a customs official insisting on searching your bag,
alarmed by the imagery of a heavy-metal T-shirt, or distressed
by the way a mother snaps at her child in the supermarket.
Nonetheless, you might not think that the law should provide a
remedy in such cases. But the threshold at which such feelings
become grounds for making a finding of 'anti-social behaviour'
remained unclear.

'Anti-social' has two quite different meanings. The first is
'opposed to sociality, averse to society or companionship':[8] thus
we might call anti-social someone at a party who refuses to
speak to anyone but glowers in a corner, sipping his vodka. The
second meaning of 'anti-social' is far wider: 'opposed to the principles on which society is constituted', or 'persons or actions
devoid of or antagonistic to normal social instincts or practices'.[9]
Early Christians were prosecuted by the Roman Empire on
the grounds that their behaviour was anti-social:[10] this was
correct, in the sense that they sought to overturn established
social practices. From Jesus to Gandhi and Martin Luther King,

many people have thought that battling against social norms was the right thing to do. Therefore, to use 'anti-social' as a condemnation requires a further unspoken supposition that what is 'normal' is also desirable. Confusion may arise because 'anti-social' in this second sense often contains a leakage of the first sense, an assumption that if one is opposed to social norms, one must be a personally dislikable character. But, of course, one can be 'anti-social' in the second sense while being gregarious and kind.

With Asbos, the meaning of 'anti-social' clearly leans towards the second definition, either opposed to society as a whole or opposed to certain 'normal' social practices. But a judgement of 'anti-social behaviour' can arise from the perceived harassment, alarm, or distress of, in the language of the Crime and Disorder Act, 'one or more persons' – i.e., possibly only one person. How might it be decided that the feelings of one person were in relevant harmony with those of society as a whole, or that they were perfectly in tune with what was generally considered 'normal'? Might some people not be unusually sensitive or picky about the behaviour of their fellow human beings? Say I think that people who cough and sneeze on public transport without covering their mouth and nose are behaving antisocially, because they spread infection to their fellow passengers by means of airborne mucus. Would I be justified in demanding that Asbos be issued against all such persons? What if I think that it is 'anti-social' to talk loudly on one's mobile phone in a café – is an Asbo the correct approach there? In some cases, furthermore, it might be within the powers of those feeling harassed, alarmed, or distressed to avoid the upsetting stimulus. In the case of the young Scottish woman served with an Asbo for being seen in her underwear, for instance, one might reasonably suggest that her neighbours ought simply to stop peering in at her windows if they don't like what they see.

The 'anti-social' concept is also shaky because it appears to assume only two levels of social organisation: the individual and society as a whole, with nothing in between. Yet what one often finds is a range of smaller social groups, each competing to label the other 'anti-social'. This problem was evident in a 2004 Home Office report, which advised the government against creating a category of 'youth nuisance' under the rubric of 'anti-social behaviour'. What is 'youth nuisance'? It is a general term for teenagers hanging around on street corners. But, as the report pointed out in deadpan style: 'while it is recognised that a group of young people can appear intimidating to members of the public, gathering in a group is not in itself necessarily anti-social'.[11] Boys and girls who seek out each other's company, indeed, are rather obviously being *social*. Of course, social gatherings can turn into criminal conspiracies, or gang rapes, depending on the subsequent behaviour of the group. Teenagers loitering on street corners might deliberately intimidate other citizens. But then again, they might not. To define their coming together as a group *per se* as 'anti-social' is nonsensical. Undeterred, however, the British government went on to cite 'youth nuisance' as a problem of 'anti-social behaviour',[12] and constables had the power to 'disperse' groups of youths if they thought their behaviour was 'likely' to alarm passers-by.[13]

Perhaps, though, these quibbles about the vagueness of the term 'anti-social behaviour' were all irrelevant. Alun Michael at one point sought to deflect such annoying questions posed by his fellow MPs, by denying that 'anti-social behaviour' really meant anything at all. 'I was asked whether the terms "anti-social behaviour" added anything to the Bill,' Michael told the committee. 'Legally, it does not, but it is an essential label that sets out clearly and succinctly what the provision is about: preventing anti-social behaviour.'[14] This is a classic example of the logical fallacy of *petitio principii*, or begging the question. According to Michael, 'anti-social behaviour' in itself meant nothing 'legally', but it served to explain that the point of the law was to prevent 'anti-social behaviour'. But what was this 'anti-social behaviour' that must be prevented, if the term itself had no legal weight? Oops. Let's hurry on. Michael admitted instead that the phrase was merely a 'label': in other words, a catchy phrase of propaganda. To enshrine a legally meaningless PR catchphrase in national legislation might be considered a recipe for confusion and misunderstanding, rather than something that would 'clearly and succinctly' inform the public. So it proved to be.

Understandably, the committee had continued to prod Michael as to what 'anti-social behaviour' might really mean. At one stage he had suggested that it consisted of 'activities that ruin the lives of individuals, families or communities'.[15] However, the ruining of a life may be just as subjective a matter as 'anti-social behaviour'. People sometimes complain that their lives were ruined when they were dumped by a lover. In subsequent years many other glosses of 'anti-social behaviour' were offered, all just as uselessly vague. It was 'unruly behaviour', offered a government review.[16] It was 'thoughtless, inconsiderate or malicious activity', wrote the minister for crime reduction in 2003,[17] neglecting to think that if being 'thoughtless' really were grounds for locking people up, there would have to be an unprecedented expansion of prisons. Perhaps it was better to define what 'anti-social behaviour' *wasn't*: it was the opposite, according to Tony Blair, of 'proper behaviour'.[18] That cleared everything up.

Back in 1998, in a fit of creativity, Alun Michael had finally come up with the alternative phrase 'sub-criminal behaviour', a novel legal concept. The commission scrutineers were none too impressed. MP Edward Leigh pointed out: 'Behaviour is either criminal, in that it infringes an Act of Parliament and a provision clearly laid down, or it is not. There is no such thing as sub-criminal behaviour; there is behaviour and criminal behaviour.' Michael's response was this: 'Sub-criminal behaviour is behaviour of a level that may be criminal, but to be actually described as such it would have to be proved to be so before a court.'[19] This was a fascinating argument. Normally, the law presumes innocence: to overcome this presumption, it must indeed be 'proved . . . before a court' that the accused has committed a crime. But according to Michael, there existed a grey area of 'sub-criminality' whereby people were not presumed innocent just because there was no proof that they were criminals. In attempting thus to water down the long-established tradition of presumption of innocence, it could be said that Michael was acting in a powerfully anti-social manner.

The blatant Unspeak of 'sub-criminal behaviour' burned brightly but briefly: it did not survive in the text of the subsequent Act. But Michael also took a second tack in fielding criticism of his government's legislation: that debates and quibbles about what 'anti-social behaviour' really meant would be proven irrelevant, because the courts would always interpret the legislation in a way that led to reasonable judgements. Let us look, then, at some examples of how the courts did subsequently use Asbos.

In 2004, a thirty-nine-year-old man was convicted for having breached the terms of his Asbo. The order in question had 'prohibited him from entering Birmingham city centre, using or engaging in any threatening, abusive, offensive, intimidating, insulting language or behaviour, or engaging in violence or damage against any person or property within the city centre'.[20] He had been seen on a city-centre closed-circuit television camera, where he 'appeared to be asking for money and acting in [an] aggressive manner when money [was] refused'; he subsequently 'spat in an officer's face when in [the] police station following arrest'. The man was sentenced to forty-five months in prison. Had it been reasonable to ban him from ever going into the centre of Birmingham? Was nearly four years in prison a reasonable punishment for begging, even 'aggressive' begging?

The editor of *Criminal Law Week* thought not. The length of 'imprisonment for conduct which *per se* was either not criminal at all or, to the extent that it was criminal, was non-imprisonable, merely serves to highlight the true nature of the anti-social behaviour legislation as a *Vagrancy Act* for the 21st century,' he wrote.[21] The Vagrancy Act of 1824 had provided for the imprisonment of 'incorrigible rogues', for a period wholly out of proportion to the specific act that had led to their arrests.

Similarly with Asbos. American judges, too, had made similar criticisms of long 'three strikes' sentences: 'the triggering offense must, within some degree, be substantial enough to bear the weight of the sentence it elicits.'[22] 'One of the principal abuses' of the Asbo legislation, the *Criminal Law Week* editor wrote elsewhere, was:

> the re-writing of the penalty section of the statute book, so as to convert non-imprisonable behaviour into imprisonable behaviour and to increase the maximum penalties for offences that are imprisonable, but with maximum penalties of less than five years. [. . .] [T]he prospect reveals itself of the prisons filling up with unlicensed or uninsured drivers, with joyriders, prostitutes, beggars, shoplifters, the drunk and disorderly, and the like – the old 'incorrigible rogues' law, dusted down, given a new name and some 21st century spin.[23]

We should note that the editor writes of the 'abuses' of Asbos. In some cases, Asbos had been used with success to tackle clearly aggressive and violent behaviour, such as intimidation of the elderly on council housing estates, or to keep in check ugly disputes between neighbours. In cases where it could be clearly determined that genuinely high levels of 'harassment, alarm or distress' were being caused, the Asbo might be an effective tool. But detailed independent research on positive Asbo outcomes, and what proportion they made of the total number of orders imposed, was not forthcoming. This was hardly surprising, given that the government's refusal to define 'anti-social behaviour' or 'harassment, alarm or distress' often led the courts to interpret those concepts extremely widely. On the one hand, the issuing courts piled up prohibitions willy-nilly, as with the bans on sarcasm, 'grass', and underwear; on the other, the sentencing courts imposed disproportionate punishments for breaching those prohibitions in relatively trivial ways. This had all been predictable, perhaps, from the deliberate vagueness of the legislation: Asbos positively invited 'abuses' precisely because of the transparently Unspeak way in which they had been defined. Facetious or overly onerous terms in Asbos contributed to the fact that, by summer 2005, 42 per cent of all Asbos were being breached,[24] a figure which cast considerable doubt on the extent of their deterrent power.

There were, moreover, serious cases where it was arguable whether the Asbo's terms were in the real interests of anyone. Take an example from 2005: a twenty-three-year-old woman, who had tried three times to kill herself by jumping into the River Avon in Bath and had on each occasion been rescued, who had also been found 'hanging by her fingertips' from a railway bridge and 'loitering at the top of multi-storey car parks', was given an Asbo.[25] The terms of the order forbade her from going to any railway track, river, watercourse, or canal in the whole of England and Wales. She was also forbidden from 'loitering' on bridges and from going to a multi-storey car park alone. Arguably, to attempt suicide is 'anti-social' in both senses: it is unsociable, and bespeaks dissatisfaction with society as a whole. But the woman was banned in future from doing things that could in no way be described as anti-social.

Magistrate Pamela Gwyther told the woman: 'You are not to dip one toe, not one finger, in a river or canal.'[26] This seems an excessively harsh thing to say to a person who is evidently unhappy. Not only are you not allowed to throw yourself into a river again, but you can't even dip a toe or a finger: you have, in effect, forfeited any right to normal enjoyment of such places. The personal aggressiveness of this command is also incompatible with the underlying fact that the Asbo wasn't really about the woman at all: it was about other people. Its terms stated that she must not do anything 'which could cause alarm or distress to the public'.[27] Never mind the distress that she was in. Upholding the Asbo on appeal, a judge later emphasised that 'rescuers also needed protection'.[28]

The Asbo thus criminalised a wide range of ordinary activity, such as paddling in a stream or standing on a bridge to watch the sunset. Meanwhile, the public could safely go about their business in the knowledge that they would not again have to suffer the particular form of 'distress' occasioned by witnessing an act of attempted suicide. If one thinks that the true interests of society are served by attempting to help troubled people, rather than simply ordering them not to be unhappy in our back yard, then this Asbo itself was profoundly anti-social. We may at least be thankful that Asbos did not exist in the eighteenth century, since one would doubtless have been slapped on Mary Wollstonecraft after she attempted suicide by jumping off Putney Bridge.[29] After she was rescued, no one thought to take revenge by banning her from the riverside, even though as a pioneering feminist writer she was a powerfully 'anti-social' force. (Instead, she was eventually driven to France by George III's outlawing of 'seditious' meetings and writings.)

In the wide and often fatuous prohibitions on behaviour imposed by Asbos, it seemed that the British government and courts were extending their role into that of managing day-to-day morality. It would have been perfectly in tune with the language and assumptions of Asbos, for example, to target adultery. After all, adultery is 'anti-social' in that it acts in opposition to the social norm of monogamous marriage. It also may cause 'alarm and distress' not just to the spouse whose partner is unfaithful but to that spouse's friends and family, thereby getting around the 'not of the same household' clause, and so fitting perfectly the law's description of 'anti-social behaviour'. Why not impose Asbos on every newlywed couple forbidding them from committing adultery, so that if one of them does, you can send them to prison? That would surely be an excellent deterrent against cheating. Why not go further and declare obese people to be 'anti-social', since they do not conform to socially preferred body types as seen on television, and might cause distress to people sitting next to them on an aeroplane? Why not impose Asbos on opposition politicians, since they do not agree with the way the country is currently run, and surely alarm many people who find them canvassing on their doorsteps? The possibilities are endless.

Yet it is not clear that most people really do want the law to govern all aspects of their behaviour. All crime is anti-social, but not everything we might call anti-social should be a crime. There is a host of excellent reasons why law should not be entirely coextensive with morality. If all our actions were governed by fear of state retribution, the idea of moral or virtuous behaviour for its own sake would be degraded. More importantly, people in large democratic countries can, and very often do, have reasonable disagreements over moral questions. Indeed, the existence of 'moral law' is commonly understood by liberal westerners to be a feature of *other* places, of societies whose principles are not readily admired – of places where, for example, adulterous women are stoned to death, as in Iran, Pakistan, and the United Arab Emirates.

The requirement that the law should extend to all areas of morality, indeed, is a characteristic of religious fundamentalism. In July 2005, a bill tabled by a coalition of religious parties in Pakistan's North-West Frontier Province called for a new government department to 'discourage vice and encourage virtue', adherence to whose strictures would be ensured by a 'moral police force'.[30] Opposition politicians called this 'Taliban-style extremism'. Meanwhile, the drafters of the new Iraqi constitution missed deadline after deadline to finalise the document over the summer of 2005, in part because different factions could not agree on the extent to which Islamic law, shariah, should be supreme in the land: whether it should be 'the fundamental source' or only 'a source' of Iraq law.[31] Nor is this exclusively a religious phenomenon. During the Terror in revolutionary France, Robespierre equated justice with virtue, and *incivisme* – lack of civic virtue, or in other words, 'anti-social behaviour' – became a crime.[32]

Such examples are very different from Asbos, you might say. And assuredly they are. But only in degree; not in kind. The germ of the idea that no part of the moral life should go ungoverned by the state is already present in the practice, now enshrined in British law, of punishing 'anti-social behaviour'.

The concept's scope looked set to widen ever further as Tony Blair called in September 2005 for the increased use of 'Parenting Orders', according to which law-enforcement agencies would instruct parents on what to do with children who showed signs of beginning to 'go off the rails'.[33] Failure to comply with the order could result in a parent's prosecution and a fine of up to £1000.[34] It was not explained how further impoverishing parents who were already likely to be poor would improve their children's behaviour.

The American commentator Christopher Caldwell, observing the beginnings of a similar trend in the US, argued that all such initiatives were 'attempts to promote sentiments of community when such sentiments do not arise spontaneously'.[35] Indeed: what better way to conjure up a sense of social cohesion than the historically tried-and-tested method of demonising those who are deemed not to fit in, those who are 'anti-social'? Meanwhile, perhaps according to the principle that if you speak about it often enough it must exist, the language of 'community' itself had become another powerful term of Unspeak.

'Go to any community'

'Community' is among the most perfect political words in English. It can mean several things at once, or nothing at all. It can conjure things that don't exist, and deny the existence of those that do. It can be used in celebration, or in passive-aggressive attack. Its use in public language is almost always evidence of an Unspeak strategy at work.

The word's political force is rooted in a powerful sense of people being nice to each other. 'Community' derives from the Latin *communitatem*, which meant the quality of fellowship, shared relations or feelings.[36] Medieval Latin usage concretised the word, so that it meant specifically a body of people sharing such feelings in common. Thus the English term came to mean not just any group of people, but a group of people who thought of themselves as a group. Connotations of fellowship, cooperation, trust, and mutual help combined to make 'community' denote something like the ideal social organisation of human beings. The motto of post-revolutionary France, *'Liberté, Egalité, Fraternité'*, carries in its third term something very similar to this ideal notion of 'community': a brotherhood of man. Among the very earliest English uses of the term, in 1587, was the observation that humans everywhere ought to be 'united by the communitie of their kind',[37] though unfortunately they were not.

Just as intermediate levels of organisation between society and the individual complicated notions of who was 'anti-social', there is not one universal 'community' but numerous sizes and types of groupings of people that can be called 'communities', with varying levels of fidelity to the word's original meaning. Often the word is used to label a mere geographical area. Writing in late 2004, for example, Tony Blair defended his government's record by instructing voters:

> Go to any community in this country – particularly those that had the roughest time in 18 years of Conservative government – and you will see the impact of progressive government.[38]

Being told to 'go to' a community, the reader will naturally have assumed that a community is a place. But what kind of place is it? The city of Liverpool surely is not a community, any more than the island of Manhattan. A suburb of London, say Brixton – is that a community? Or does it need to be even smaller, a subset of a suburb, just a few streets square? Even in such a small area, are we to assume that all the residents really comprise a 'community' of cooperative friendliness, basking in a genuine *esprit de quartier*, as the French say? Well, that is indeed what we are invited to think. Blair could have written simply 'Go to any place', but in using the word 'community' he subtly imported all the feel-good notions of mutual help and understanding that the word implies.

The difficulty of drawing the conceptual boundaries of any one 'community' within a vast modern city is a symptom of the fact that, as often used politically, the term 'community' is saturated with nostalgia for forms of life that no longer exist. If you had to draw a picture of a 'community', you would probably come up with an idealised country village ('It takes a village,' noted Hillary Clinton) of a few hundred inhabitants at most: a place with a square, a tavern, and cheerful farmers, a place where, as in the TV series *Cheers*, everybody knows your name. Such modes of life are rare in Los Angeles or London. And a homogeneously friendly community is not automatically found in the country any more than it is in the city. So to describe a local area as a 'community' is to express a wish about how the people living there should behave, regardless of how they actually do behave. (Can there be a community of the anti-social?)

Used in this way, then, 'community' maps political desire on to geography. But there are other possible forms of 'community', that depend not on shared location but on shared interests. Guilds of craftsmen, athletics clubs, or specialist internet forums whose members discuss the implications for quantum physics of *Buffy the Vampire Slayer* may all be thought of as 'communities', even though their members are widely dispersed. (This sense of community, still implying virtuous cooperation, may then be appropriated by other groups who wish to be regarded in a positive light. And so businesspeople, usually in cut-throat competition with each other, will present themselves in a united front as the 'business community' when it comes time to lobby against corporate tax rises or an increase in the minimum wage.) Indeed, though all uses of the word 'community' codify a kind of idealism, this sense of common interest or sympathy is probably the most robust. It may be appropriate, for example, to say that users of the London Underground temporarily became a 'community' after the July 2005 bombings; or to say that the siege of Sarajevo sought to destroy a particular kind of 'community', in the sense of a way of life that was not predicated on ethnic differences.

But words are used in many different ways. As with 'anti-social', the fact that 'community' has a reasonable meaning does not prevent it from being used in other, more argumentative senses. If we examine the phrase 'the international community', for example, we find that its inbuilt notions of global fellowship and multilateral agreement express a very particular wish about how the countries of the world should act with respect to each other. 'International community' itself is a form of Unspeak, mapping political desire on to geopolitics. For this reason the phrase is regularly subjected to scorn – 'the so-called international community', wrote Justice Antonin Scalia;[39] 'a fiction called the international community',[40] said Michael Ignatieff – by those who find such a harmonious ideal naive.

In the domestic sphere, 'community' really begins to earn its Unspeak stripes when the sense of shared interests is projected on to people whom the majority considers 'other'. The gay community, the black community, the Jewish community, the Muslim community: thus are all gay, black, Jewish, or Muslim people regularly forced to coalesce into homogeneous groups by the language of US and British politicians and news media. At first this form of language looks unexceptionable: it merely adds the warm and fuzzy connotations of 'community' in what might be thought a welcoming or respectful fashion. But if it is respectful, it connotes respect for what is irremediably alien. To say that Jewish people, taken all together, form a 'Jewish community' is to say that they are separate, that they associate among themselves but keep themselves aloof from others, and it implies further that, by virtue of being Jewish, they all think alike.

As Ian Mayes, readers' editor (ombudsman) of the *Guardian*, notes, this use of 'community' tends to imply 'that there isn't a diversity of opinion'.[41] 'The principle is the same one,' Mayes adds, as when 'we try to dissuade people from talking about "the disabled" or "a diabetic", which tries to define the whole by the part.' Similarly, 'gay community' or 'black community' defines the people so labelled entirely in terms of their gayness or blackness. To the extent that we can be said to be members of 'communities', we are members of many at once: for example, the community of one's workmates, or sports team, or TV show discussion forum. But people described as 'the gay community' or 'the Muslim community' are allowed to belong to only one, which defines their whole identity.

This use of 'community' is mirrored in another feel-good term that may in fact hide a darker meaning: 'tolerance'. If people congratulate themselves on 'tolerating' others, it may be because they already find them uncongenial in some way. One tolerates a friend's annoying habit, or a mild toothache. To tolerate is not to embrace. George W. Bush displayed the weasel use of 'tolerance' when asked, during the third Presidential debate in 2004, whether he thought that homosexuality was a choice. 'I don't know, Bob. I just don't know,' Bush said, playing for time. Then he found the appropriate homily: 'I do know that we have a choice to make in America, and that's to treat people with tolerance and respect and dignity.'[42] This might be read as meaning: gay people deserve tolerance, sure – but that doesn't mean we have to *like* them. We tolerate what we despise, as the hippo tolerates the flea. *We* will 'tolerate' *their* 'community', as long as it doesn't impinge upon ours. Of course, one is not morally obliged to feel warm and fuzzy towards those whose rights one is nevertheless prepared vigorously to defend. But to congratulate oneself for one's 'tolerance' is sometimes actively to display distaste.

Consider, by contrast, how relatively rarely one hears of 'the heterosexual community' or 'the white community', or even 'the Christian community'. In the US and Britain, to be white, heterosexual, and Christian is the default position, and so carries the privilege of not having to be defined by a limiting 'identity'. Only those who do not fit the white, heterosexual, Christian template are described as forming 'communities', and in this way the word already bespeaks a kind of contempt for people who are somehow 'other' and so naturally will huddle together for warmth and mutual reassurance. It is further assumed that,

in such an embattled position, 'their' interest will be more mil-
itantly homogeneous than 'ours'.

It will often be reported, indeed, that a 'community' is
demanding, or opposing, some political action, as though black
or gay people operate like bees, with a hive mind. What is really
happening in such cases is that self-appointed or elected or
media-christened 'community leaders' are speaking to reporters
or politicians, and their views are taken as representative of the
entire group. And they may even, like all politicians, fight
among themselves for primacy. Stephen Whittle, head of editorial policy at BBC News, says that there are often many different
'people competing to be, at least in media terms, the "leader of
the community"'.[43] But the people whom they claim to represent often resist the reification of their 'community' in this way.
'There is no such thing as the Muslim community,' Asim
Siddiqui, chairman of a group of Muslim professionals, told the
Observer.[44] 'There are communities.'

Yet, especially in television news, producers are not interested in having three Muslims carefully and soberly explaining
the nuances of differing opinions among Muslim citizens, as
one might easily see three white, heterosexual people arguing
the toss about some subject which, by virtue of the fact that
they are white, heterosexual people, is assumed to be neutral
and of interest to people of all ethnicities and sexual habits.
What producers want instead is one person who can by visual
or aural synecdoche represent all Muslims, and so that is what
they get. BBC World radio news presenter Kirsty Lang explains
how it works: 'In the context of a very short news story, there
just ain't time' to represent differences of opinion, she observes.
She describes the typical situation facing a journalist: 'Very
often, you're in a hurry looking for a quote, and you take the
quote from the first person you ring up from your list of "community leaders in Brixton".'[45] Politicians, too, will fall into this
kind of shorthand trap. Discussing Britons' variety of religious
and ethnic affiliations in the wake of the London Underground
bombings of 7 July 2005, Tony Blair said:

If you talk to, as I say, the majority of the Muslim community here, or the Hindu community here, or the Sikh community here, or the Jewish community here, or the Chinese community here, any of those communities integrate very intensely but they still keep their own culture alive and their own identity alive, and I don't think that's a problem.[46]

Of course, there was no sense in which Blair could possibly have talked to 'the majority of the Muslim community', or that many Hindus, Sikhs, Jews, or Chinese, for that matter. Certainly he would have talked to some 'community leaders', though it would be interesting to know if he asked them how they derived their authority to speak for so many other Muslim or Chinese people. In his incontinent use of 'community', Blair was perpetuating the fiction that all Muslims or Sikhs or Jews in Britain ('here' clearly meant the same as 'in this country' earlier in the speech) were united in one mind. Contrarily, in a denunciation of the 'glib, facile word', former *Guardian* editor Peter Preston sought to limit 'community', if it must be used at all, to small neighbourhoods:

I can, with endeavour, find Bangladeshi communities in the East End, Saudi communities just off the Edgware Road, Pakistani communities in Bradford and Indian communities in Leicester, plus huddles of Afghans and niches of Iraqis, all of them with mosques and imams but none of them part of a wider 'community'.[47]

Even so, Preston was himself perpetuating, only on a smaller geographical scale, the notion of a 'community' necessarily being a group who would congregate in 'huddles': other, afraid, defensive.

'They' have their own communities, but they interpenetrate with 'our' community, so it is said, in ways which would make for a confusing scribble if you attempted to draw the appropriate Venn diagram. 'Most people understand,' said Tony Blair,

'that you can have your own religion and your own culture but
still feel integrated into the mainstream of a community.'[48] This
'mainstream' was rather vague: was it the local neighbourhood
in question, or was it a fictional national 'community', the non-
community that was the white Anglo-Saxon community?
Perhaps only a tiresome literalist would demand to know what
'our' community was. It was easy to recognise it as long as it
did not contain too many of 'them'.

Community spirit

This modern political emphasis on 'community' was not initiated by British leaders dreaming of a lost rural England. President Bill Clinton got there earlier, exhorting Americans in his
1993 inaugural address: 'Let us all take more responsibility,
not only for ourselves and our families, but for our communities and our country [. . .] I challenge a new generation of
young Americans to a season of service [. . .] keeping company
with those in need, reconnecting our torn communities.'[49]
Clinton continued to harp on this theme throughout his time
in office, reminding his audience of the devastation that
would follow from the loss of what he wished existed: 'If
we have no sense of community, the American dream will
continue to wither.'[50] On other occasions he let the word
stand alone, using it in a tremblingly phatic way that was
emptied of all specific meaning: 'Old-fashioned Americans for
a new time. Opportunity. Responsibility. Community.'[51] This
must have reverberated in people's minds as a kind of rhetorical slam-dunk. For in 2005 the Democratic Party, jealous of
the well-oiled Republican propaganda machine, unveiled the
results of much hard thinking about how best to 'frame' their
'message'. The new slogan? 'Prosperity. Opportunity. Community.'[52] Pretty radical. Clinton's 'responsibility', it was presumably thought, might scare people who didn't want to be
responsible; let's offer them 'prosperity' instead, for who does

not want to be rich? And good old 'community' was still going strong.

Where had Clinton himself learned the magic power of the c-word? Apparently from the sociologist Amitai Etzioni, professor at George Washington University, whose 1993 book *The Spirit of Community* was 'spotted on President Clinton's desk', who was described as 'a favoured guru of the Clinton administration',[53] and who had also reportedly been influencing the thinking of Tony Blair and Gordon Brown, not yet in power, on the other side of the Atlantic.[54] Etzioni's thinking, which was known as 'communitarianism', envisioned families, schools, churches, and civil organisations taking over much of the state's work. In practice this meant, among other things, more equivocal support for the poor, as Etzioni explained when discussing Clinton's policies in 1993:

> The welfare reform that Clinton favors – demanding that those on welfare either find work or repay their debt through service to the community – further illustrates the direction he is moving. There is debate as to at what point does demanding responsible behavior from welfare recipients turn into cruel punishment (e.g., cutting payments if a woman on welfare conceives more children), but the message is unmistakable: social responsibility will be encouraged with more than warm words: it will be underwritten with special incentives and, perhaps, even penalties.[55]

'Reform' has long been a useful term. Oddly, it contains two contradictory senses, as Raymond Williams noted: '(i) to restore to its original form; (ii) to make into a new form'.[56] Neither of those actions necessarily implies making what is re-formed better, and yet 'reform' also inevitably carries a sense of amelioration. Williams argues that this is owed to the first sense of restoration, because an earlier condition or state of affairs was consistently assumed to be 'less corrupted', and notes that the English Reformation of the sixteenth century 'had a strong sense of purification and restoration, even when it needed new forms and institutions to achieve this'.

Modern political senses of 'reform', on the other hand, have played a clever trick. They transfer the positive implication of reform-as-restoration on to the other meaning of reform as mere change. The result is a sense of 'reform' which implies that anything new must automatically be better than what came before. It is not new – radical English democrats in the eighteenth century were called 'reformists'. But now any change may be called a 'reform': the word symbolises the central non-idea of all 'modernising' rhetoric. (Said Tony Blair: 'Jesus was a moderniser.')[57] Blair's 'House of Lords reform' consisted not of returning to an even more archaic Lords but gradually eliminating hereditary peers and stuffing their benches instead with political appointees. Clinton's 'welfare reform', too, represented a change, but not one that was unarguably better for those on welfare.

And the word 'reform' is so good at what it does that all political parties claim to be in the reform business: George W. Bush's attempts in 2004 and 2005 to privatise pensions in the US were argued under the rubric of 'social security reform', with the added rhetorical trick that the social-security system was claimed to be in a 'crisis', so that to reform it would be not just a change for the better but a kind of heroic intervention. Meanwhile, according to *The Economist*, 'labour-market reform' is the preferred term for restructuring pensions to dissuade people from retiring early. What kind of 'reform' might this entail? Well, 'Germany has recently made a welcome start by cutting jobless benefits.'[58] Welcome to some, no doubt, but not evidently to the jobless.

Just call any proposed change a 'reform', indeed, and people may assume that it will be an improvement, even if all you are doing is getting rid of people who disagree with you, or trying to save some federal dollars so you can give them back in electorate-pleasing tax cuts.

The very word 'reform' thus argues efficiently in favour of

itself, whatever it actually is, in paradigmatic Unspeak fashion. As used by communitarians and their political disciples in phrases such as 'welfare reform', however, it represented not an offer but a demand. In the 'communities' that would blossom after such 'reform', there could be no rights without responsibilities, a web of mutuality. Etzioni argued that 'for the ship of state to progress, everyone must pull the oars'.[59] He emphasised the idea of 'social responsibility',[60] which became a key phrase of New Labour rhetoric.[61]

Evidently this notion of 'community' laid the groundwork for the Blair government's later legislation against what was considered 'anti-social'. As Jack Straw explained to Parliament in 1998, Asbos had at first been proposed as 'community safety orders', before the snappier name was found.[62] To complete the circle of logic, Anti-Social Behaviour Orders were then justified by appeal to – what else? – the sanctity of community. We needed to be protected, insisted Blair in 2004, from 'anti-social behaviour within our communities'.[63] It was the enemy within. It was *George A. Romero's Land of the Dead*, with the 'anti-social' playing the roles of the zombies. The community could survive only as long as it was regularly purged.

Also a threat to the fictionally homogeneous 'community' in Britain were 'asylum seekers', those seeking to stay in the country on the grounds that they were persecuted in their place of origin. The term 'asylum seeker' had gradually replaced 'refugee', shifting the emphasis from what a person was fleeing to the demands he was making on the country he arrived in. It was safe to call people 'refugees' as long as they remained elsewhere in the world (as, for example, those displaced by the 2004 Asian tsunami); but as soon as they arrived on British shores they became 'asylum seekers'.

Moreover, they were often described as 'bogus asylum seekers': a rabble-rousing piece of nonsense. There could be no such thing as a 'bogus asylum seeker': whatever one's motivations, one was simply an asylum seeker up until the time when one's request for asylum was either granted or denied; the idea of a 'bogus asylum seeker' destroyed any presumption of innocence or sincerity. The term 'bogus asylum seekers' was first employed by ministers of the Conservative government in the mid-1980s, during controversy over the admission of Sri Lankan Tamils.[64] The phrase was found to play so efficiently to public prejudices that it was enthusiastically adopted by the incoming Labour government in the late 1990s, when it was used regularly by then Home Secretary Jack Straw.[65] Newspapers that traded eagerly in fearmongering adopted the phrase as their own: the *Daily Mail* reported approvingly of Straw's plan for 'bogus asylum seekers' to be 'thrown out to prevent them from disappearing into the community'.[66] The idea that they might 'disappear' into the 'community' pictured people from foreign lands as an invisible infection, an epidemic virus. Perhaps the *Daily Mail* was still furious at the fact that the French had disappeared into the community a millennium earlier: it must not be allowed to happen again.

The increasingly hysterical concentration on asylum seekers in British politics was often code for simple racism, appealing to a fear of being overrun. Labour Home Secretary David Blunkett conjured an image of the children of asylum seekers 'swamping the local school'.[67] According to a 2005 poll, Britons on average believed that 21 per cent of the entire population was comprised of immigrants; the actual figure was 8 per cent.[68] 'The asylum-seeker issue has been great for us,' chuckled the leader of the neofascist British National Party.[69]

A more sophisticated treatment of the concept was evident in a Conservative poster visible on billboards in Britain during the 2005 election campaign. In a typeface that mimicked the handwriting of the barely literate, the poster read: 'It's not racist to impose limits on immigration.' Below was the Conservatives' campaign slogan: 'ARE YOU THINKING WHAT WE'RE THINKING?' First, the words implied that the Labour government did not already 'impose limits on immigration', which was false. Second, the phrase 'It's not racist' functioned deliberately to introduce the idea of a racist sentiment, just as the words 'I'm not a racist but . . .' invariably precede a statement of bigotry. 'It's not racist' worked in combination with the nose-tapping appeal to something unspoken but sincerely thought: are you thinking what we're thinking? The poster as a whole could thus be translated: We think there's nothing wrong with being racist; in fact we are racist, just like you; but we all know that we cannot publicly admit to being racist; so let's just deny that we are racist while continuing to think the same old racist thoughts. The poster as a whole was a brilliant piece of Unspeak, appealing to and endorsing a silent 'community' of resentful xenophobia: the hate that dare not speak its name.

Anti-social behaviour orders, in the meantime, were defended by Home Office minister Hazel Blears on the grounds that they helped to 'rebuild confidence in communities'.[70] Yet perhaps the 'confidence' enjoyed by a 'community' that threatened to transfer certain of its members into a community of prison inmates for being sarcastic or sitting down on a riverbank was not an untrammelled moral good. And one might have been forgiven for continuing to lack 'confidence' that 'community' itself was anything more than a promiscuous term of Unspeak.

In exposing the tricksiness of 'community' talk a decade earlier, Stephen Holmes, professor of political science and law at the University of Chicago, had pointed out: 'Members of the Ku Klux Klan, too, have "a commonality of shared self-understanding". Shared self-conceptions or aspirations or allegiances are not thereby intrinsically admirable.'[71] Indeed: just as being anti-social is not intrinsically wrong unless you accept the extra hidden premise that society is already how it should be, so being social is not intrinsically a virtue: there may be 'communities' of neo-Nazis, or plotters of terrorism, or sexual torturers of children, who are not made admirable simply by grouping together. Theorists of 'community', Holmes argued, 'surreptitiously import moral approval into ostensibly descriptive categories such as "group loyalty", "collective aims", and "social bonds".'[72] The surreptitious importing of moral approval (or disapproval) into a supposedly neutral name is, of course, a primary characteristic of Unspeak.

So it had always gone with the most blatant political uses of 'community' to try to engineer a positive response to a policy. Even before Clinton, Blair, and Etzioni, Margaret Thatcher's government, which was not known for indulging in the rhetoric of social cohesion, had attempted to defuse widespread loathing of its new 'poll tax' by renaming it the 'community charge'.[73] The mental-health policy christened 'care in the community', meanwhile – first announced, aptly, in 1984 – had resulted in the evacuation of 'large numbers of mentally ill people from institutions, without providing an adequate alternative':[74] in other words, the phrase chose not to acknowledge the large-scale release of patients from asylums, and instead promised 'care' that was not sufficiently forthcoming. The cosy ideal of the caring 'community' was in marked contrast to the subsequent neglect or even persecution of those thrown on its mercies.

Later on, a second-class cadre of policemen was introduced by Blair's Home Secretary, David Blunkett, under the name 'community support officers': they would contribute, he said, to the 'endeavour [. . .] to face down the antisocial and thuggish behaviour that bedevils our streets, parks and open spaces'.[75] CSOs were much cheaper than real policemen, went out on the beat after only four weeks' initial training, and were advised to avoid 'dangerous situations', according to an undercover reporter who trained as such an officer.[76] Walking away was a novel way to 'face down'. But never mind: the very repetition of their name – 'community support officers' – sounded pleasantly reassuring in Parliament and on TV. Everyone loves support, just as everyone loves a community. And CSOs, furthermore, were introduced by the Police Reform Act,[77] so they must be a good thing.

The faith community

Happily the word 'community' is so semantically promiscuous that George W. Bush could carry right on using it when he took over from Clinton, as with his programme named 'Faith-Based and Community Initiatives', which involved giving religious organisations access to federal welfare funds. 'As we improve our communities, we improve our nation,' Bush explained, in a direct echo of Clinton's language.[78] Bush even managed to refer to 'the faith community', which was strange given the historical fact that different religions, and different factions of the same religion, had not always worked together harmoniously. But since Bush had 'faith', and held weekly Bible-study sessions in the White House,[79] there was at least one 'faith community' centred on him.

It was a curious feature of political rhetoric, indeed, that nearly all politicians appealed implicitly to something like a 'faith community' in the vocabulary they used to express their opinions. Rather than saying 'I think' that something is the case, Bush and Blair, for example, consistently preferred to say 'I believe'. What does this apparently trivial decision accomplish? Well, it encases the speaker in an armour of faith. If you 'think' something, you may just be mistaken. Moreover, to say 'I think' implies the kind of cold ratiocination that may dent a politician's likeability rating in polls. If he claims to 'believe' something, on the other hand, whether he is right or wrong on the issue in question, he is automatically virtuous, because he is at least sincere: he *believes*. Thus George W. Bush said in July 2005: 'I believe that we will succeed in Iraq',[80] which expressed a noble optimism and could not in principle be refuted by any subsequent events. Even if success in Iraq (howsoever defined) was not forthcoming, that could not dent the purity of Bush's faith. Opposition politicians played the same game. The phrase 'I believe' was used thirty times by both Bush and John Kerry in their third Presidential debate in 2004, compared with thirty-two instances of 'I think'.[81] Thus the debate was a contest of faith as much as of reason.

Similarly, Tony Blair, facing a hostile television audience and attempting to justify the upcoming Iraq war, said in early 2003: 'I think it's my job as Prime Minister, even if frankly I might be more popular if I didn't say this to you or said I'm having nothing to do with George Bush, I think it's my duty to tell it to you if I really believe it, and I do really believe it. I may be wrong in believing it but I do believe it.'[82] Notice how he moves from saying 'I think' to insisting more powerfully that 'I believe'. And so faith trumps truth: 'I may be wrong', but who cares if I am wrong or not as long as 'I do believe it'?

You can also, usefully, say you 'believe' something for which you intend to offer no evidence, as when Blair claimed: 'I believe the vast majority of those on the centre-left now believe in the new personalised concept of public services.'[83] Here he even offered two 'beliefs' for the price of one. Not only did he 'believe' that a 'vast majority' of ill-defined people agreed with him, he 'believed' that those people 'believed in' his policy. The idea that a policy is something to be 'believed in', rather than to be argued about and rationally accepted or rejected, converts politics itself into faith. People who 'believe in' a policy might indeed be described as a 'faith community'.

What is the opposite of a 'faith community'? Reporter Ron Suskind learned the answer when in summer 2002 he met a 'senior adviser to Bush', who provided him with what has become a justly famous explanation of US policy in that era:

> The aide said that guys like me were 'in what we call the reality-based community,' which he defined as people who 'believe that solutions emerge from your judicious study of discernible reality.' I nodded and murmured something about enlightenment principles and empiricism. He cut me off. 'That's not the way the world really works anymore,' he continued. 'We're an empire now, and when we act, we create our own reality. And while you're studying that reality – judiciously, as you will – we'll act again, creating other new realities, which you can study too, and that's how things will sort out.[84]

This may fruitfully be read in parallel with the words of Hannah Arendt, who defined totalitarian thinkers specifically as having 'extreme contempt for facts as such, for in their opinion fact depends entirely on the power of the man who can fabricate it'.[85] In this aide's words, the word 'community' maximises its potential to be patronising, even pitying, contrasted as it is with the chest-beating of 'empire'. The 'reality-based community' is pictured as embattled, timid, probably gathering in 'huddles', like the Afghans found by one intrepid journalist in Britain.

But if the Bush administration was not 'reality-based', on what exactly did it base its acts? On, we must suppose, faith. And indeed, the Bush administration did not lack for impressive displays of 'faith' in contradiction of ascertainable realities. Another realm in which 'the judicious study of discernible reality' was held in contempt, for example, was that of science.

3

Nature

Climate change

Sometimes there are smoking guns. In the arena of science, there is plain evidence of political groups and corporate interests mulling over the right Unspeak strategies. US pollster Frank Luntz, for example, has produced a range of documents advising Republicans on the kind of persuasive political language they should use. One such memo, leaked in 2003, treats the language of environmental policy. A section headed 'Winning the Global Warming Debate' reads in part:

> The terminology in the upcoming environmental debate needs refinement [. . .] *It's time for us to start talking about 'climate change' instead of global warming* [. . .]
>
> 1. *'Climate change' is less frightening than 'global warming.'* As one focus group participant noted, climate change 'sounds like you're going from Pittsburgh to Fort Lauderdale.' While global warming has catastrophic connotations attached to it, climate change suggests a more controllable and less emotional challenge.[1]

This is an example of what Luntz, elsewhere in the document, called the strategy of 'redefining labels'. According to this view, 'global warming' sounds sinister and menacing: it may conjure a picture of a red-hot planet Earth, swathed in hellfire. 'Climate change', by contrast, is what happens when you go on holiday, or switch on the air-conditioner at home, or the 'climate control' in your sports-utility vehicle. Notice also that 'climate change' modestly takes no position on the direction or quality of any possible change. It might get warmer, but then again it might get cooler, avoiding droughts; or rainier, which would be nice for the garden; or we might just have a picturesque dusting of snow every Christmas.

In fact this rhetorical contest had already been won in the international arena more than a decade earlier. In the late 1980s, the scientific talk had been of 'global warming' due to increased atmospheric concentrations of greenhouse gases. The UN convened panels and working groups to discuss the problem, and for a time the phrases 'global warming' and 'climate change' (as in the name of the Intergovernmental Panel on Climate Change (IPCC), set up in 1988) coexisted. But within a few years, the phrase 'climate change' had replaced 'global warming' as the official general name for the phenomenon.

We can pinpoint quite precisely when this took place. In December 1988, the UN General Assembly passed a resolution entitled 'Protection of global climate for present and future generations of mankind', which mentioned both 'global warming' and 'climate change'.[2] A year later, the UN passed another, identically named resolution. It continued to talk of 'climate change', but now all mention of 'global warming' had mysteriously disappeared.[3] By the time of the 1992 UN Framework Convention on Climate Change, this had been entrenched: the convention mentions even the idea of 'warming' only once, and 'global warming' nowhere at all.

Why did this shift happen? Because states with oil interests, including Saudi Arabia and the US (then as now the world's biggest contributor to global warming), had specifically lobbied for the elimination of the phrase 'global warming' in agreements.[4] The mention of 'warming' seemed to enshrine as fact the theory that burning fossil fuels was largely to blame for the heating of the planet. 'Climate change' instead gestured vaguely at an unspecific problem, without pointing the finger of blame directly at any particular industry. For the same reason, Saudi Arabia had demanded that treaties refer only to 'greenhouse gases' and not specifically to 'carbon dioxide' – the gas, emitted when fossil fuels were burned, that was the major contributor to global warming.[5] The Soviet Union and China joined in continuing Saudi efforts during 1990 to 'weaken' the language of assessments, and the US contributed an amendment saying that 'information' was 'inadequate'.[6] Meanwhile, the Reagan and Thatcher governments had opposed any mention of the concept of 'populations' in the global-warming agreements,[7] the effect of which was to suppress discussion of the fact that global warming would impinge directly on the lives of large numbers of people.

It should be noted that there is also a scientific reason to prefer the term 'climate change' in some contexts. If the melting of polar ice caps releases too much water into the oceans, the warm Gulf Stream current (part of what is called the thermohaline circulation) could be turned off, making Britain's weather much colder.[8] Thus drastic local cooling can occur; depending on the interaction of vastly complex systems, a local climate might either heat up or get colder. A particular area, therefore, can 'change' in either direction; but always as a result of the mean temperature of the planet having increased – in other words, because of global warming.

Some people even thought that 'global warming' was not frightening enough – it sounded 'too cosy', according to one newspaper letter-writer.[9] (On one day of IPCC negotiations in August 1990, in fact, the US delegation had floated the idea of replacing the term 'climate change' with the highly specific 'global warming at the surface of the Earth', which sounded minimally catastrophic.)[10] Jeremy Leggett, former professor of earth sciences at Imperial College, London and chief scientist at Greenpeace during the 1990s, goes further: 'I have never considered global warming a scary enough term. If I could have designed the language, I'd have gone for global overheating, climate chaos, or maybe climate meltdown.'[11] But even if 'global warming' is not scary enough, polling by the Brookings Institution in the US confirmed Frank Luntz's assessment that 'climate change' was even less frightening.[12]

'Climate change' was unarguably more vague. Besides its ability to point in both directions, the noun form of 'change' also seemed to be agnostic as to whether any change was anthropogenic – whether it was man's fault at all. After all, the climate had 'changed' many times over the earth's geological history, for example during several ice ages, before humans were around. This indeed is how the IPCC defined 'climate change': any variation in the climate, attributable to either 'natural internal processes or external forcings'.[13] But in a subtle disagreement on terminology that was not reflected in public discourse, the UN Framework Convention on Climate Change used 'climate change' specifically to mean change caused by man; natural change was instead called 'climate variability'.[14] The effect was that UNFCC reports allowed themselves to mean 'global warming' when they said 'climate change', without actually using the troublemaking former term, and making it possible for their use of 'climate change' to be interpreted in the agnostic fashion in which everyone else meant it.

It is clear that in the phrase 'global warming', after all, the word 'warming' implies an agent doing the warming. And once you accept that human beings might be the cause of the problem, again you will eye sceptically those with an interest in burning coal, oil, and gas. Thus the preference for the term that seems to assign no blame, 'climate change', works to support the notion, eagerly propagated by the Bush administration, that there is a controversy about whether there is warming, and if there is, whether humankind is to blame at all. Luntz's memo, indeed, encouraged an appeal to uncertainty: 'Should the public come to believe that the scientific issues are settled, their views about global warming will change accordingly. Therefore, *you need to continue to make the lack of scientific certainty a primary issue in the debate.'* That first sentence is wonderfully revealing: it means, essentially, that if the public knew the truth, they would not accept your policies. So you need to hide the truth from them.

Curiously enough, this was also the strategy of oil companies. In 1998, for example, the American Petroleum Institute, working with Exxon, Chevron, and Southern, created an internal 'Global Climate Science Communications Action Plan', a programme for a multi-million-dollar media offensive. In it, they noted that if people were told that there was scientific uncertainty, they were more likely to oppose US ratification of the Kyoto Protocol, according to which more than 140 countries of the world had agreed to timetables and mechanisms for reducing overall greenhouse-gas emissions. 'When informed that "some scientists believe there is not enough evidence to suggest that (what is called global climate change) is a long-term change due to human behavior and activities," 58 percent of those surveyed said they were more likely to oppose the Kyoto treaty.'[15] The API's 'Action Plan' thus concludes that 'Victory Will Be Achieved When [. . .] recognition of uncertainties becomes part of the "conventional wisdom".' Obediently, George W. Bush cited the 'incomplete' state of scientific knowledge when announcing in April 2001 his country's withdrawal from the Kyoto negotiations.[16] Of course scientific knowledge is always incomplete: that is what drives research. But that is a long way from saying it is wrong, or even controversial.

Industry's attempt to publicise the fictional debate on global warming was, however, abetted by structural biases in the media, on both sides of the Atlantic: 'The problem lies with the media's obsession with entertaining us with a good bust-up between two warring sides,' said Fiona Fox, director of the Science Media Centre. [. . .] 'This means the public gets a manufactured debate. The *Today* programme [on BBC Radio 4] is a classic example. It seems incapable of running a piece on new climate research without asking those in the denial lobby [. . .] to come along to spice up the action.' [17]

Some of those in the 'denial lobby' turned out to be financially motivated. Stephen Whittle at BBC News recalls that, on one occasion, 'The BBC got rather caught by some American bloke appearing on [a news] programme to discuss these things and who wished to cast a large question mark over the whole question of global warming. It turned out that he was actually being paid by an oil company.'[18] Other deniers had a rather shaky grasp of science. The British pundit Peter Hitchens, for example, wrote: 'The greenhouse effect probably doesn't exist. There is as yet no evidence for it.' To this, George Monbiot offered the following unimprovable riposte: 'Perhaps Mr Hitchens would care to explain why our climate differs from that of the moon.'[19] The greenhouse effect described how the earth's atmosphere trapped heat.[20] The dumping by human beings of carbon dioxide and other pollutants in the atmosphere did not create the greenhouse effect, but it did accelerate it. Hitchens had also appealed to one set of data much cherished by a handful of sceptics with more expertise: that although measurements of the earth's surface temperature showed clear rises in the previous few decades, there seemed to be no such rise in atmospheric temperatures.[21] This objection was finally laid to rest in 2005, when three articles in the journal *Science* showed that the placement and functioning of weather-balloon sensors in the 1970s had resulted in erroneous data and satellite readings had been misinterpreted: in fact, the atmosphere too had warmed.[22]

There was, in short, no controversy. The vast majority of scientists, including those whose work was studied by the Intergovernmental Panel on Climate Change, and those on a review panel of the National Academy of Sciences set up by Bush himself and including 'some well-known sceptics', agreed that the earth was warming significantly and that most of the effect was man-made.[23] A review of 928 articles on the subject published in scientific journals between 1993 and 2003 showed that 'None of the papers disagreed with the consensus position'.[24] Announcing proof of the warming of the oceans in 2005,

Scripps Institution of Oceanography member Tim Barnett declared: 'The debate over whether or not there is a global warming signal is now over, at least for rational people.'[25]

Sir David King, chief science adviser to the British government, summed up the matter succinctly in 2004: 'The current state of climate science is that it's now accepted that we have global warming. It's now accepted that this is largely due to anthropogenic effects. That part of it is not up for argument any more.'[26] By then the phrase 'global warming' seemed to carry a spark of illicit thrill, because it took a clear position on scientific fact. The effect of the long hegemony of the studiedly neutral 'climate change', indeed, was eventually to make the more honest alternative seem almost biased. This phenomenon added great rhetorical force to a 2004 article by John Browne, group chief executive of BP, which freely acknowledged the fact of 'global warming' and discussed how best to tackle it.[27] If the head of one of the largest oil companies in the world was talking about global warming, perhaps there was something to it after all.

Politicians, however, continued to prefer the usefully vague 'climate change'. Tony Blair, for example, used the phrase even while dismissing the notion of a controversy about the facts. 'It would be false to suggest that scientific opinion is equally split,' Blair wrote in 2005. 'It is not. The overwhelming view of experts is that climate change, to a greater or lesser extent, is man-made and, without action, will get worse.'[28] Blair, who had ratified the Kyoto treaty and taken a relatively enlightened stance on the issue, was right; but the situation was already even graver. Global warming was going to get worse even if action was taken: even if all global emissions were cut to zero overnight, the earth was already 'committed' to another '30–40 years of global warming based on existing levels of greenhouse gases'.[29] Perhaps Blair thought it impolitic to mention this because it would smack of defeatism: and indeed it was still urgently necessary to cut emissions so as to mitigate as far as possible future disasters. Unfortunately, however, Blair failed to persuade

George W. Bush to commit to any concrete measures on global warming at the 2005 G8 summit.[30]

The Republican strategy of claiming that there was a controversy was cunning, because it took a grain of truth before falsifying it. There were differences among scientists – but they consisted mainly of differing projections about the scale of the coming catastrophe. Owing to the extreme difficulty of predicting the interaction of climate systems decades in advance, there were different forecasts as to how much sea levels would rise, which coastal cities would be destroyed, and how much of the earth's surface would be rendered uninhabitable. Those who favoured taking no remedial action would point at such disagreement and claim that it applied to the subject as a whole: extrapolating from areas of uncertainty in the science to an argument that *all* of the science was uncertain.

In a technical sense, the science of global warming was uncertain, in that all science is provisional and able to be overturned by new evidence. As one writer put it: 'If it wasn't uncertain, it wouldn't be science.'[31] But this did not mean that the main facts about global warming were up for grabs. There was also considerable uncertainty among physicists as to how the theory of gravity could be reconciled with quantum mechanics. But this did not give anyone reason to doubt that if you dropped an apple it would fall to the ground.

Intelligent design

In August 2005, George W. Bush gave his official imprimatur to a similarly cooked-up 'controversy', which centred on the teaching of biology in US high schools. It represented a miraculous victory for those who opposed the science of evolution, and who now called their alternative scheme 'intelligent design' (ID). The idea behind ID, familiar from the mid-nineteenth-century arguments over Darwin, was that some biological structures were so complex that they could not have occurred through evolutionary processes, and must instead have been 'designed' by an 'intelligence'. This kind of argument used to go by the name of 'natural theology'. Its most famous early exponent was the theologian William Paley, who argued in this way: if we see a watch, we infer the existence of a watchmaker; so when we see complex life, we should infer the existence of a God.[32]

ID kept the same creationist argument, but changed the angle of attack by substituting vocabulary. Gone was any explicit mention of theology or God, replaced by the usefully vague 'intelligent'. That adjective also had a secondary use: when one hears the phrase 'intelligent design theorists', it is perhaps tempting to understand 'intelligent' as referring to the theorists themselves, as well as to the design. By contrast, IDers tended to refer to their opponents – that is, biologists – as 'neo-Darwinists', as though scientists around the world were desperately clinging on to an old and unfashionable idea. This appellation handily ignored the existence of the twentieth-century revolution in the genetic understanding of evolution, and also imputed to scientists an idolatrous reliance on one man, Darwin, as though he were the false god of an 'evolutionist' religion.

The phrase 'intelligent design' itself was first popularised in a notorious 1987 American biology textbook called *Of Pandas and People*, earlier drafts of which had referred approvingly instead to 'creationism' and 'creationists' before the new jargon was simply dropped in.[33] The term was quickly adopted by religious sympathisers, and gradually gained traction through the 1990s. Its cheerleaders creatively employed many tricks of language-twisting and code-phrases to gain ever more publicity for their cause, culminating in two major trials in 2005, in Kansas and Pennsylvania, that hinged on the question of whether ID should be taught alongside evolutionary theory in high-school biology classes.

When addressing audiences of fellow believers, proponents of ID were quite frank about their motivations. 'Intelligent design' was engineered as a weapon in the war between Christianity and godlessness. The famous 1999 'Wedge Document' that was leaked from the carefully named pro-ID organisation the Discovery Institute, set it out explicitly. 'Design theory promises to reverse the stifling dominance of the materialist worldview, and to replace it with a science consonant with Christian and theistic convictions.'[34] One of ID's founders, Phillip Johnson, expressed the essentially religious nature of the concept thus: 'There's a difference of opinion about how important this debate is. What I always say is that it's not just scientific theory. The question is best understood as: Is God real or imaginary?'[35] Another ID advocate, William Dembski, wrote: 'Any view of the sciences that leaves Christ out of the picture must be seen as fundamentally deficient.'[36] ID's proponents were motivated to criticise evolution not for its scientific content, but because they believed the view of life as having arisen from natural processes robbed the world of meaning. 'Intelligent design theory' would rectify this catastrophe by basing school discussions of biology firmly on Christian principles.

However, there was the pesky obstacle of the US Constitution to contend with, particularly the Establishment Clause that prohibited the government from promoting religion, and which had led the Supreme Court to strike down previous attempts at teaching creationism in science classes. ID's novel approach to this problem was to deny that it was religious, and instead to claim for itself the status of science, so that it should be taught alongside evolutionary biology.

ID's claim to be science was implicit in its self-description as a 'theory'. In the parlance of science, a 'theory' is not just a casual guess, but a well-established understanding that accords with the present evidence and reliably explains or predicts features of the natural world. On the other hand, IDers regularly referred to evolution as 'just a theory', appealing to the ordinary-language sense of 'theory' as meaning a mere guess: in this way, you might have a theory about why your friend acted the way she did last Thursday; or you might even sarcastically deride another friend's opinion by saying 'That's just your theory'. So ID carefully worked the same word in two directions: appropriating the technical sense of 'theory' for itself, and demoting it to the casual sense for the enemy.

Evolution makes predictions – for example, about what kinds of fossils should be expected to be found at different strata of rock, including intermediary forms such as the winged dinosaur *archaeopteryx*; or about the results of genetic experiments in the laboratory, including the evolution of drug-resistant bacteria – and they are repeatedly confirmed by observation. Evolution also has majestic explanatory force, in accounting for the features of current life on the planet. It can inspire awe; but IDers felt that awe was their turf. So for ID, evolution was 'just a theory'. 'Intelligent design', on the other hand, was purportedly a 'theory' in the sense of a robust, scientific theory, and yet, weirdly, it did not do much explaining or predicting. Officially, for example, it did not hold even a view as to who the mysterious designer was. All of its proponents believed that the designer was the Christian God, but since to admit this would be to admit that ID was disguised religion, and so unfit to be taught in science lessons, they preferred to leave the official theory vague.

Michael Behe, author of one of the celebrated ur-texts of popular ID, *Darwin's Black Box*,[37] was asked to confirm this at the Dover Area School District trial in Pennsylvania during October and November 2005, where a group of parents were suing to overturn the district's decision to use the ID bible, *Of Pandas and People*, in biology class. Their counsel, Eric J. Rothschild, asked Behe: 'You believe [the designer is] God, but it's not part of your scientific argument?' Behe responded: 'That's correct.'[38] In other words, ID as a 'theory' observed some biological feature and said: this must have been designed, but we have no idea who designed it, and we are not even interested in finding out. Actually, they were certain they knew.

As well as pretending ignorance as to the identity of the

designer, ID also had nothing to say about how the purported design actually happened. What were the physical mechanisms by which the designer fiddled with molecules so as to produce his desired animals? ID offered no answers, not even any hypotheses. In Dover, Michael Behe defended this odd reticence by comparing it to astrophysics. Rothschild asked Behe to confirm the statement that 'intelligent design does not describe how the design occurred'. Behe responded: 'That's correct, just like the Big Bang theory does not describe what caused the Big Bang.' The comparison was vastly erroneous. Big Bang theory describes what caused the universe as it appears to us now, offers a massively detailed description of what happened during the Big Bang itself, and does indeed have ideas about what caused it.[39]

As it happens, the theory of the Big Bang was first proposed by a Catholic priest, Georges Lemaître, who wrote that his idea remained 'entirely outside of any metaphysical or religious question'.[40] The Vatican, indeed, officially took the view that God was the 'cause of causes', setting the universe in motion to operate according to natural laws, and that religion was therefore compatible with robust scientific theories, including evolution.[41] The fundamentalists of ID, on the other hand, hated what they saw as the ideological consequences of evolution too much to adopt such a view. Yet their competing 'theory' of 'intelligent design' was completely silent on what happened during the hypothesised design, or even when it happened. It just must have happened, right? Don't ask me how.

In general, for a 'scientific theory', ID was curiously reluctant to answer scientific questions. Why did, for example, the mysterious Intelligent Designer give vertebrates, including humans, a flawed eye with a blind spot, but bless the humble squid with a different type of eye that suffered no such problem? ID studiously avoided the question. Why did the Intelligent Designer give humans an organ, the appendix, which resembles a withered version of that for digesting plant matter in other animals but serves no function in people except occasionally to poison them? What principle of intelligent design causes five-month-old human foetuses to grow a thin coat of fur all over their bodies while still in the womb, where it is not cold, and then lose it before they are born into the world, where it might well be cold?[42] Don't ask.

ID's strategy was instead to focus on unanswered problems. As with any scientific field, areas of evolutionary biology are incompletely understood. To scientists, these areas suggested new research, experiments, and hypotheses. To IDers, they represented a chance to claim that these questions would *never* be answered by science. We cannot currently explain how this part of a bacterium evolved, they would reason, so it must have been created by an intelligent entity. This type of argument had for centuries been known as the 'God of the gaps'. It is easy to do: you simply find a gap in current understanding and claim that it can only be filled by positing God.

Modern IDers used exactly the same idea, only now dressed up in pseudo-scientific terminology. William Dembski coined the phrase 'complex specified information' to denote information – such as that encoded by the human genome – that in his view could in principle not have come about through natural causes. (Sometimes he described it as 'souped-up information', though the flavour of the soup remained obscure.)[43] Michael Behe, meanwhile, promoted the notion of 'irreducible complexity', according to which some biological systems could not in principle have evolved, since if you remove any one part they no longer work.[44] Both phrases amount to the logical fallacy of proof by definition. I make up a technical-sounding phrase that really means 'designed'. I say that some biological feature can be described by this phrase, and then try to argue that *therefore*, that feature must have been designed. But this is only an illusion of logic: the inference follows directly from the way I have carefully stacked the linguistic decks. In fact, in their a priori ruling-out of scientific explanation, the phrases 'complex specified information' and 'irreducibly complex' are both just rhetorical appeals to ignorance.

In Behe's case, this was dramatically illustrated during the Dover trial. One of his favoured examples of 'irreducible complexity' at the time was the immune system of vertebrate animals, so Eric J. Rothschild stacked in front of Behe a pile of books he had previously lent him, that Rothschild claimed represented the leading research into the topic, with titles such as *Evolution of Immune Reactions*, *Origin and Evolution of the Vertebrate Immune System*, *The Natural History of the Major Histocompatibility Complex*, and so on. Behe had not read any of them. 'I am quite skeptical,' he opined, 'although I haven't read them, that in fact they present detailed rigorous models for the evolution of the immune system by random mutation and natural selection.' Rothschild was incredulous. 'You haven't read the books that I gave you?' he asked. 'No,' Behe replied. 'I haven't.'[45] Apparently, it is not necessary to know everything the enemy thinks. It suffices to insist that whatever they think must be wrong. ID's inbuilt prejudice against *any* type of naturalistic explanation for its favoured talking-points, and so its inescapable religiosity, could not have been more clearly demonstrated.

Vacuous though they were, ID's jargon-phrases of 'complex specified information' and 'irreducible complexity' did have the undeniable virtue of sounding sort-of-scientific. And in this way they could function as stealthy stalking-horses for the prime idea of ID itself. Following similarly farcical court hearings in May 2005, the Kansas State Board of Education drafted a new version of its Science Standards, which claimed in its prefatory 'Rationale' that it did not include 'Intelligent Design'. However, attentive reading revealed the following passage later on: 'Whether microevolution (change within a species) can be extrapolated to explain macroevolutionary changes (such as new complex organs or body plans and new biochemical systems which appear irreducibly complex) is controversial.'[46] See that little 'irreducibly complex' smuggled in there? That, as noted, is code. It is used by no one except proponents of ID. What it really means is 'intelligently designed'. What is more, the terms 'microevolution' and 'macroevolution' themselves are ID fictions, expressing the strategy of accepting some parts of evolutionary science because the evidence is so overwhelming, and focusing highly selectively on a few examples. Kansas education functionaries had once again become the laughing stock of the civilised world during the trial. Perhaps it would be more politically efficient to adopt ID by stealth, using its special code-language to reassure the initiated.

It was time to conduct an experiment. I decided to test the hypothesis of ID-by-stealth, and wrote to each member of the Kansas Board. Two of the minority disagreeing with the new draft, Sue Gamble and Bill Wagnon, replied in agreement with my analysis.[47] Of the majority who were pushing the new draft, only Kathy Martin replied. She wrote that the new Science Standards document did 'not support or repudiate Intelligent Design'. 'Please explain to me,' Martin requested, 'why "irreducibly complex" could not be used when referring to scientific data/evidence being studied by scientists.'[48] Once I had explained this, she responded a second time, very graciously, to wish me luck in my 'search for truth'. On 8 November 2005, by a vote of six to four, the board approved the new standards.[49]

It might be accounted a problem with the God-of-the-gaps argument that, as scientific understanding advances, questions are answered, and so gaps filled in, without reference to God. But this should not dissuade the light-footed creationist, who can simply hop over to another gap. The human eye, an apparently miraculous device for seeing, was once the cherished favourite of those inferring divine design from perceived complexity. By 2004, however, the eye's evolutionary pathway was remarkably well understood.[50] In any such case, the antidote is misdirection and irrepressible forward momentum. Look over here, another gap! When Michael Behe's own examples of 'irreducible complexity', such as the blood-clotting cascade in vertebrates, were convincingly refuted by biologists who pointed out simpler clotting mechanisms and proposed detailed pathways of evolution,[51] he simply came up with new ones.

Reassuringly, the day when there would be no more gaps to fixate on continued to seem a long way off.

In sum: 'intelligent design theory' was remarkably free of explanatory or predictive content, and not even willing officially to speculate on the identity or behaviour of the 'designer' that it proposed, instead being negatively parasitical on areas of uncertainty within real science. During the Dover trial, Michael Behe was forced to admit that ID did not fit the definition of 'science' given by the National Academy of Sciences, and that his own definition of 'theory' as applied to ID was so generous that under it, astrology would also qualify as a scientific theory.[52] In general, ID proposed no experiments that would confirm or refute it, and it created no substantial new data, simply adopting a defeatist philosophical position on the same data available to all biologists.[53] ID was not in fact a theory at all.

Even this defect, however, was not insurmountable. William Dembski, for one, adopted the remarkably original argument that ID should be taught in schools precisely *because* it was so poor in content – or, as he put it, not 'mature'. Only by teaching ID in biology classes, he wrote, could we be assured of having a 'next generation' of 'scholars' to investigate the topic.[54] This was particularly revealing because, if 'intelligent design' had really been a controversy within science, it would have already been a rapidly expanding field, as young researchers flocked to fruitful new areas of research to attempt to make their name. Despite more than a decade of publicity, at the end of 2005 this was just not happening. The number of articles endorsing ID in the peer-reviewed scientific literature remained, depending on how you counted, somewhere between vanishingly small and exactly zero.[55]

Patently, such 'controversy' as existed was not a scientific controversy at all. The players in the ID 'controversy' were scientists on the one hand, most of whom felt it a poor use of their time to respond to anti-scientific attacks upon their work, and evangelical Christians on the other. ID was not science but crypto-creationism.

Yet, by continuing to abuse the word 'controversy', as well as other terms such as 'theory' and 'science' itself, the IDers remained in the ascendant. Astrophysicist Lawrence M. Krauss observed, with a kind of admiration: 'They've really in many ways won the public-relations battle with a brilliant slogan, which is "Teach the controversy". Because it implies that there is a controversy. When in fact in science, in the scientific literature, there's no controversy. But by saying that they've managed to convince the public that somehow it's a debate between two ideas that are virtually equal, when in fact they're not.'[56] And so in August 2005, George W. Bush endorsed the neocreationists' claim that there was indeed a 'debate': 'Both sides ought to be properly taught [. . .] so people can understand what the debate is about. I think that part of education is to expose people to different schools of thought.' To this, ABC presenter Ted Koppel responded, with perfectly pitched irony: 'Well . . . yes. But not all schools of thought deserve the same level of attention.'[57]

The Dover trial judge eventually ruled against the IDers, but they had won in Kansas, making the score 1-1 for 2005. Bush's blessing was a crucial victory for the strategy we might call Manufacturing Dissent. It works like this: shout loudly enough, and get enough publicity, and you can sow confusion and the illusion of controversy where there was none before. ID, remember, stands for intelligent design. But initials are versatile things. ID also stands for ideological dissatisfaction. And implicit deism. And intellectual dishonesty.

Sound science

Just as the 'Discovery Institute' was a scientific-sounding verbal cloak for religious fundamentalists, a base from which to promote the imaginary 'controversy' about evolution, so the supposed 'controversy' about global warming was stoked by industry lobby groups with crudely Unspeak names. The Global Climate Coalition, the Information Council on the

Environment, and the Greening Earth Society were all PR fronts for US coal and utility companies, and campaigned against environmental regulation. There was even something called the Advancement of Sound Science Coalition, funded by oil, chemical, car, and tobacco companies.[58] The phrase 'sound science' itself was a clever piece of Republican propaganda, common in discussions about stem-cell research, employee health, and food safety as well as global warming. It too had been recommended by the Luntz memo: 'Sound science must be our guide.'

The purpose of the slogan 'sound science' was to instil fear and distrust of science. The adjective 'sound' inevitably conjured a picture precisely of another, *unsound* kind of science. And so those scientists who made up the planetary consensus on global warming were by definition 'unsound': reckless mad professors advancing an alarmist ideology. 'Sound science', on the other hand, described the views of the handful of sceptics who agreed with policy.

The real nature of 'sound science' could be deduced again from Luntz: while claiming that 'sound science must be our guide', he also wrote: 'The best solutions to environmental challenges are common sense solutions.' But 'common sense' is the opposite of science. Any appeal to 'common sense' recommends a complacent acceptance of the intuitions and prejudices of the general public. If those intuitions and prejudices were sufficient to understand the world, there would be no need for a cadre of trained and specialised scientists at all. There is nothing commonsensical, for example, about the fact that light can behave both as a wave and as a particle. Common sense told us that the earth was flat. If you decide what is 'sound science' by testing it against 'common sense', then sound science is just anti-science.

A curious defence of 'common sense' published by a science journalist in the *New York Times* considered contemporary quantum gravity and superstring theory, and noted that their claims were currently untestable. With the air of a QED, the author concluded complacently: 'Common sense thus persuades me that these avenues of speculation will turn out to be dead

ends.'[59] If only, the reader will have sighed, theoretical physicists the world over were as sensible as this man. But in
assuming easily that what was currently untestable would
remain untestable, and declaring that 'common sense' therefore told him that zany-sounding theories were 'dead ends', the
writer was just confirming that common sense was anti-science:
for the implication was that superstring and quantum-gravity
theorists should just give up on their projects. Actually, many
powerful theories have only been tested by experiment long
after their inception. The idea of the Greek philosopher
Democritus that all matter was made up of atoms, for example,
was not testable in the fifth century BC, but that does not mean
it was a 'dead end'. Shutting down investigation on the basis
of a 'common sense' hunch is not a reliable route to lasting
understanding.

The phrase 'sound science' had been born when the
Advancement of Sound Science Coalition was originally set up
in 1993. It was created by tobacco firm Philip Morris 'to fight
against the regulation of cigarettes'.[60] And the Bush administration's use of 'sound science' continued this tradition.
Refusing to enact Clinton's plan to regulate the levels of arsenic
in drinking water to the level used by the European Union,
Bush demanded some 'sound science', even though the
Environmental Protection Agency had already been studying
the toxicology of arsenic for seventeen years.[61] The Department
of Health and Human Services appealed to 'sound science' in
denying the findings of a World Health Organization report
showing that fast food encouraged obesity.[62] A Vice-Presidential
panel urged more drilling for oil and gas in Alaska according to
the principles of 'sound science'.[63] Twenty American Nobel lau-
reates were among the signatories of a 2004 report which
detailed how the Bush administration, while appealing to
'sound science', had consistently falsified scientific findings in
order to support its own policies.[64]

Campaigning for the presidency in 2000, Bush had pledged
to regulate power plants' emission of carbon dioxide. Once in

office, he declared that he would not do that after all. The White House spokesman explained that Bush was committed to a 'multi-pollutant strategy', but that 'CO_2 should not have been included as a pollutant during the campaign. It was a mistake.'[65] Carbon dioxide was the major contributory factor to global warming, and yet, the American public were asked to believe, calling it a pollutant had been a 'mistake'. The legislation that Bush subsequently proposed, giving polluters a free pass on carbon dioxide, was called the Clear Skies Act. This was intended to replace the existing Clean Air Act, rhetorically altering a specific promise about cleanliness to a merely aesthetic vision of clearness. 'Clear skies' may still be filled with invisible pollutants. And in fact the provisions of the Clear Skies Act were less onerous to industry than those of the law it replaced.[66]

Four years later, it was alleged that the chief of staff for the White House's Council on Environmental Quality, Philip A. Cooney, had changed the language of several official reports on climate science so as to soften their conclusions and introduce doubt where there was none.[67] Cooney had previously been employed as a lobbyist for the American Petroleum Institute. The week after the allegations about his actions at the White House hit the news, Cooney resigned. He was immediately given a job by ExxonMobil.[68]

Perhaps the Bush administration's stance could be explained by simple political short-termism, in which the profits of the fossil-fuel industry counted for more than vague threats of future devastation. After all, Bush famously took no interest in how he might be regarded by history, because by then, 'We'll all be dead.'[69] But there was also evidence of a longer-term view within the government, according to which the possibility of catastrophic global warming was accepted, and considered to have a bright side: because it would enhance the global hegemony of the United States. According to a 2003 Pentagon report, 'the United States could likely survive shortened growing cycles and harsh weather conditions without catastrophic losses. [. . .]

Even in this continuous state of emergency the U.S. will be positioned well compared to others. [. . .] the U.S. itself will be relatively better off and with more adaptive capacity.'[70] In other words: sure, global warming was going to be bad for everyone, but it was going to be worse for America's enemies than for itself, so why worry? Best keep this a secret, though: all uses of the term 'global warming' were deleted from a 2003 report of the Environmental Protection Agency.[71]

In 2005, the British television interviewer Trevor McDonald pointed out to George W. Bush that pollution in the US had 'increased amazingly since 1992'. Bush shot back: 'That is a totally inaccurate statement.' McDonald insisted: 'It's a UN figure.' Bush's response? 'Well, I just beg to differ with every figure you've got.'[72] Ingenious: not only do I deny what you have told me, but I will deny everything that you *could* tell me in future. A perfect illustration of the principle of 'sound science'.

Energy

Meanwhile, there were tangential contests of Unspeak among those who did not deny the facts of global warming but did disagree on what to do about it. One buzzphrase that arose was 'sustainable development', which was used in two very different senses by opposing groups, because it left vague by what metric sustainability might be measured. Environmental groups meant by 'sustainable' a holistic approach by which life as we know it might be sustained. Scientists talked about 'sustainable cities' to mean cities that would not be destroyed by flooding in the wake of global warming.[73] But to others, 'sustainable' meant a financial approach by which the oil industry as we know it might be sustained: sustainability was the minimum amount of environmental care that was affordable by those whose activities harmed the environment.[74]

Another strategy consisted in the wholesale replacement of one vocabulary with another. Talk of the 'environment' was considered an irritant to be brushed aside. Thus George W. Bush stated: 'I believe nuclear power answers a lot of our issues. It certainly answers the environmental issue, and those people who are concerned about whether or not we can continue burning coal.'[75] Concern for the environment was just a single 'issue': a simple question that could be 'answered'. More use of nuclear power would reduce carbon emissions, but global warming was not the only way in which humans could harm the environment. Given the problems of transporting and storing radioactive waste that would remain dangerous for hundreds of thousands of years, perhaps Bush's 'answer' to 'the environmental issue' was simply: Fuck the environment.

It was better, perhaps, to avoid talk of the 'environment' at all, because the word could already be argued to reify a holistic concept of an interconnected biosphere. Still more perilous were concepts such as 'conservation': a big no-no, according to the Luntz memo. More politic for a certain audience was the vocabulary of 'energy'. 'Energy' is something everyone likes: it's positive, it's get-up-and-go, it's an almost metaphysical virtue. However, in government phrases such as 'energy policy' and 'energy security', the term meant one thing only: oil.

> [F]or former oilmen like Bush and Vice President Dick Cheney, the equation of 'energy' with 'oil' couldn't have been more transparent. The United States must 'explore for energy,' Cheney asserted. Clearly, the former CEO of Halliburton was not suggesting his colleagues go hunting for sunlight to shine on solar PV panels.[76]

Former US Department of Energy official Michelle Billig confirmed the point in 2004, when she recommended that 'the U.S. government should create a national energy council'[77] – not to investigate other sources of 'energy', but just to be on the lookout for possible interruptions in the global oil supply. Indeed, energy-as-in-oil trumped the woolly lexicon of tree-huggers, as Cheney had made clear in 2001: 'Conservation may be a sign of personal virtue, but it is not a sufficient basis for a sound, comprehensive energy policy.'[78] A 'sound policy' is obviously based on 'sound science'; both of them are superior to mere 'personal virtue'.

Natural resources

Such viewpoints could nonetheless be given an ethical makeover by appeal to the concept of 'natural resources', which at first glance may help to endorse our use of what it denotes. State Department spokesman Adam Ereli claimed in 2005 that the government was concerned 'to act in ways that secure resources, natural resources, for future generations'.[79] US federal spending on environmental matters is counted under the heading 'Natural resources and environment':[80] 'natural resources', among which are counted oil, coal, and gas, the use of which harms the environment, come before the environment itself. Etymologically, a 'resource' is something that springs up again. But reserves of fossil fuels are finite, and when the last of them are sucked from the ground there will be no more for millions of years. To describe oil as a 'resource', then, covers up the fact of its inevitable exhaustion.

But the concept of 'natural resources', first recorded in the writings of the eighteenth-century economist Adam Smith,[81] is also Unspeak for a larger idea: that everything in the natural world is there to be used by man, and is valuable only to the extent that it finds a place in the human economy. In the early nineteenth century, areas that were not farmed or built upon, yet might nevertheless be teeming with life, began to be termed 'waste lands'. The idea of 'natural resources' is similar: everything in nature is exploitable; not to exploit it would be a waste. Another US lobby group with a blatantly misleading name, for example, was the American Forest Resource Alliance, which was set up 'to fight proposed federal laws to protect ancient forests'.[82]

At least 'resource' is less incorrect when applied to forests, since if they are properly managed and replanted, trees will spring up in the place of those removed and turned into coffee tables, or indeed books. On the other hand, forests may just be razed by enthusiastic logging and never grow back, in which case it turns out that they were not automatically a 'resource' after all. Similarly, a species of fish that is fished to extinction is quite plainly an ex-resource. This etymological observation might be taken to suggest that the idea of a 'resource' implies a duty of proper care, of human beings as stewards rather than owners of the world. Yet as generally used, the notion of a 'resource' connotes an almost sacred right to exploitation, with no blowback – a view which may be encouraged by a literal reading of God's granting 'dominion' over all earthly life and the planet itself to Adam and Eve.[83]

British MP Robin Cook explained the recklessness of the 'resource' view in the following way:

> The market is incapable of respecting a common resource such as the environment, which provides no price signal to express the cost of its erosion nor to warn of the long-term dangers of its destruction. Yet every participant in the market will experience a loss in their quality of life if the cumulative effect of their activities is to degrade their common environment.[84]

Of course, environmental degradation will affect all human beings and all animals, not just 'every participant in the market'; and thinking of the environment as a 'resource', as Cook termed it, is a symptom of the problem that he was decrying. Probably Cook realised this, however: he was addressing his argument to the blithe consumers of 'natural resources', and casting it in their own vocabulary.

To call what will not necessarily spring up again a 'resource', then, calms any shadowy anxieties about degradation, and also implies our right to do as we wish with it. Adding the term 'natural' reinforces this latter point, suggesting not just a right of use but the healthy duty to use. What is 'natural', after all, must be good for us and the planet as a whole. 'Natural resources' are part of Nature's gracious bounty; and to use them is only natural.

Consider a further Unspeak use of the concept of 'nature' in the term 'natural gas'. Since 'gas' already meant gasoline in the US, the burnable gas trapped under the earth's surface was christened 'natural gas': the addition of the term 'natural' had the further helpful effect of making gas seem somehow purer and cleaner than other fossil fuels, even though oil and coal were just as natural. Fossil-fuel companies deliberately played on this deceptive language in advertising new drilling for gas as a virtuous development. A 2005 ChevronTexaco advertisement described natural gas as being 'one of the most environmentally friendly fuels in the world. It produces almost no emissions of sulfur dioxide or particulates and leaves no solid waste behind, which means less impact on air and water quality.'[85]

A sceptical reader might have observed that the advertisement, for what it also called a 'cleaner fuel', made no mention of carbon dioxide, the main contributor to human-caused global warming. And for good reason: this 'cleaner', 'environmentally friendly' fuel emits only 29 per cent less carbon dioxide than oil for the same heat output, and actually gives off 20 per cent more carbon monoxide.[86] Furthermore, when 'natural gas' leaks into the air, its main ingredient, methane, is a far more potent greenhouse gas than CO_2. According to a 1999 US government report, methane amounted to only 0.5 per cent of US emissions but was responsible for fully 10 per cent of the total emissions' greenhouse effect.[87] 'Natural gas' was, after all, no friend to nature.

The template of 'natural resources' must, further, be to blame for the modern barbarism of the corporate term 'human resources'. To call human beings 'resources', firstly, is to deny their existence as individuals, since any one person will not spring up again once worn out; instead, people are 'resources' only insofar as they are thought of as a breeding population, like rabbits or chickens. 'Human resources', first recorded in 1961, eventually succeeded the term 'man-power' in business parlance:[88] the effect was merely to replace a crude sexism with a more generalised rhetorical violence. People considered as 'human resources' are mere instruments of a higher will. Compare the Nazi vocabulary of 'human material' (*Menschenmaterial*) and 'liquidation' (*liquidieren*, recasting murder as the realisation of profit):[89] if 'natural resources' evinces merely a blithe disregard for the environment, 'human resources' contains an echo of totalitarian Unspeak.

The grain of Nature

Still, we all loved 'nature'. Of all words, wrote the urbane philosopher David Hume, 'there is none more ambiguous and equivocal'.[90] In the twenty-first century it remained one of those terms wrestled over by everyone, regardless of their attitude to what it denoted, because it automatically evoked pleasant feelings. It worked in the same way as the splendidly Unspeak name of environmental group Friends of the Earth, or even Greenpeace – for who did not like green stuff, or peace?

'Nature' was a hotly contested term, too, in debates over biotechnology. Was the genetic engineering of crops or embryos an example of man playing God, interfering with 'nature', indulging in 'unnatural' perversity? Or was it, on the contrary, simply the latest stage in 'nature's' understanding of itself? Even if you thought the term 'nature' was unhelpful, it was hard to get away from it completely. In a report on genetically modified crops, a British think tank, the Nuffield Council on Bioethics, stated:

> The 'natural/unnatural' distinction is one of which few prac-
> tising scientists can make much sense. Whatever occurs,
> whether in a field or a test tube, occurs as the result of natural
> processes, and can, in principle, be explained in terms of natu-
> ral science.[91]

The authors, having decided that the natural-versus-unnat-
ural distinction is senseless, nonetheless found themselves
appealing to a concept of the 'natural' in order to defend
science. But their claim that everything done by science is perforce 'natural' allowed the conclusion that, say, grafting a
human ear on to a mouse's back is perfectly natural. This may
strike some people as a stretch. Yet it is merely a version of the
old idea that, since humans are part of nature, anything they do
must be natural: it is in principle impossible for their actions to
be unnatural.

But if 'natural' describes everything that occurs in the universe, including the behaviour of people, it follows that it is
impossible for *anything* to be unnatural. As Hume pointed out,
even if a supernatural miracle occurs, then it has emerged in the
realm of empirical reality, and so could be considered 'natural'
too. 'Natural science' does not imply any notion of 'unnatural'
science but only distinguishes itself from social science or political science. Meanwhile, there can be no other kinds of
'processes' apart from what the Nuffield authors call 'natural
processes', since they happen in fields and test tubes alike. Used
like this, the term 'natural' loses its primary antonym and so
ceases to contain any real meaning at all, apart from a residual
intimation of virtue.

Once 'natural' is thus emptied of discriminatory meaning, it
may happily be used in biotech PR. Another Unspeak smoking
gun, for example, comes from the Asian Food Information
Centre, a company funded by the biotech food and agriculture
industry whose mission is to 'provide sound science-based
information on nutrition, health and food safety across the Asia
Pacific region'.[92] (Clearly, 'sound science' gets around these

days.) In a 2001 report entitled 'Food Biotechnology: A Communications Guide to Improving Understanding', it advised companies on the right sort of PR language to use when describing genetically modified food. Sure enough, 'natural' was among their recommended 'Words to Use', along with 'better', 'field', 'heritage', 'tradition', 'wholesome', and even 'organic'.[93] (All food is 'organic' in the sense that it is made up of organic chemicals, but that might not be what shoppers read into the term.) 'Words to Lose' include 'alter', 'chemical', 'DNA', 'genes', 'laboratory', 'patent', and 'technology'. Spot the pattern: all terms that smack of *science* are to be discarded. 'Sound science' demands that the workings of science be swept under the carpet. Instead, producers of genetically modified food should speak only in terms of wholesome, traditional nature.

Even the term 'genetically modified' itself was soon for the chop. It had originally been the Unspeak replacement for 'genetically engineered': the teleological concept of engineering implied ground-up creation and so perhaps 'playing God' by scientists, as well as an unpalatable association with machinery or weapons. Modification, on the other hand, connotes mere tinkering, on a smaller scale, and, implicitly, for the better. In an excellent book on the language of biotech debates, linguist Guy Cook interviewed many scientists and representatives of the biotech industry and found that, for these reasons, they 'were quite unanimous and explicit in their preference' for the term 'genetically modified' instead of 'genetically engineered'.[94] Moreover, 'genetically modified' is usually shortened in PR and the media to GM, so that any potentially worrying implications of science in the term are compressed out of existence. After all, GM can also denote General Motors, or a grandmaster in chess.

But the Asian Food Information Centre was already speeding ahead on the road of Unspeak, and they recommended changing the language once again. A new report in 2004, on the reaction of people in the Philippines, China, and India to different terms (in English, Mandarin, and Hindi respectively), found that even the 'modified' part of 'genetically modified' struck people as meaning 'unnatural' and 'strange'.[95] An improvement was 'genetically enhanced': because the focus-group participants said that 'enhanced' sounded 'positive', and even as though the food were 'more nutritious'. Best of all, though, was the shiny new term 'biotechnology foods'. The mention of technology was softened and rendered virtuous with the reassuring prefix 'bio-'; while genes (a Word to Lose) could be forgotten. 'Biotechnology foods' sounded 'life-affirming' to the survey's respondents. It even sounded 'natural'.

Opponents, on the other hand, continued to appeal to the concept of the natural, while meaning something quite different. Outlining his pre-millennial '10 Fears for GM Food', Prince Charles wrote:

> Are we going to allow the industrialisation of Life itself, redesigning the natural world for the sake of convenience and embarking on an Orwellian future? And, if we do, will there eventually be a price to pay?
>
> Or should we be adopting a gentler, more considered approach, seeking always to work with the grain of Nature in making better, more sustainable use of what we have, for the long-term benefit of mankind as a whole?[96]

It must be admitted that Charles, while adopting a threadbare disguise of merely asking questions, was weighting those questions rather heavily. Few people, however excited by the possibilities of biotechnology, would put their hand up and cry: 'Yes! I want to industrialise Life itself and embark on an Orwellian future!' Notice also Charles's loading of the second question with the holistic use of 'sustainability'. His distaste for 'redesigning the natural world', moreover, implied that the world had already been *designed* in a certain way, in a way that was perforce good, for we had no right to change it. And the person who designed it, as we know from the dishonest neocreationists touting 'intelligent design' in the US, can be none other than God – for whom, indeed, 'Nature' is often just an alternative name, used to avoid scaring the horses.

Charles's further implicit recommendation is that we should always 'work with the grain of Nature'. The metaphor of carpentry (working with the grain of the wood) evokes a rustic, harmonious idyll. Taken seriously, the call to work with the grain of Nature becomes a radical Luddite manifesto. After all, by 'Nature', Charles does not mean the whole universe and all the actions of the humans within it, as the Nuffield Council on Bioethics used the term. If humans should work with 'Nature', then they are by definition not part of it. On this understanding of 'Nature', it is violently opposed by much of modern science. A doctor who saws through a patient's sternum in order to try to revive a failing heart is, we might say, working rather obviously *against* the grain of Nature. A dentist who scrapes out the nerves at the root of a molar and implants a titanium post is fighting against Nature's plan for teeth. Lasers, like the one in your CD player, exist nowhere in Nature. A space probe is launched atop an enormous rocket in order to overcome the reluctance of terrestrial objects to leave the planet's gravity well: a reluctance wisely ordained by Nature.

'Can [. . .] that offend great Nature's god / Which Nature's self inspires?' asked Alexander Pope, a couplet which James Boswell derided for its 'flimsy superficial reasoning'.[97] Prince Charles clearly agreed: one could indeed cause offence, as long as one believed in Nature's 'god'; or, like the ancient Greeks, in nature as a vast organism with an intelligence of its own.[98] (We borrowed the late-classical Greek word for nature, *phusis*, to name our science of 'physics', but the word no longer carries the same metaphysical assumptions.) But if one sincerely believes that one should always 'work with the grain of Nature', then one is committed to turning the clock back by at least several centuries, if not to the time when we were all swinging from trees and eating berries. That, perhaps, was the last time that 'Nature' was in perfect harmony with human beings.

Human nature

Ideological appeals to 'nature' also abounded in the phrase 'human nature'. In this expression, the war between man and the environment was internalised: there was assumed to be a core of innate, 'natural' humanness, and a person could choose to work with its grain, in Prince Charles's language, or against it. Sometimes it was thought that this nature was virtuous, so that various forms of vicious behaviour could be condemned on account of the belief that they ran counter to 'human nature'. At other times this 'nature' was specifically God-given, and in a Christian context referred to man's fallen state, the ineradicable stain of original sin. Thus Thomas Aquinas used it (in Latin: *natura humana*), and thus Tony Blair, in his statement on the death of Pope John Paul II, referred to the latter's experience of 'what was wrong in human nature'.[99] George W. Bush declared explicitly that 'the Author of Life wrote [. . .] our common human nature'.[100]

Theologists have the advantage of a metaphysics, according to which this 'nature' is implanted by God, and so they can claim to be sure about aspects of it. Absent any such foundational certainty, the problem with invoking 'human nature' is that, given the enormous variety of humans, any such assertion as to their 'nature' is bound to be a generalisation that omits or implicitly denounces certain individuals. David Hume wrote *A Treatise on Human Nature*, supposing that such a 'nature' was open to empirical investigation, like the 'nature' of plants and animals. When he wrote 'An affection betwixt the sexes is a passion evidently implanted in human nature',[101] he accurately pointed out that most people express heterosexual preferences, but did not account for homosexuality. One might decide to infer from Hume's sentence, after a little thought, that homosexuality must be contrary to 'human nature'; and then, if it is so contrary, that it must be morally wrong. Thus, according to Republican Senator Rick Santorum, 'homosexual acts' are 'deviant', they 'undermine the basic tenets of our society and the family', and should be considered in the same category as 'man on child, man on dog'.[102] From the idea that certain behaviour is 'deviant' – statistically in the minority, not 'normal', against 'nature' – Santorum elicits a whole line of apocalyptic moral reasoning, accompanied by a vivid dumb-show of pornographic marionettes.[103]

Moral arguments from claimed observations about a 'human nature' have hardly been thin on the ground ever since Aristotle defended the practice of slavery by asserting that some human beings were slaves by nature.[104] Conservatives in particular have often claimed there to be an inescapable and unimprovable 'human nature', so as to argue that any newfangled thinking which runs counter to that 'nature' must needs risk catastrophe. In a 2004 book, historian John Lukacs bemoaned the 'myopia of liberals [. . .] about human nature', using the phrase repeatedly thereafter, but without ever explicitly giving an account of it.[105] There were clues, however, in his generalisations: for instance that, apparently, 'people are moved by (and at times even worship) evidences of power, rather than by propositions of social contracts'.[106] As is the fate of most claims about 'human nature', this one was at least as false as it was true. It is not obviously the case, for example, that 'people' in general really were more 'moved' by the 2003 American invasion of Iraq (an evidence of power), than by the American Bill of Rights (a proposition of a social contract). Indeed, if you tied Lukacs's statement down to any set of empirical facts, it began to look very shaky. But it was given rhetorical force by the implicit appeal to 'human nature'.

In order to counter such pessimism about the practicability of new forms of society, in contrast, Marxists and some existentialists had regularly argued there to be no such thing as 'human nature' at all. Taken to mean that there was nothing innate about human behaviour, this was just as untrue as the reifying claims about 'human nature' on the other side of the argument.[107] But modern ideologues on both sides were not really concerned about the facts: they were more likely to invoke 'common sense'.

As it continued to be used at the end of the twentieth century, the idea of 'human nature' was dressed up verbally as a quasi-scientific understanding, but really used just as code for a generalised pessimism about human affairs. 'Human nature' was an ancient inheritance of selfishness, greed, and violence. It was a counsel of despair. In this sense the term was available to all political viewpoints. The siege of Sarajevo, for example, was taken to symbolise 'the depravity of human nature'.[108] When unleashed, 'human nature' would inevitably become the engine for a historical tragedy.

4

Tragedy

A tragic mistake

On 22 July 2005, Jean Charles de Menezes, a Brazilian electrician living in London, was chased on to an Underground train by police, who then shot him seven times in the head and once in the shoulder. They had suspected him of complicity in the previous day's attempted bombings, because he lived in a block where another apartment was under surveillance, and he was allegedly wearing an unseasonably warm jacket, perhaps hiding a belt of explosives. (His cousin later said he had been wearing a denim jacket.[1]) In fact Menezes was innocent of any involvement and had not been about to blow himself up. As the Metropolitan Police Service put it the next day: 'We are now satisfied that he was not connected with the incidents of Thursday, 21 July 2005. For somebody to lose their life in such circumstances is a tragedy and one that the Metropolitan Police Service regrets.'[2]

Thus began a veritable orgy of tragedy-talk by officials and commentators. 'Tragedy' has long been a most useful term of Unspeak. For what is a tragedy? It is a work of fiction, devised by a godlike author. It plays out before us, with implacable logic, for our moral edification. But we are not actually involved in it, and cannot change the outcome. The spectators are not at fault when a tragedy occurs, any more than you blame the theatre manager for the death of Hamlet.

Who, then, to blame for the death of Jean Charles de Menezes? You might suppose, from reading the police statement, that Menezes himself was in error, having been careless enough to 'lose his life'. According to the first theoretician of tragedy, Aristotle, the tragic hero must be doomed by his own tragic error, or *hamartia*. It was presumably just such an error to run away from undercover policemen, if that was what the victim actually did. Hence the tragedy in this case may be seen to be that of Menezes himself. Such was the insinuation of the police's coolly distancing language. Their announcement that they were 'now satisfied' that he was not a terrorist further insinuated, in icily sinister fashion, that it was the victim's fault not to have 'satisfied' them of his innocence sooner: and indeed that anyone who could not so 'satisfy' the police on demand, at the very least by being dressed appropriately for the climate, might expect to be shot. Aristotle said that a tragedy should inspire pity and fear in the audience; the police felt only a lukewarm 'regret'. And they were clearly only spectators, since there was no mention of their having killed Menezes, who instead somehow mislaid his health with no outside help. Tony Blair subsequently corrected this unfortunate implication with the most passive, no-blame language possible, referring to 'the death that has happened',[3] as though, perhaps, it had been the result of natural causes.

It could be that Home Secretary Charles Clarke was also accusing the victim of *hamartia* when he called the shooting 'an absolute tragedy for Mr de Menezes and his family'.[4] Alternatively, the odd construction 'a tragedy for' might imply a performance put on especially for the victim and his relatives; in that case, it was all too unfortunate that Menezes had somehow broken through the fourth wall and become an unwilling participant in the drama.

Another option was to suggest that the graver mistake had actually been made by the police in shooting to death a man innocent of any crime: so the Muslim Council of Great Britain called this a 'terrible, tragic mistake'.[5] But then if the mistake belongs to the police, it might be a *hamartia*, and so the tragedy itself might be theirs too. The police had in place a shoot-to-kill policy in regard to suspected suicide bombers, a policy that had been in effect in secret since 2002.[6] Now, when its existence was revealed, the term was hastily retooled with the somewhat more unwieldy name 'shoot-to-kill-in-order-to-protect', according to Metropolitan Police Commissioner Ian Blair;[7] or, as former Prime Minister John Major subtly shortened it, 'shoot-to-protect',[8] thereby avoiding any distasteful mention of killing at all. The policy's official code name was Operation Kratos.[9] *Kratos* was a word borrowed from ancient Greek and so had aptly tragic resonances; it meant, appropriately, 'power'.

Tony Blair pleaded: 'I think it is important [. . .] that we understand that had the circumstances been different and, for example, this had turned out to be a terrorist and they had failed to take that action, they would have been criticised the other way.'[10] Yes; but the circumstances were not different. Blair attempted to reframe the debate in the most euphemistic manner: apparently the real scandal was the fact that the police had been 'criticised', rather than that an innocent man had been killed. Now, few people should like to be a police officer working under the Kratos principle, with the duty to make split-second decisions about whether the person pursued may be about to detonate an explosives belt. The officers involved may have been traumatised by their actions. But to regard the incident as their tragedy had the effect of relegating the man killed to a walk-on role in a drama of heroic-but-flawed law-enforcers.

All the more so if the killing were characterised more widely, as the tragedy of society as a whole. Thus London mayor Ken Livingstone: 'This tragedy has added another victim to the toll of deaths for which the terrorists bear responsibility.'[11] Tragedy here is a kind of impersonal machine – an arithmetical machine, for adding tolls of deaths – hovering over everyone. It has been set in motion, or authored, by 'the terrorists'. Neither Menezes nor the police are at all to blame in this most generous definition of 'tragedy': as an epic conceived by supervillains who 'bear responsibility' even for deaths physically performed by their enemies.

And so it went. Under the onslaught of tragedy-speak, it became ever more difficult to make out the person of Jean Charles de Menezes, shot repeatedly in the head, fading into the rhetorical distance.

Fence

The use of 'tragedy' to avoid accepting responsibility or pointing the finger has long been widespread. In 1988, the killing of three Palestinian villagers by an Israeli soldier was deemed a 'tragic incident' by the army, who declined to prosecute the perpetrator.[12] In the same year, meanwhile, PLO leader Yasser Arafat disdained any mention of acts of terrorism committed by his group, instead using the words 'tragedy' or 'tragic' five times in a speech to the United Nations.[13] Not only specific incidents but entire conflicts can be called tragedies, and the Israel–Palestine situation as a whole is particularly apt to be described as one. So wrote outgoing *New York Times* public editor Daniel Okrent in 2005: 'Who can be dispassionate about an endless tragedy? [. . .] Each day's reports in The Times are tiny fragments of a tragic epic.'[14] Okrent's power to predict the future, and so ascertain that the 'tragedy' would indeed be endless, was impressive, and his marriage of tragedy with another literary form, epic, no doubt demonstrated the extent of his passion. Like Homer's *Iliad*, an epic was bound to be a tale of blood-soaked heroism, in which no one was really at fault, but all were the playthings of the gods. Less thrilling to the moral imagination but more demonstrable, however, was the fact that Israelis and Palestinians had been engaged in one of the most intense and multifaceted contests of Unspeak in modern times.

In 2002, Israel began constructing what it called a 'security fence'[15] around its territory. The term 'fence' evokes thigh-high slats of wood, painted white, around the borders of a pleasant suburban garden, or a decorative wrought-iron structure. (The Modern Hebrew term for the structure, *gader*, has the same connotations of something 'usually made of wire (barbed wire is *geder tayil*) or wood',[16] as opposed to a wall.) The Israeli fence was rather more complex, consisting of, at various parts along its length, roads, trenches, guard-towers, thermal-imaging cameras, a steel-and-barbed-wire electrified fence, and an eight-metre-high concrete wall.[17] Therefore, to call the entire structure a 'fence' was deliberately misleading propaganda. It became known in Arabic as 'the Wall',[18] and was thus referred to in English by some commentators, though that appellation too was deliberately misleading propaganda, since in many places it was not a wall. In Britain, BBC News told its presenters not to use the term 'wall' for the structure as a whole; but they were allowed to say 'fence', which was also inaccurate.[19] How to get around this problem? Some opted to use both names at once: 'fence/wall'.[20] George W. Bush called it a fence when standing next to Ariel Sharon, but a wall with then-Palestinian Authority Prime Minister Mahmoud Abbas.[21] Meanwhile, one photograph of a section that was a wall, from Agence France Presse, carried the splendidly ironical caption 'concrete fence'.[22]

A further idea was implied by the epithet 'security' in the original designation 'security fence': that the structure was being built only to keep Israeli citizens safe. Certainly one reason for it was to prevent suicide bombers from crossing over from the West Bank into Israel and blowing up civilians; as a spokeswoman for the Israeli Embassy in London put it: 'to impede the terrorists' access to Israel'.[23] Some writers accepted this argument while indicating their displeasure by using the competing noun, calling the thing a 'security wall'.[24] In an apparent concession to the fence/wall controversy, some official Israeli communications began to refer to the 'security barrier' instead. 'Barrier' might have looked like a more neutral term for the structure *in toto*, but that word, too, always has a connotation of defence from danger or contamination, as in flood barrier, or blood-brain barrier. And so the word 'barrier' worked to enhance the other half of the term: the claim that its motivation was solely 'security'. Yet the structure did not simply enclose pre-1967 Israeli territory but encroached far into the occupied West Bank. Under the proposed final route of the barrier in spring 2005, according to a report that continued nonetheless to use the soothing, suburban noun 'fence': '9.5 percent of the territory of the West Bank would end up on the Israeli side of the fence [. . .] and 230,000 Palestinians would be living in enclaves surrounded on three sides by the fence.'[25]

Some Palestinians had therefore renamed the structure the 'Apartheid wall', attempting to align themselves in international sympathy with the oppressed black population of South Africa during apartheid rule. This propaganda term was also adopted, for instance, by retired British MP Tony Benn.[26] Others contested the idea of security as the sole motivation in different ways. Chris McGreal, Jerusalem correspondent for the *Guardian*, explained in an internal memo that he had sometimes chosen to write '"security" barrier', with scare quotes around the first term only: 'to convey the idea that the dispute is not whether it's a fence (where it is) but whether it's about security. It signals that there are legitimate questions over the government's claim that this is driven by security considerations when there are good reasons to believe that the barrier is also (or mainly) political, marking out a future border and grabbing land.' In 2004, the International Court of Justice noted that the barrier's construction involved the demolition of Palestinian homes and 'led to increasing difficulties for the population concerned regarding access to health services, educational establishments and primary sources of water', and that if it became permanent, it 'would be tantamount to *de facto* annexation'. The ICJ concluded that it was 'contrary to international law'.[27]

Finally, the state of Israel was driven to concede in a court case that security was not the only reason for the structure. *Ha'aretz* reported:

> Israel has acknowledged for the first time that not just 'security' considerations were instrumental in determining the route of the West Bank separation fence.
>
> Responding to a petition brought to the High Court by the residents of the Palestinian village Azun in the northern West Bank, the state asked for the fence to be left on its original route, previously ruled to be unsuitable, as it would be very expensive to move. [. . .]
>
> In its principal ruling on the issue last year, in the Beit Surik affair, the High Court determined that the state has no authority to build a fence for 'political' considerations, such as appending land to Israel. [. . .] Until now, the state has claimed that the fence was a short-term measure, and it was possible to move or dismantle the barrier.[28]

The reporter continued to use the terms 'fence' and 'barrier' interchangeably, but notice what had happened to the secondary term: it was no longer a 'security fence' but a 'separation fence'. It was not that the claim of security as a motivation had been disproven or abandoned – the structure had reduced the number of suicide attacks within Israel – but that security had been shown not to be the sole motivation.

A general lesson is here exemplified. It is that political acts are commonly overdetermined: there are many reasons for them. Contests of Unspeak ensue when each side attempts falsely to simplify the facts by claiming that only one motivation exists: so, on one side, the 'fence' was purely for 'security'; on the other, the 'wall' was a tool of 'apartheid'. The designation's eventual evolution into 'separation barrier' was something of an improvement, even if the phrase was a crude tautology. Both sides could at least agree that its effect was indeed to separate one side from the other, though 'barrier' still implied that its

function was to protect the Israelis from the Palestinians, and
not vice versa.

Merely calling the thing by a different name did not ease the
grievances of Palestinians affected by its route. 'It's certainly a
problem to the extent that it prejudges final borders, confiscates
Palestinian property or imposes further hardship on the
Palestinian people,'[29] said a US State Department spokesman in
July 2005. Less than a week after conceding that it had other
considerations besides security in building the structure, meanwhile, the Israeli government decided to 'cut off 55,000
Palestinian residents of East Jerusalem from the rest of the
city'.[30] It was part of what was called the 'Jerusalem envelope'
project.[31] It was a strange 'envelope' that could be constructed
out of concrete and steel. Envelopes, of course, are there to be
pushed, and the Jerusalem envelope was no exception: 'Out of
the 130 kilometers of the fence in the Jerusalem area,' *Ha'aretz*
reported, '102 kilometers are on West Bank territory, to a depth
of up to 10 kilometers.'[32]

A further, ingenious trick of Unspeak was employed to
justify the appropriation of land in East Jerusalem: people
whose land was cut in two or entirely annexed were deemed
nifkadim, or 'absentees'. Israeli law had decreed 'absent' anyone
who, during its War of Independence more than half a century
previously, found themselves at any time on Palestinian territory not controlled by Israel or on the land of another Arab
state:

> An absentee was anyone who, on or after 29 November 1947
> (the date of the United Nations General Assembly resolution
> to partition Palestine) [and before 2 December 1948] had been:
> (a) a citizen or subject of one of the Arab countries at war
> with Israel; (b) in any of these countries, or in any part of
> Palestine outside the jurisdiction of the regulations; or (c) a cit-
> izen of Palestine who abandoned his or her normal place of
> residence. Technically, this included virtually all Arabs who
> vacated their homes during the war, regardless of whether

they returned [. . .] [T]ens of thousands of Arab Israeli citizens [were] classified as absentees, assuming the paradoxical legal identity of 'present absentee'.[33]

A fine paradox, 'present absentees' (*nochihim nifkadim*). Though they were right there, they were absent. They were phantoms, unpeople – rather like the CIA's 'ghost detainees', whom we shall meet in Chapter Seven. One such present absentee was a farmer named Johnny Atiq, who in 2004 saw the 'separation barrier' constructed through his olive groves so that 40 trees remained on his side and 150 on the Israeli side. The Israeli army subsequently told him that those trees now belonged to Israel. *Ha'aretz* reported that he was amazed to discover that 'he is an "absentee" living physically 100 metres from his olive trees'.[34]

The phrase 'present absentee', a giddy apex of Unspeak, expresses a wish that the enemy should not even exist. In the same way, Israel's government and press cooperated after the outbreak of the second Intifada in October 2000 in spreading the message that there was 'no partner' for peace negotiations, the continuing existence of Yasser Arafat notwithstanding.[35] Such rhetorical fantasies are common on both sides. The Arab League countries, including Libya and Syria, officially recognised the existence of the state of Israel (within its pre-1967 borders) only in 2002; in 2005 Hamas leader Mahmoud al-Zahar was continuing to insist that 'in the long term Israel will disappear from the face of the earth'.[36] Conversely, some Israelis and supporters of Israeli policy have always refused even to use the term 'Palestinians', preferring simply 'Arabs', because to say 'Palestinians' might already imply that the people so named have some just claim to statehood. Thus, for instance, American preacher Pat Robertson referred contemptuously to 'so-called Palestinians'.[37]

Instead, generalisations were made about 'the Arab'[38] – to name one's enemy in the singular, of course, legitimises collective punishment, for 'the Arab' must be responsible for any act by an individual Arab. Former Israeli Prime Minister Ehud Barak claimed that Arabs could not distinguish between truth and lies: 'They don't suffer from the problem of telling lies that exists in Judeo-Christian culture [. . .] There is no such thing as "the truth".'[39] Essentially, this is to say that all Arab speech is Unspeak; that they do not exist in the civilised continuum represented by 'Judeo-Christian culture', that they are ineffably other. Such epistemological contests were even evident in heated disagreements over what a man's own name meant: Mahmoud Abbas was also called, by Israelis and Palestinians alike, Abu Mazen, but for very different reasons. 'Abu Mazen' means 'father of Mazen', and is a common honorific in Arab societies, where sons are highly prized: it is a 'kunya, a nickname that most often refers specifically to one's offspring'.[40] On the other hand, pro-Israeli commentators routinely referred to 'Abu Mazen' as Abbas's 'nom de guerre',[41] thus darkly hinting that he was or had been involved in acts of terrorism.

If one accepts that one's enemies do in fact exist, perhaps they are disqualified in some subtler way from equal consideration. Israel Zangwill had coined a well-known slogan to promote the founding of Israel in the late nineteenth century: 'A land without a people for a people without a land.'[42] This phrase was often subsequently misquoted in anti-Zionist writings as 'A land without people', missing the indefinite article.[43] This subtle falsification enabled some to make a comparison of early Zionism with the racist attitudes of the colonial English in America and the Dutch in South Africa, to whom native Americans or Africans did not qualify as human beings at all. But in Zangwill's particular slogan, the difference represented in 'without a people' is crucial. The specific claim was not the blatantly false one that the territory was unpopulated, nor that those living there were not human, but that they did not constitute 'a people': in other words, it was argued that they had no conception of nationhood in a modern western sense. Therefore, they would presumably not mind leaving their land and moving to other Arab countries. It was in this sense that Golda Meir, later to be Israel's Prime Minister, told historian Tony Judt in the 1960s that he could not speak of 'Palestinians' since 'they did not exist'.[44] However, the grammar of Meir's formulation shows well the ease with which rhetoric can slip from one claim – long highly contested by Palestinians themselves – about the self-image of a 'people', to another, darker claim, evident in the phrase 'present absentees', about people whose existence one finds uncongenial not really being there at all.

If those living on a piece of land are not really 'a people', or legally not actually there, the land may be considered ripe for 'settlement', another well-entrenched term of Unspeak. Settlement conjures an idea of virgin, unpopulated territory: an image of building log cabins in the wilderness. But the fortified and heavily guarded towns called 'settlements' that Israel built on territory it had occupied since the 1967 war were not all founded on vacant sand dunes. Some began life as purely military outposts;[45] and from 1977 onwards 'settlements' began to be deliberately constructed for strategic purposes in 'heavily populated Palestinian areas', a decision that former Prime Minister Ehud Barak characterised in 2002 as 'a major historical wrong turn' for Israel.[46] The Modern Hebrew term for the 'settlements' in the West Bank and Gaza was *hitnakhlut*, 'a word of biblical origin which means roughly "settling down on one's patrimony"'.[47] The official Arabic term for the 'settlements' was *musTawtanaat*, a neutral term for a collection of dwellings, though some Arabic speakers preferred to call them *Must'amaraat*, which has the sense of colonies established by invaders.[48]

'Settlement' also has a useful secondary sense of 'agreement', but Israeli settlements were deemed illegal by the UN Security Council[49] and the International Court of Justice,[50] opinions that Israel itself, and post-Carter US administrations, refused to accept. While still governor of Texas, George W. Bush had returned from a 1998 helicopter tour of East Jerusalem 'settlements' in the company of Ariel Sharon and said: 'What struck me is the tiny distance between enemy lines and Israel's population centers.'[51] He apparently did not understand that the 'population centers' (another item on the rich menu of euphemism) had been deliberately built that close to 'enemy lines'; that Sharon as foreign minister was telling 'settlers' to 'run, grab hills'.[52] In 2002, attempts were made in the Israeli and US media to delete the shop-soiled euphemism 'settlements' from the lexicon entirely and replace it with the even more euphemistic 'neighbourhoods', where you might indeed expect to see white picket fences.[53]

Road map

A freeze on 'all settlement activity' by the Israelis, as well as a halt to acts of terrorism by the Palestinians, were among the acts demanded of both sides in Phase 1 of the 'road map' to a projected final peace, first so dubbed by George W. Bush in June 2002 and elaborated in an April 2003 document by the quartet of the EU, the US, Russia, and the UN.[54] The course of subsequent events, during which neither side hurried to fulfil its obligations, made clear the way in which this curious metaphor of a 'road map' was all too accurate. For a road map describes a particular territory but does not commit you to going in any particular direction. It does not prevent you from driving around in circles, or stopping off for a prolonged break at a motorway service restaurant. 'Road map' quickly became a general term for any projected solution to a problem. Meanwhile, Palestinians continued to kill Israeli civilians in suicide bombings and rocket attacks, and Israelis continued to shoot stone-throwing teenagers[55] and fire missiles from helicopters in the rough direction of Hamas leaders.[56]

The road map was also sometimes pictured as a vehicle itself. And so, everyone having rapidly agreed that the road map was 'stalled',[57] like a recalcitrant Citroën ('we hit a bump in the road,' Bush later improvised),[58] Ariel Sharon's government unveiled in 2004 a unilateral plan of 'disengagement' from Gaza and a small part of the West Bank. This would entail the evacuation of 9000 'settlers' from a total of 240,000.[59] The neutral sense of the English 'disengagement' mirrored the Modern Hebrew term, *hitnatkut*, although Sharon had originally referred to the plan as *tochnit ha-hafrada*, or 'the separation plan', before realising that 'separation sounded bad, particularly in English, because it evoked apartheid'.[60] During the 'disengagement' in August 2005, all 1500 vacated Israeli homes in Gaza were demolished[61] (though Ehud Barak had promised Yasser Arafat in 1999 that any settlements emptied under a peace agreement would be available to house Palestinians).[62] Israel maintained, meanwhile, that it would keep control over Gaza's airspace, offshore waters, and the majority of its border crossings.[63] Separation would indeed be the effect.

US Department of State spokesman Adam Ereli claimed that the 'disengagement' would be 'a real step forward in advancing the road map'.[64] However, a former chief of Mossad reported that it was 'a way to bypass the road map'.[65] No one, it seemed, could quite agree where this car was heading. In 2004, Sharon's aide Dubi Weissglas had reassured the 'settler' contingent by describing the Gaza plan in the Israeli press as a 'bottle of formaldehyde': 'It supplies the amount of formaldehyde that's necessary so that there will not be a political process with the Palestinians.'[66] The image of formaldehyde, in which dead tissue is preserved, implied the death or erasure of the road map rather than its 'advancement'. Riffing further on the road-map metaphor, Weissglas said: 'The American term is to park conveniently.' Before that interview appeared in full, Weissglas had responded to criticism occasioned by advance publication of some of his comments by changing his story, telling Israel Radio: 'There is no intent [. . .] to freeze the political process. There is a definite intent not to have a peace process with the Palestinian Authority in its present state, with those engaged in mad terror.'[67] But the question of when the Palestinian Authority would no longer be 'in its present state', and so qualify as a negotiating partner, was put off into an indefinite future.

The replacement of Yasser Arafat with Mahmoud Abbas as president in January 2005 did not elicit any official acknowledgment that this 'state' had changed, only the lament that 'Abu Mazen is a disappointment'.[68]

Meanwhile, preparing for the Gaza 'disengagement', Israel cemented its presence in the West Bank by continuing to build new houses there for its Jewish citizens,[69] appealing to a concept of 'natural growth of settlements', as though bulldozers, cranes, and concrete were part of a fertile ecosystem, and even though such 'natural growth' was explicitly disallowed by the road map. According to one Israeli commentator, the problem was that, even by April 2005, 'in Sharon's mind the road map has not yet kicked in, and indeed will not kick in until the Palestinians take the steps they are called upon to take; namely, ending violence and dismantling the terrorist infrastructure'.[70] Israel considered itself in a 'pre-road map' phase,[71] and the Palestinians had to meet all their road-map requirements before Israel met any of its own.[72] After the Gaza 'disengagement', the *New York Times* saluted Sharon's 'statesmanship', expressing the hope that he had given 'a sign of readiness to negotiate'.[73] In fact Sharon had reiterated that he would not halt new building in the West Bank.[74] The road map, it appeared, was still in formaldehyde.

Sir Harold Walker, former UK ambassador to Iraq, explains further: 'Sharon, very often when he says he's committed to the road map, says "We are committed to the road map," then he says, "according to its sequence." Now, that is code. It may mean nothing to the person listening, who thinks it means "We're committed to the road map according to its sequence", but what it means for Sharon is "We're not committed to it; we don't have to do a thing about it, until the Palestinians control their terrorists."'[75] And so the road map became a satiric tango of faux-politeness: you first; no, *you* first. Another useful application, then, of the road-map metaphor: for you may even sit in your car with the engine off, looking sceptically at your road map, before deciding to drive somewhere else entirely.

Sacred space

All this is often justified by a leap into the realm of metaphysics. After the Six-Day War in 1967, one Rabbi Kook Jr. referred to the land occupied by Israel as 'liberated', and explained: 'We are returning to our home, to the inheritance of our ancestors. There is no Arab land here, only the inheritance of our God.'[76] In 2003, Pat Robertson repeated the idea for an American audience: 'God promised the land of Israel to the Jews thousands of years ago. He won't let anyone take it away.' [77] Well now, what can compete with the promises of God? Only, perhaps, the promises of another God. And so it goes. American scholar of the Middle East Juan Cole wrote in 2005 that the route of the barrier through Jerusalem constituted 'land theft on a massive scale [. . .] theft on a stage of sacred space that affects the sentiments of over a billion people. Whether Westerners like it or not, Jerusalem is considered by Muslims their third holiest city, and Israeli theft of the whole thing drives a lot of them up the wall.'[78]

It is unclear whether the image of Muslims being driven up the wall was a heavy joke about refusing to call the barrier a 'fence'; what is more notable is that Cole, in writing approvingly of Muslims' 'sacred space', somehow forgot to mention that the space is allegedly just as 'sacred' to Israel. This kind of talk is just a playground game of My-God-Is-Better-Than-Your-God. Rational observers should have no business endorsing one side's claims of what is 'sacred' in preference to another's. In its most vicious form, this encourages, for example, the resurgence in the Arab Middle East of the blood-libel of the Protocols of the Elders of Zion,[79] or the following words from a 2001 sermon by Rabbi Ovadia Osef: 'May the Holy Name visit retribution on the Arab heads, and cause their seed to be lost, and annihilate them [. . .] It is forbidden to have pity on them. We must give them missiles with relish, annihilate them. Evil ones, damnable ones.'[80] It would be better to refuse to encourage the cynical exploitation of

mythic fictions by demagogues on all sides. The reader, however, may not care to hold her breath until this phenomenon
ceases.

Competing myths of what is sacred tend, further, to encourage the view that a conflict is 'ancient' and so insoluble, as in
this exchange about Israel between Dick Cheney and Larry
King:

> Cheney: You don't want to be pollyannish about it. President
> Clinton's right, this is a very, very tough nugget. These issues
> go back for generations.
> King: Centuries.
> Cheney: Absolutely.[81]

Centuries? Why not go the whole hog and say millennia? In
fact, the 'issues' of land and occupation go back much less far,
most of them having taken their present form in the second
half of the twentieth century. But to acknowledge that might be
to acknowledge the possibility of a political solution. Best to
say it is tragic, epic, sacred, ancient. The associated concept of
a 'cycle of violence', according to which an atrocity by one side
is always represented as a 'reprisal' or 'retaliation' for a previous atrocity by the other, evinces a similar attitude of
helplessness: in the face of an infinite historical regress, when
there is always an event further back in the past to cite as justification, one may feel unable to come to any judgement as to
what should be done now. The media collude in a rhetorical
presentation of the problem as 'intractable'.[82] It is just 'a self-
perpetuating tragedy',[83] and so one's only duty is to express
noble sympathy.

This, indeed, has been a much-exploited rhetorical strategy
by those wishing to do nothing. It has proved useful in many
other situations than Israel–Palestine. Also tragic and with
ancient roots, for example, were developments in the Balkans in
the 1990s, which gave to the world one of the most repugnant
terms of Unspeak yet invented.

Ethnic cleansing

The enemy are filth: removing them is an act of hygiene. So the Nazis spoke when calling the deportations and mass murders of Jews by the name *Säuberungsaktion*, 'cleaning process'. Areas thus voided of Jews were termed *Judenrein*: 'cleaned' or 'purified' of Jews. The organisation which supplied gas to the death camps was called the German Association for the Extermination of Vermin.[84] Similar metaphors were used by others: the fascist Croatian commander Viktor Gutić, in a speech to Franciscan friars in 1941, referred to 'the prearranged, well-calculated plan for cleaning our Croatia of unwanted elements',[85] and a month later referred to 'Serbian dirt'.[86] The verb that Gutić used for 'cleaning', *cisjenje*, was the same as in the Serbo-Croat phrase *etnicko ciscenje*, which was fatefully translated into English in August 1991, when it was reported that Croatian leaders declared that Serbia's aim under Slobodan Milosevic was 'the *ethnic cleansing* of the critical areas that are to be annexed to Serbia'.[87]

'Ethnic cleansing', as the phrase rapidly spread in English, accomplishes several rhetorical tasks. Firstly it reifies a notion of easily distinguishable 'ethnicity'; then it implies that some ethnicities are dirtier or more corrupted than others, that they constitute infectious filth or vermin. The use of 'cleansing', rather than the more normal 'cleaning', has an extra connotation in English of spiritual and not just physical purification. Thomas Cranmer's 1548 Communion Prayer-Book, for example, asked God to 'cleanse the thoughts of our hearts',[88] and it is probably this implication of virtue that leads modern cosmetics companies to advertise 'cleansing products': washing one's face is next to godliness. This imputation is made clearer still in one of the French versions of the euphemism, *purification ethnique*, where 'purifying' has an inescapably metaphysical aspect. Thus to engage in 'ethnic cleansing' is an act of not just physical but also moral hygiene.

To use the phrase 'ethnic cleansing' oneself is to acquiesce in each hateful stage of this argument. To call 'ethnic cleansing' the mass murders, rapes, concentration camps, and other horrors of the former Yugoslavia in the early 1990s was to reinforce the perpetrators' scheme of self-justification. So much was evident to some observers very early on. Jean de Courten of the Red Cross referred carefully to 'so-called "ethnic cleansing"' in an address to the UN in 1992.[89] Shortly afterwards, the UN General Assembly made its position clear, referring in a resolution to the 'ethnic cleansing' committed by Serb forces in Bosnia-Herzegovina, using the phrase always in scare quotes, and culminating in a reference to 'the abhorrent policy of "ethnic cleansing", which is a form of genocide'.[90]

Genocide was the elephant in the room that the US and Britain, along with many other countries, did not want to acknowledge. For signatories to the 1948 UN Genocide Convention, in which the word was first legally defined, were bound immediately to intervene, with force if necessary, when genocide was determined to be occurring. Such intervention in the former Yugoslavia was considered politically undesirable by those most able to perform it. And so it was necessary to deny that genocide was happening. Luckily, there was this phrase 'ethnic cleansing' lying around: so the enemy euphemism was blithely adopted and used regularly by the Bush and then Clinton administrations, and the Major government, in order to express a certain amount of disapproval while justifying the decision to do nothing to stop it.[91] The adoption of the phrase 'ethnic cleansing', in short, constituted verbal collaboration in mass murder.

This was made easier by a widespread misunderstanding, or deliberate falsification, of what 'genocide' actually meant. It was regularly assumed or stated that it meant nothing less than a programme of mass killing on the scale of the Holocaust: that millions of murders, systematically performed, were necessary to justify the label of 'genocide'. This was simply false, as anyone knew who actually consulted the text of the Genocide Convention. Its Article 2 reads:

[G]enocide means any of the following acts committed with
intent to destroy, in whole or in part, a national, ethnical, racial
or religious group, as such:

(a) Killing members of the group;
(b) Causing serious bodily or mental harm to members of the
group;
(c) Deliberately inflicting on the group conditions of life cal-
culated to bring about its physical destruction in whole or
in part;
(d) Imposing measures intended to prevent births within the
group;
(e) Forcibly transferring children of the group to another
group.[92]

The clear intent of 'in whole or in part', as well as the enu-
meration of crimes that were not murders, was that genocide
did not mean only monstrous acts on the scale of the Holocaust:
indeed, if the signatory nations were to wait until millions of
killings had been committed, the Convention would be useless,
since its function was explicitly to 'prevent' genocide from happening. This, moreover, is the reason why the term 'genocide'
itself was chosen by the Convention's drafters instead of
another proposed term, 'extermination', because the latter
would have, as one of the framers noted, 'limit[ed] the prohibited crime to circumstances where every member of the group
was killed'.[93] General Radislav Krstic, one of the Bosnian Serb
commanders who oversaw the deliberate massacre of more
than 7000 Bosnian Muslims at Srebrenica in 1995, did not succeed in killing every Bosnian Muslim man, woman, and child;
nevertheless, he was convicted of genocide by the International
Criminal Tribunal for the Former Yugoslavia. The conviction
was later reduced to that of 'aiding and abetting in genocide',
owing to legal tergiversations over the concept of 'intent'; but
the word 'genocide' remained.[94]

A further effect of the euphemisation of genocidal crimes
under the heading 'ethnic cleansing' was, very cunningly, to

imply that one kind of act not specifically mentioned in the Genocide Convention – mass deportation – was the only process that 'ethnic cleansing' denoted. In other words, if you first accept the covering up of murder and other violent acts by the term 'ethnic cleansing' and grant that phrase an autonomous legitimacy, you may later read back into the phrase 'ethnic cleansing' only a less violent kind of crime. Linguist Ranko Bugarski noted that *'ethnic cleansing* [. . .] was replaced in some negotiations between Serbian and Croatian leaders with the improbable expression *humane transfer of populations'* – which decision would seem to be an acknowledgement that 'ethnic cleansing' was understood by both sides to cover rather more actions than a simple 'transfer', humane or otherwise.[95] As London School of Economics professor of international relations Fred Halliday points out:

> The word 'cleansing' has a sinister polysemic character, appearing to stop short of killing or genocide, with mere displacement, but also echoing the twentieth-century word 'purge' – a euphemism, as in Soviet Russia, for mass murder. In all of these cases a significant proportion of those 'cleansed' were actually killed, not least to encourage the others to leave.[96]

Reading 'ethnic cleansing' only as displacement was the fallacy to which Brent Scowcroft, George H. W. Bush's National Security Advisor, appealed when he described the situation in retrospect: 'In Bosnia, I think, we all got ethnic cleansing mixed up with genocide. To me they are different terms. The horror of them is similar, but the purpose is not. Ethnic cleansing is not "I want to destroy an ethnic group, wipe it out." It's "They're not going to live with us. They can live where they like, but not with us."'[97] In fact, in all too many cases, 'ethnic cleansing' really meant 'They're not going to *live*', full stop.

Part of the problem may have been that 'genocide' itself was too successful a word. The man who coined it, lawyer Raphael

Lemkin, had deliberately engineered it so as to sound as powerful as possible, to connect 'the word', as he wrote in one of his
notebooks, inextricably to a 'moral judgement', to make it an
'index of civilization'.[98] And though it was subsequently
defined by the UN so as to include crimes of much lesser scale
than the Holocaust, its etymology kept alive the opposite implication: from *genus* (race, kind) and *caedere* (cut, kill), it seemed
to picture the annihilation of an entire kind. Indeed this was
how Lemkin himself had first defined it in 1944: 'By "genocide" we mean the destruction of a nation or of an ethnic
group.'[99] This tension between what the word 'genocide'
itself seemed to imply and its actual legal definition in the
Genocide Convention, made genocide-denial eminently possible. Continuing arguments over the mass slaughter of nearly
one million Armenians in Turkey in 1915,[100] which had inspired
Hitler's 'Final Solution' ('Who today still speaks of the massacre of the Armenians?' he asked in 1939),[101] followed the
same pattern. Many decades later, the Turkish government
would allow only talk of 'incidents'[102] or 'events'.[103] In 2004,
historian Norman Stone wrote from Ankara to the *Times Literary
Supplement* to deny 'Armenian nationalist claims that a "genocide" as classically defined had taken place'.[104] Of course there
existed no 'classical' definition of this twentieth-century word.
In fact, Lemkin had been inspired to begin his campaign for
the criminalisation of genocide precisely by the suffering of the
Armenians.[105]

In a kind of rhetorical pincer movement, meanwhile,
recourse to the term 'genocide' had been discouraged in Serbia
itself by a campaign to cheapen the word and render it empty
through overuse:

> The word *genocide* was bandied about so much in preparation
> for the revision of history that its meaning simply evapo-
> rated [. . .] As a consequence it became possible to describe the
> death of a few soldiers as *local genocide*, and on Sarajevo TV a
> person was said to have committed *genocide and even theft*.

Perhaps most tellingly, a poster at a Belgrade gathering of angry clients of a savings bank gone bankrupt appealed to 'Stop the genocide over our pockets!'[106]

'Genocide' was thus stretched to breaking point in both directions: with some using it to denote small-scale crimes and others demanding it be reserved only for a new Holocaust, it became very difficult to use the word according to its true meaning. Thus was created the semantic space into which the brutal euphemisers and their apologists eagerly leapt with 'ethnic cleansing'.

The phenomenon was to recur during international discussions about Rwanda, where in 1994, 800,000 people were murdered, mostly with machetes, in the space of a hundred days. US officials made lamenting noises about 'ethnic cleansing'; again the word 'genocide' was avoided since it was thought to imply a duty to intervene. That a rapid enlightenment as to what was actually going on was possible is evident from the experience of Roméo Dallaire, commander of the UN peacekeeping forces in Rwanda at the time, whose repeated warnings were ignored by Washington. He told author Samantha Power:

> To us in the West, 'genocide' was the equivalent of the Holocaust or the killing fields of Cambodia. I mean millions of people. 'Ethnic cleansing' seemed to involve hundreds of thousands of people. 'Genocide' was the highest scale of crimes against humanity imaginable. It was so far up there, so far off the charts, that it was not easy to recognize that *we* could be in such a situation.[107]

Then, Dallaire said, he looked up the text of the Genocide Convention itself. 'I realised that genocide was when an attempt was made to eliminate a specific group, and this is precisely what we saw in the field ... I just needed a slap in the face to say, "Holy shit! This is genocide, not just ethnic cleansing."'

President Clinton and his advisers, however, either were not given such slaps in the face or were blessed with impressively thick skin.

Such confusion of terminology persists in those who lack the initiative displayed by Dallaire to find out for himself, or want deliberately to muddy the waters. In 2003, Michael Ignatieff administered a sorrowful slap on the wrist to a perpetrator of genocide by writing: '[Slobodan] Milosevic [. . .] was wrong in believing that he could use any means, including attempted genocide and ethnic cleansing, to repress' the Kosovars.[108] First, 'wrong' reduces Milosevic's crimes to the category of a mistake; second, the idea of 'attempted genocide' betrays the erroneous opinion that genocide is total destruction, and ignorance of the fact that any 'attempt' at such destruction already constitutes genocide; and third, the addition of 'and ethnic cleansing' perpetuates the euphemistic falsehood that this is a separate and lesser category of crime. In fact, 'ethnic cleansing' never became a recognised crime in international law. The 2002 Rome Statute of the International Criminal Court nowhere uses the vicious term, speaking only of 'genocide' and other 'crimes against humanity'.

Nonetheless, the pattern seemed to be repeating itself once again in the international response to the genocide in the Darfur region of Sudan. In April 2004, the UN Under-Secretary-General for Humanitarian Affairs, Jan Egeland, described the situation as one of 'ethnic cleansing'.[109] UN Secretary-General Kofi Annan was even more fastidious, claiming only that it was 'bordering on ethnic cleansing'.[110] But then a strange thing happened. A US Congress resolution in July stated explicitly that 'genocide' was happening in Darfur; then Secretary of State Colin Powell used the term; and George W. Bush himself called Darfur a 'genocide' in a speech to the UN.[111]

What happened next? Faced with an actually occurring humanitarian crisis of far greater gravity than had been invoked to justify the 2003 invasion of Iraq, the US did nothing. Sudan's military-intelligence establishment was, after all, an ally of the

CIA, who flew its chief to Washington for secret meetings.[112] Noting that the US statements had not necessitated any forceful intervention, other officials, such as the German defence minister and the British Foreign Secretary, felt free to follow suit in deploring the 'genocide' so as to demonstrate their noble ethical standards.[113] By early 2005, it was estimated that more than 300,000 people had died in Darfur;[114] the international response had been to dispatch about 700 troops of the African Union, in order 'to monitor a nonexistent ceasefire'.[115]

And so the word 'genocide', long taboo since it was thought to confer an automatic duty to act, was now shown to have no magical power. In finally using the word officially and denying any consequential obligations under the 1948 Convention, the West had perhaps killed 'genocide' once and for all.

Biblical proportions

The genocides in Bosnia and Rwanda, apart from being misdescribed in the most sinister and disingenuous manner as 'ethnic cleansing', were also blamed, in further handwashing rhetoric, on something dark and interior to victims and perpetrators alike. Bill Clinton alluded to the Yugoslavian crisis in his 1993 inaugural address with the phrase 'ancient hatreds'.[116] His Secretary of State, Warren Christopher, spoke the next month of a 'cauldron of ancient ethnic hatreds' in the Balkans;[117] later that year, Clinton saw him and raised him by speaking of 'many' such 'cauldrons of ethnic, religious, and territorial animosity' in an address to the UN.[118] What do you do with a cauldron? You certainly don't jump in, since you would just be cooked along with its contents. You put a lid on it, perhaps, and hope it simmers down.

A cauldron is also often said to belong to a witch: it speaks of black magic, bubbling evil. It was therefore a metaphysical problem, not a political one. In a cauldron, too, the ingredients are all mixed up together, boiling away: thus one could avoid distinguishing between perpetrators and victims. Meanwhile, the concept of 'ancient ethnic hatreds' argued that such 'hatreds' could somehow persist in an entire people across centuries: passing down from one generation to the next, in the blood, in the very DNA. It is an image of racial disease, of contamination, and so fits right in with the hate-speech of 'ethnic cleansing'. Racist connotations were even more blatantly in evidence when the genocide in Rwanda was ascribed to 'ancient tribal hatreds'.[119] In fact, numerous authoritative studies have shown that, in both the former Yugoslavia and Rwanda, fear, racial hatred, and hysteria were deliberately and systematically whipped up by governments and the media.[120] Bugarski comments: '[I]t was only through the protracted and vicious abuse of language in the service of propaganda and war that a sufficient amount of interethnic hatred could be generated to make traditionally good neighbors – indeed, frequently members of the same ethnically mixed family! – get at each other's throats.'[121] Never mind that, though. Sporadic battles and atrocities in the past could be knitted together into a homogeneous narrative of 'ancient conflict'. Evidently, hatred coursed through the veins of entire peoples. 'Slowly the poison the whole blood stream fills [. . .] The waste remains, the waste remains and kills.'[122]

Ancient, bloody and insoluble? It must be a 'tragedy'. So indeed they spoke. Clinton's Secretary of Defense, William Perry, said in 1995 that Bosnia was a 'tragedy', 'a place where paradise and innocence ended long ago'.[123] The remarkable language, alluding to the story of the Fall in Genesis, could mean nothing other than that the sufferings of those being murdered, raped, and tortured far away were their own fault: the result of some original sin, for which they had been expelled from the Garden of Eden. Similarly, Perry called the genocide in Rwanda 'a human tragedy of Biblical proportions'.[124] Surely it would be tragic hubris for mere humans to intervene in a Biblical tragedy, which plays out according to the mysterious plans of God himself. Only at the end of August 1995, after the renewed siege of

Sarajevo and the massacre at Srebrenica had made inaction politically untenable, did Nato intervene forcefully in Bosnia.

Subsequently, the situation appeared to be repeating itself in Kosovo: this 'tragedy', it seemed, would not die. What kind of power could finally overcome its ancient, sacred, inexorable force? Only an even more sacred force. And so it was that, in an irony not lost on those who loathed the Milosevic regime but were not sure that long-range bombing which destroyed much civilian infrastructure was the best possible remedy,[125] the 1999 Nato military action in Kosovo was christened 'Merciful Angel'. Clearly, an 'angel' trumps any earthly debates about genocide or 'ethnic cleansing': the latter may safely be forgotten, while we bask in the radiating image of heaven-sent deliverance. All kinds of cognitive dissonance may be resolved, indeed, with a finely tooled operation name.

5

Operations

Just Cause

It was known by the planning nickname 'Blue Spoon'. Panamanian dictator Manuel Noriega, formerly a valued employee of the CIA, had annulled the results of the May 1989 election and, in December, announced that a state of war existed with the US. The next day, Panama forces shot dead a US Marine not in uniform. President George H. W. Bush decided to invade the country. The attack began on 20 December. Noriega hid in the Vatican Embassy, at which US forces blasted deafening rock music. He surrendered on 3 January. The name for this little war, announced to the US public after it had begun, was Operation Just Cause.

Thus was inaugurated the contemporary strain of propaganda in which military adventures are given self-justifying public names. The original SOUTHCOM operation nickname, Blue Spoon, did not really mean anything. You might take a long spoon to sup with the devil, but why a blue one? In fact there was a whole series of military exercises and operations beginning with the term 'blue', including Blue Crab and Blue Tiger.[1] But Just Cause was obviously different. No reasonable individual could be against a 'just cause': the question of whether the invasion of Panama really was a just cause would, it was hoped, be shut down in advance by its very name. Since no authorisation for the invasion had been sought or granted

from the UN Security Council, it was perhaps even more necessary to describe it unilaterally as 'just'. The stated objectives of
the war included to arrest and extradite Noriega on drug
charges (despite the Drug Enforcement Agency having praised
him, just three years previously, for his 'vigorous anti-drug traf-
ficking policy'), and the old standby, to restore freedom to the
citizens of the country being invaded. Some commentators,
though, noticed that on 1 January 1990, a large part of the
administration of the Panama Canal, so important to US trade,
was due to be handed over to Panama itself, and wondered
whether perhaps the US government's action was driven by
eagerness to install a government friendly to its own interests.[2]
However, American TV news programmes enthusiastically
adopted the phrase 'Just Cause' to denote the events,[3] and the
pleasant sense of righteousness induced by this slogan worked
to drown out criticism, which was dismissed irritably by one
columnist as 'this static on the left'.[4]

Operation Just Cause was the first US combat operation since
the Korean War whose public name was chosen specifically 'to
shape domestic and international perceptions about the mission it designated',[5] according to military historian Gregory
Sieminski. But the importance of the right mission name – and
the negative publicity effects of the wrong one – had been
known long before. In January 1966, the US 1st Cavalry Division
began an operation in Vietnam that had the codename 'Masher',
the idea being to sweep across a plain and crush the enemy
against waiting Marines. Unfortunately the name 'Masher' was
widely reported in the US media, and a furious Lyndon B.
Johnson complained that it did not connote the right 'pacifica-
tion emphasis'. General William Westmoreland, who was two
years later to convene a 'nuclear study group' to see if he could
drop an atomic bomb on a North Vietnamese division,[6]
enlarged on Johnson's reasoning, explaining that 'the connotation of violence' in the codename Masher 'provided a focus for
carping war critics'. The operation was rapidly renamed 'White
Wing'.[7] Since white wings are traditionally supposed to belong

to angels, or doves of peace, those annoying 'connotations of violence' were effectively whitewashed. The poignant hope that this little coup of Unspeak would quiet the carping war critics proved, however, to be a vain one. Similarly, the mere fact that Israel called its 1982 invasion of Lebanon by the name Operation Peace in Galilee did not succeed in persuading all onlookers that peace was its true motive.

Winston Churchill is credited with naming the Normandy landings in the Second World War Operation Overlord, perhaps the most thrilling and morale-enhancing military nickname ever devised, for an invasion that had originally been planned under the far-from-inspirational name Roundhammer.[8] The doubling of power terms – not just a lord but an *over*lord – perhaps conveyed the idea that, though the Nazis were currently 'lords' of Europe, they would have to submit to a superior authority. (The choice of a phrase that expressed the desired outcome was subsequently copied, less cleverly, in actions such as the 1993 US mission in Somalia, called Operation Restore Hope. A sort of magical thinking, according to which names are destiny, was severely injured in that operation's disastrous end.) Churchill later set out his own rules for naming operations, among which is this: 'Operations in which large numbers of men may lose their lives ought not to be described by code words which imply a boastful or overconfident sentiment.'[9] Perhaps Overlord itself breaks that stricture, but it might be thought a forgivable instance.

Later givers of names, however, ignored Churchill's warning against hubris altogether. For the first Gulf War, General Norman Schwarzkopf chose the boring name Peninsula Shield. Then someone noticed that this might imply that the intent was simply to protect Saudi oil rather than to liberate Kuwait, and so the name was changed to Desert Shield, and finally Desert Storm.[10] With 'Storm', the US-led coalition painted itself as an irresistible force of nature before which all resistance would be annihilated, a posture that Churchill might well have called 'boastful'. The second Iraq war, meanwhile, was for a time

called Operation Iraqi Liberation,[11] until an eagle-eyed func-
tionary spotted that this spelled OIL. It certainly would not do
to encourage a new generation of carping war critics to suppose
that the opportunity to wean itself off dependence on Saudi oil
figured in US strategic calculations. So the name was hastily
changed to Operation Iraqi Freedom, thereby avoiding the link
to black gold but keeping the handy implication that the only
reason for the invasion was a purely philanthropic one. (The
ramifications of exporting 'freedom' to Iraq will be examined
more thoroughly in Chapter Eight.)

The naming of operations in the twenty-first century has represented an apex of selective justification and jingoism.
CENTCOM originally dubbed the US invasion of Afghanistan
Operation Infinite Justice, until Muslims pointed out that,
according to their religion, only Allah could dispense infinite
justice.[12] It was changed to Operation Enduring Freedom,
another phrase expressing a wish as to the result: for who could
be certain at the operation's start that the 'freedom', whether it
was supposed to belong to Americans or Afghans, would
indeed endure? It also contained a grammatical ambiguity that
proved rather a hostage to fortune. You could read it as meaning
that the freedom brought to Afghanistan by US troops was
something to be endured rather than enjoyed: the same kind of
pun as had previously been exploited in, for example, the title
of Ian McEwan's novel, *Enduring Love*. Human Rights Watch
appropriated the phrase in this ironical way in its report
'Enduring Freedom', about the excessive violence practised by
American forces in Afghanistan.[13] By contrast, the British military, once notable for its sick sense of humour – a mine-laying
operation in Yemen in 1964 had been dubbed Operation
Eggshell[14] – was now rather more subtle. UK involvement in
Enduring Freedom was given the classily classical name
Operation Veritas. Did calling it by the Latin for 'truth' mean
that the intent was to find out the truth, or that the British were
going along with it because its public justification – that Al
Qaeda operated in Afghanistan – was on this occasion true?

Any notion of certitude about truth or freedom was absent from the British involvement in the subsequent war in Iraq, which was called Operation Telic. From the Greek *telos*, meaning end or purpose, the effect of Telic was perhaps to say that there was indeed a purpose in invading that country, while remaining agnostic as to what that purpose actually was, and looking forward to the day when the purpose was accomplished and forces could be withdrawn.

Public American names for actions in occupied Iraq showed no such reserve, but seemed rather to increase in bellicosity as the situation deteriorated. Operations Iron Hammer or Resolute Sword had a 'punitive' ring, wrote former British minister Robin Cook, implying 'that even senior officers [saw] their objective as intimidating Iraqis rather than winning them over'.[15] There were, moreover, unfortunate echoes: Iron Hammer was the exact English equivalent of *Eisenhammer*, a Luftwaffe plan to destroy Soviet generators in 1943.[16]

Operation names in the 'war on terror' as a whole followed a pattern of rhetorical inflation and inevitably diminishing returns: what Churchill would have criticised merely as 'boastful and overconfident' gave way to names that were in danger of spiralling into pure nonsense. Operation Epic Fury was an intelligence operation supporting Enduring Freedom:[17] if it hoped to borrow the glamour of Homer's Achilles, the exemplar of epic fury, it may be supposed that the namer did not remember that the Greek hero's rage was inspired by the death of his male lover, since the US military was not noted for its enlightened attitude towards homosexuality. Meanwhile, an Army project to provide portable electronic devices adopted the brash biblical allusion of the name Genesis II[18] (the codename Genesis I is not recorded, presumably reserved for the divine operation that created the universe; the sequel was thus of similarly cosmic importance); and an 'advanced concept technology demonstration' in 2001–2 was christened Krimson Sword,[19] which recalled, no doubt by tasteless accident, the Ku Klux Klan's habit of spelling as many words as possible with an initial K. (It is particularly strange to remember, in the age of the 'war on terror', that white supremacists call their bible the Kloran.)

Operation names, wrote Churchill sternly, 'ought not to be names of a frivolous character [. . .] They should not be ordinary words often used in other connections.'[20] In reading through William Arkin's *Code Names*, a massive compendium of both public 'nicknames' and classified codenames used by the US in recent decades, one sees that the sheer number of operations indulged in by that country after the Second World War eventually rendered these rules unworkable. A more relaxed attitude was possible, too, in choosing names that were not intended to be released to the public. Patent absurdities among these include Comfy Sword, Utopian Angel, Flexible Anvil, and even, for a Marine exercise in Saudi Arabia, Infinite Anvil, on which one perhaps makes shoes for infinitely large horses. Occasionally, too, one must suspect deliberate mischief. A 1990s rocket-launch programme was awarded the somewhat rococo designation Zodiac Beauchamp, perhaps as a tribute to rock band Zodiac Mindwarp and the Love Reaction, whose 2003 live album was named *Weapons of Mass Destruction*. A joint US–United Arab Emirate exercise in 1999 was given the name Iron Fist, possibly by a PlayStation-owning military joker, since Iron Fist is the name of a post-apocalyptic martial-arts tournament in the popular game series Tekken.[21] And there can be no possibility of coincidence with the name of a US–German air-combat exercise in 2001: it was called Millennium Falcon.[22] Well, if you're going to name a missile-defence project Star Wars, as Ronald Reagan did in the 1980s, why not go the whole hog? Osama bin Laden can be Darth Vader. Still, the name was an odd choice in this context: for in *Star Wars*, the *Millennium Falcon* was a smuggler ship that aided a small band of rebels in defeating a mighty military empire. Surely some mistake?

By mid-2005, however, there were signs that America's public operation names, having run the gamut of enraged hammers, vengeful anvils, and infinite furies, had begun to shout themselves hoarse. Perhaps the budding of a new, more lovable strain of propaganda was evident in the name for the newest stage of Operation Iraqi Freedom. As part of the battle for 'hearts and minds' in the occupied country, US pilots were instructed to drop parachute-wearing cuddly toys on to the streets of Baghdad. It was announced as Operation Teddy Drop.[23]

Surgical strike

An 'operation' can also be a surgical procedure, and indeed this medical sense predates the military usage by nearly four hundred years.[24] It is not certain that the first uses of the word in its modern military sense in the early eighteenth century were the result of a conscious borrowing from medical language, however, since other, more thematically neutral meanings of 'operation' – functioning, work, practical action – were already available. But in phrases such as 'surgical strike', which became a slogan of the Gulf War in 1991, the language of war clearly appropriated medical vocabulary. Why should this be so? It is possible to consider surgery in terms of physical intervention with saws, scalpels, and needles, a form of violence that serves a greater good: hurting some parts of the body so as to restore the whole to health. If surgery is a war against disease or dysfunction, it is the ideal example of a just war. No bleeding-heart liberal is on the side of the bacillus. To turn the metaphor around and use images and terms from medicine in describing actual war could in this way have the effect of justifying the military action in question.

Three specific implications arise from the use of the metaphor 'surgical' for military activity. The first is that the attack is precise. Just as we hope a surgeon will perform a procedure with the minimum possible damage to surrounding tissue, a 'surgical strike' is presumably one that is perfectly targeted and practises restraint, using the least amount of violence necessary to achieve the objective. The military metaphor usefully conflates precision with delicacy, the latter being a quality which few missiles possess. Even if a 500-pound bomb is 'surgical' in that it lands within centimetres of its intended target, it will spray indiscriminate destruction far and wide. The second, related implication is that, since modern surgery is performed on the unconscious, anaesthetised body, a 'surgical strike' will cause no pain or suffering.

The *Oxford English Dictionary*'s first recorded reference to 'a so-called "surgical" strike' is in the context of John F. Kennedy's government debating whether to launch an immediate air attack on the Cuban missile sites in 1962.[25] It subsequently became a common euphemism in Vietnam, where, according to one writer, 'surgical strike' meant 'chasing and mowing down peasants from the air by spraying them with 8,000 bullets a minute'.[26] The US bombing of Libya in 1986 was announced as a 'surgical strike':[27] bombs landed on Qaddafi's compound (killing his three-year-old adopted daughter), on a naval training school, on the French Embassy, and on a residential neighbourhood in Tripoli, killing an entire family and many others.[28] In all more than a hundred civilians were killed, perhaps to be written off as complications arising from surgery, or the result of a regrettable iatrogenic ('caused by the doctor') illness. Subsequently, the rhetoric of 'surgical strikes' was employed widely in the 1991 Gulf War, and television news outlets eagerly replayed the videogame-style missile's-eye-view clips of weaponry whizzing around city corners as though they represented the entire arsenal; the Pentagon later revealed that a mere 7 per cent of the ordnance dropped on Iraq was made up of the kind of guided bombs that could be accurately targeted.[29] Nonetheless, the operation had certainly worked to restore health, if only to Americans themselves: President George H. W. Bush announced that the success of his war had cured the 'Vietnam syndrome'.[30]

But 'surgical strike' has a third implication, this time about who the targets are. If the attack is surgery, it follows that what is being attacked is disease. The enemy are no longer human beings, but an impersonal sickness that must be eradicated by whatever means necessary. This idea has its forebears in talk of 'sanitising' targets in Vietnam, and the description of Jews as vermin or virus in Nazi Germany, along with that regime's euphemism of 'cleaning' for mass murder, which later transmuted into the abominable phrase 'ethnic cleansing'. Put this notion together with the concept of surgery and you are, it seems, irresistibly drawn to the modern version of such dehumanising language, which is to say that the enemy is a cancer. 'We need to make a decision on when the cancer of Fallujah needs to be cut out,'[31] a senior US officer was reported as saying in September 2004, which remark was characteristic of much rhetoric in the second Iraq war.

One reason why cancer is the epitome of frightening disease is because a tumour may spread, or 'metastatise', to different places in the body. Thus, to designate as a 'cancer' a group of enemies is already to make an argument about the urgent necessity for taking forceful action now, since the problem will only get worse later. Cancerous cells are those that have forgotten how to die: it is the job of the army to remind them. Both communism and terrorism had been routinely described as 'cancers' since the 1980s for this reason: if unchecked, it was implied, they were likely to creep silently around the world. And use of cancer imagery, along with an updated version of the Nazi infection trope, is common in contemporary apocalyptic anti-Semitism, such as the claim by Gaza cleric Ibrahim Mdaires that 'the entire Islamic nation was lost because Israel is a cancer spreading through the body of the Islamic nation, and because Jews are a virus resembling AIDS, from which the entire world suffers'.[32] This example shows how the rhetorical use of cancer imagery itself can metastatise, eventually abandoning all pretence at 'surgical' restraint. In March 2003, after Marines machine-gunned at least twelve civilians who were trying to cross a bridge in Iraq, one of the Marines told a reporter: 'The Iraqis are sick people and we are the chemotherapy. I am

starting to hate this country. Wait till I get hold of a friggin'
Iraqi. No, I won't get hold of one. I'll just kill him.'[33]

In the remark about the 'cancer of Fallujah', the sickness had
been pictured as a containable part that could be excised, leaving the rest of the population healthy. But the Marine's image
considered 'the Iraqis' in general to be 'sick people', the sickness
was cancer, and the Marines were the drugs that would cure the
Iraqis by killing them. (To a physician, chemotherapy means
any treatment with drugs, but it is used by the public to refer to
cancer treatment. As it happens, cancer chemotherapy originated when it was noticed that the chemical weapon mustard
gas, used offensively in the First World War, attacked white
blood cells; in the 1940s, physicians began testing it on patients
with advanced lymphomas.[34]) The soldier was speaking extem-
pore, and was clearly shocked by the first-ever suicide bombing
recorded in Iraq the previous week; but his style of thinking was
reflected in the more deliberate pronouncements of senior officers and commanders, and its logical endpoint was that a
perfectly healthy Iraq would be one with no Iraqis left. The run-
away nihilism of such imagery is comparable to the famous
(though perhaps apocryphal) comment attributed to a US official in the Vietnam war: 'It became necessary to destroy the
village in order to save it.'

While describing their operations as cancer treatment, US
and British forces were conducting a rather poorly controlled
form of radiotherapy by firing hundreds of thousands of shells
made of 'depleted uranium'.[35] This name itself is a term of
Unspeak, implying that it is considerably safer or weaker than
naturally occurring uranium: in fact both are mainly constituted
of uranium-238; 'depleted' uranium is only depleted in that it
contains about half the amount of the highly radioactive fissile
isotope uranium-235.[36] It is what is left over after the processing
of uranium for nuclear fuel; it may also be 'contaminated' with
uranium-236 and plutonium. In 2000, the US Energy Secretary
admitted that thousands of workers at one of the main US
depleted-uranium manufacturing plants in Paducah, Kentucky,

had suffered 'cancer and early death'.[37] Ammunition made from depleted uranium, first used in the Gulf War when between 300 and 800 tons of it were deposited on Iraq,[38] gives off highly toxic dust particles on impact which 'can be blown around and inhaled by civilians for years to come'.[39] It has been blamed for a tenfold increase in birth defects and cancers in areas of Iraq where its use was concentrated in 1991.[40] Inducing cancer in the Iraqi population would certainly be a novel means of curing it.

One journalist finessed the imagery of disease by hiding it in a term of jargon with which few readers could have been familiar, reporting in April 2004 how forces had begun 'debriding Fallujah of its guerrillas'.[41] Debriding, more properly 'débridement', means 'the removal from a wound, etc., of damaged tissue or foreign matter';[42] or 'the surgical removal of lacerated, devitalized, or contaminated tissue'.[43] Thus the guerrillas in the town of Fallujah represented 'damaged' or 'contaminated' tissue, or even 'devitalized', a synonym for necrotic or dead tissue. If they were indeed already considered dead, then the surgical procedure would be a simple matter of clearing away dead matter for the good of the town as a whole. The implements chosen for this delicate operation included helicopter-fired missiles and '500-pound GBU-12 laser-guided bombs'[44] launched from fighter aircraft. Marines blocked the roads leading to the city's only two hospitals:[45] metaphorical surgery was the only acceptable kind. Subsequent estimates of the number of Iraqis killed by the 'debriding' ranged from 264 to 600.[46] Even so, it was considered necessary to conduct another assault on that city eight months later, whose code-name, Operation Phantom Fury (more *Star Wars* echoes), showed no residual trace of surgical care.

One purpose of débridement is to prevent an infection taking hold: so, like the image of cancer, its use in a military context represents a fear of the spread of disease. For other purposes, however, it may be useful to claim that the spread has already happened: that the infection is system-wide, and so all measures

may be justified in order to save the patient. In this way Daniel
Senor, a senior adviser to the Coalition Provisional Authority,
defended the attack on Fallujah by saying: 'It is critical that we
cleanse the Iraqi body politic of the poison that remains here
after 35 years of Saddam Hussein's totalitarian rule.'[47] This
remarkable image had clearly been agreed at the top, for in the
same week CPA chief Paul Bremer had said on NBC: 'There is
a lot of poison built up in the Iraqi body politic.'[48] The 'body
politic' was a much-worked-over image in medieval and Ren-
aissance thinking, often used to furnish a 'natural' justification
for emerging ideas of the nation, its parts all working in harmony. This standard image is offered, for example, by a citizen
in Shakespeare's *Coriolanus*: 'The kingly crowned head, the vigilant eye, / The counsellor heart, the arm our soldier, / Our
steed the leg, the tongue our trumpeter.'[49] Now, to say that Iraq
in 2004 actually had a 'body politic' was more wish than fact.
Nonetheless, if it existed, and if it was poisoned, it was no doubt
necessary, as Coriolanus himself had insisted before the sena-
tors, 'To jump a body with a dangerous physic / That's sure of
death without it.'[50]

Terrific service

If the military appropriation of medical language serves to de-
humanise the enemy and recast war as the restoration of health,
another purpose is served by borrowings from the vocabulary
of bureaucracy. An example is furnished by the accounce-
ment that May 2005 in the US would be Military Spouse
Appreciation Month:

> Military Spouse Appreciation Month is this month, and there
> will be some announcements and some other activities associ-
> ated with that tomorrow and through the weekend. We,
> obviously, always talk about how we recruit soldiers, sailors,
> airmen and Marines, but we retain families, and we retain

families largely because of military spouses and the terrific service that they provide as well. We honor them, and this is the month where we will be taking particular time to honor them.[51]

Why exactly are military spouses so wonderful? Because of 'the terrific service that they provide'. Now, 'service' originally meant the condition of being a servant, and from its earliest appearances in the thirteenth century, it was also used in the sense of obeisance to a supernatural master, God.[52] So a gathering in a church was also called a service. From here the word was extended to the notion of fealty and righteous service to a king (ruling, after all, by divine right), then to loyalty to his army, then to the country as a whole. So the almost sacred idea of 'service' in the military, particularly in the modern US, has its roots in the religious meaning. But the military spouses being celebrated above are not said to be in service in this sense; they are instead *providing* a 'terrific service'. To do someone a service has long meant simply to do a favour, but to provide a service is different: it is a specifically commercial usage in the modern idiom, not recorded before the twentieth century.[53] (In 1919, a *Ladies' Home Journal* article explained to its readers the new-fangled concept of 'self-service' in a New York department store's grocery section: 'the customers, not the store, provide the service.')[54] Even if we refrain also from pointing out that 'to service' also means 'to have sex with', the notion of soldiers' wives and husbands as service providers, offering valuable logistical support, is an illuminating example of the military's instrumentalist view of human beings, even those human beings who have not volunteered specifically to be instruments.

In the same way, the service (the military) as a whole may be recast as a service industry. Missiles and aircraft are 'force packages'[55] and 'delivery systems', as though the US Air Force were just a branch of FedEx. Weapons are 'assets',[56] and the leaflets, radio shows, and other materials produced by US Psychological Operations teams are called 'products': 'It's not like selling

Coke,' one PsyOps officer told writer Jon Ronson. 'Sometimes you're trying to sell someone something that you know they might not want in their hearts.'[57] In other words, it's not like selling Coke, but it *is* 'selling' something. The verb 'to service' is also, creatively, used as a euphemism for 'to blow up'. As one artillery captain explained in the first Gulf War: 'I prefer not to say we are killing other people. I prefer to say we are servicing the target.'[58] As well as its disguising of war as a merely commercial activity, to call the launching of explosives 'servicing the target' has a further, remarkable implication. Since the barbarous twentieth-century business sense of 'servicing' to mean providing a service[59] denotes the supply of something that was explicitly requested, the artilleryman's language implied that those people who were the target were actually asking for it. He was simply fulfilling their wishes.

Servicing targets, delivering force, providing a service: war was, then, business as usual. War might once have been, as Clausewitz famously remarked, 'the continuation of politics by other means'. Now it was the continuation of commerce by other means. Wars as a whole, indeed, are often discussed in overarching economic terms, balancing victory against 'cost' or 'price'. This is how General Westmoreland remembered the Vietnam war:

> The objective in Washington was to raise the cost of the war from the standpoint of the enemy, to the point that he would come to some negotiated settlement. The attitude of the enemy was not comparable to what our attitude would have been under the circumstances. He was ready, willing and able to pay a far greater price than I would say we Caucasians would.[60]

Westmoreland's 'we Caucasians' may be fruitfully compared to Muhammad Ali's description of Vietnam as 'a white man's war'.[61] But US soldiers on the ground in Vietnam did not buy this notion of human lives as summable in terms of a 'cost' or 'price' that, as long as it was lower than some critical number, would be worth paying. Their view that human life was precious for altogether different reasons was evident in their coining of a modern slang term for killed: 'wasted'.[62]

Collateral

The weapons that are used to service targets, or as the surgical instruments in operations, are also given names that hide their real functions, since those are considered unspeakable. In Vietnam, a 'beehive round' did not contain tasty honey but was 'an explosive artillery shell which delivered thousands of small projectiles, "like nails with fins," instead of shrapnel.'[63] The Daisy Cutters dropped in the first Gulf War and Afghanistan were not tools of horticultural tidying-up but unguided 15,000-pound bombs that obliterated everything in a 250-foot radius, and which 'were dropped as much for their psychological effect as for their destructive power'.[64] An intercontinental ballistic missile developed by the US in the 1980s, which carried ten separate re-entry vehicles, each armed with a nuclear warhead representing the destructive power of twenty-five Hiroshimas, was dubbed by Ronald Reagan the Peacekeeper.[65] The name stuck.

Our weapons are surgical, or, as was first announced in the Vietnam War and later repeated enthusiastically during the first Gulf War, 'smart'. Smart weapons do not hold conversations about the films of Ingmar Bergman or the novels of Nabokov; they merely go, allegedly, where they are supposed to go. Between 7 and 10 per cent of them in fact miss,[66] sometimes by a long way: cruise missiles fired at Iraq during the 2003 war landed in Saudi Arabia and Turkey.[67] Even such 'smart weapons', however, constituted only a minority of the weapons used by US and UK forces in 1991, and about half those used during the 2003 war. Among those weapons we might consider 'dumb' are what are euphemised as 'cluster bombs', which do not drop in a tight cluster of limited radius but are designed expressly to spray their cargo of sub-munitions, or cutely named 'bomblets', over a wide distance. One such bomb regularly dropped on Iraq even before the 2003 war, as part of the enforcement of no-fly zones, was known as the Joint Stand-Off Weapon, which contained '145 anti-armor and anti-personnel incendiary bomblets' that scattered over an area the size of a football field. On average 5 per cent of them did not immediately detonate, and lay in wait as mines for years afterwards, incapable of 'smartly' distinguishing between soldier and civilian.[68] In mid-2003, after the end of 'major combat operations' in Iraq, it was estimated that up to ten thousand such unexploded 'bomblets' dropped by US and UK aircraft littered the country.[69]

Meanwhile, in the same war the US used an upgraded version of napalm that was made from kerosene rather than petrol. Cunningly it subsequently denied any use of 'napalm', because the new incendiaries were instead called 'Mark 77 firebombs'. The troops, though, undermined this cynical Unspeak strategy by continuing to call it napalm. '"We napalmed both those [bridge] approaches," said Colonel James Alles, commander of Marine Air Group 11. "Unfortunately there were people there . . . you could see them in the [cockpit] video. They were Iraqi soldiers. It's no great way to die. The generals love napalm. It has a big psychological effect."'[70]

Unrepresentative of western tactics though they remained, the development of modern laser-guided missiles and other 'smart weapons' in the 1990s had been hailed as a 'Revolution in Military Affairs'. Why? Because with smart weapons, 'only the bad guys get hurt'.[71] In other words, their well-publicised existence made war less controversial, because they allegedly reduced 'collateral damage'.

The phrase 'collateral damage' is first recorded in the 1975 'SALT lexicon' issued by the US Arms Control and Disarmament Agency to accompany the Strategic Arms Limitation Talks between the US and the USSR. It was defined

as 'The damage to surrounding human and non-human
resources, either military or non-military, as the result of action
or strikes directed specifically against enemy forces or military
facilities.'[72] (We are by now familiar with what is meant by
'human and non-human resources'.) Curiously, lexicographer
William Safire goes on to claim that 'This term was turned into
a euphemism during the Gulf War of 1991.'[73] But from birth it
was already a horrifying phrase in its euphemistic efficiency.

Damage is what occurs to objects: buildings or vehicles are
'damaged'; we do not usually say that a human being can be 'damaged', except metaphorically, to indicate an emotional problem.
To call the killing of human beings 'damage' is to deny their
personhood, their existence as individuals, and their crucial
difference from inanimate matter. Meanwhile, 'collateral'
makes us think of something happening on the sidelines, in
the wings: as it were, offstage. The phrase thus graphically
performs its own function: it evokes an image of hiddenness,
exactly as its purpose is to hide the reality of what it refers
to. It's very clever. It's also hideous. In its German form,
Kollateralschaden, it was voted 'ugliest word of the year' in
1999.[74] Yet, according to the authors of the 9/11 Commission
Report, one reason why we should despise Al Qaeda was
because: 'It makes no distinction between military and civilian
targets. *Collateral damage* is not in its lexicon.'[75] The implication
seems to be that we should be proud of our moral sensitivity
and linguistic creativity in having invented the phrase 'collateral damage' itself. One might not consider this cause for too
much self-congratulation.

It is worth noting that the 1975 SALT lexicon also defines the
concept of 'unacceptable damage', the degree of destruction
possible by a retaliatory enemy strike that is considered sufficient to deter a first strike. So whatever is described as 'collateral
damage' is by implication acceptable. It might yet be bad for
publicity, however. General Tommy Franks's remark that 'We
don't do body counts'[76] was widely quoted as evidence for a
callous attitude towards civilian casualties; in fact he was

making a different point, that progress in the Afghanistan war should not be measured by the numbers of enemy killed. And yet the number of civilians killed in the Iraq war was an embarrassing subject studiously avoided by pro-invasion commentators and politicians, except to say blandly that it was as low as possible. 'The war [. . .] was completed with dispatch and with minimal collateral damage and with minimal loss of life,' said Donald Rumsfeld in 2005.[77] What exact quantity was hidden behind the usefully vague term 'minimal'? No official was saying. The Pentagon allegedly kept data but did not reveal it to the public.[78] At the time of writing, the conservative minimum estimate of civilian deaths caused by the invasion of Iraq, according to the Iraq Body Count organisation, was 27,295.[79] Collateral. Acceptable.

Even thus euphemised and officially uncounted, collateral damage is still an inconvenient phenomenon to commanders. In early March 2003, Franks had presented George W. Bush with a list of '24 high-collateral-damage targets that could result in the killing of 30 or more civilians if struck'. Bush's response was: 'I'm not picking targets.'[80] Relating this scene, Bob Woodward pointed out: 'In the Vietnam War, President Johnson had spent hours reviewing and approving targets.' But the prospect of civilian deaths apparently made President Bush squeamish. Having ordered a war, he did not want to dirty his hands with the ugly details.

Luckily, there is an excellent way to minimise accountability for 'collateral damage'. It was used extensively in the Vietnam War, when, according to US Marine Philip Caputo, 'We were told . . . "Well, if it's dead and Vietnamese, it's VC."'[81] After US forces bombed a wedding party in Afghanistan, Donald Rumsfeld said: 'Let's not call them innocents. We don't know quite what they were.' [82] In the meantime, US Special Forces soldier Dave Diaz told a reporter how, in Afghanistan, they played 'this terminology game'. In order to justify attack, a 'mud hut' would be referred to as a 'military compound' or a 'built-up area'. If women and children were observed among a party of Taliban that forces wanted to attack, Diaz's 'guidance' would be that 'they are combatants'.[83] You can see the pattern. Rather than wring one's hands about the deaths of civilians, why not just change what you call them? Say they are not civilians after all but Viet Cong or 'combatants'. Remember: 'only the bad guys get hurt'. So anyone who gets hurt must be a bad guy. Then the whole problem of 'collateral damage' may be safely swept under the carpet.

Mass destruction

If we euphemise our own weapons and killings of civilians, we also dysphemise (if I may use an appropriately hideous word) the weapons of the enemy, giving them names to make them sound as horrible as possible. The notorious Scud missile of Saddam Hussein was actually christened 'Scud' by the West. The weapon was first developed by the Soviets in the 1960s, under the less evocative designation R-11; Nato referred to it as the 'SS-1b Scud-A'.[84] The Iraqi military later heavily modified the design, but it was useful to keep the name Scud so as to make it sound maximally brutal and disgusting.

Ballistic missiles such as the Scud are considered 'weapons of mass destruction', a term that, as used in the early years of the twenty-first century, carried an impressive payload of special pleading and disinformation. Saddam Hussein's fictional stockpiles of WMD were settled on as the excuse for war 'for bureaucratic reasons', as US Deputy Secretary of Defense Paul Wolfowitz explained afterwards.[85] Condoleezza Rice's catchy slogan, 'We don't want the smoking gun to be a mushroom cloud',[86] dropped a heavy hint that nuclear armageddon would be the price of inaction, and much speculation surrounded chemical and biological weapons. Wrapping it all up in the mantra WMD enabled everyone to forget about the details and simply trust that the Iraqi leader had amassed the most egregious arsenal known to man. The notorious 'dossier' released

by the British government in September 2002 had its title
altered, at the last minute, from 'Saddam's Programme for
Weapons of Mass Destruction' to 'Iraq's Weapons of Mass
Destruction',[87] thus changing the nature of what was described
from one man's desire to a country's imminent threat.

The cold, bureaucratic terminology of the phrase 'weapons of
mass destruction' only served to make it more frightening, as it
evoked the rational calculations of kill-ratios in moodily lit government departments. Such weapons, we were enjoined to
believe, were worse in a qualitative, not merely quantitative way
from other weapons (but no one referred to weapons of local
destruction or weapons of small destruction). One could not
imagine even the most robust defender of the use of force saying,
in an adaptation of the US gun-enthusiast's mantra: 'Weapons of
mass destruction don't kill people; people kill people.'

The apocalyptic tone of 'weapons of mass destruction' was
matched by a concomitant vagueness. How much destruction
was to be considered 'mass destruction'? No one was saying.
The kinds of chemical and biological weapons so far employed
in human warfare do not even begin to approach the devastation of which a single Peacekeeper is capable. They are much
less destructive, too, than many other kinds of weapons, such as
the US's MOAB, for Massive Ordnance Air Blast, or, in the Air
Force's affectionate nickname, Mother Of All Bombs (a sarcastic
rejoinder to Saddam Hussein's promise of 'the mother of all
battles' in 1991). Unveiled in March 2003 as the successor to the
Daisy Cutter, the MOAB contained 18,700 pounds of high
explosive,[88] and did not simply push air around; it was able to
kill all people within a 1.7-mile radius and break windows up to
five miles away, and created 'a fear-inspiring mushroom cloud'
10,000 feet high.[89] Saddam Hussein's chemical-weapon attack
on the Kurdish city of Halabja was an atrocity, but, as
Christopher Hitchens observed: 'A sustained day of carpet-
bombing with "conventional" weapons would have been more
lethal, as well as more annihilating.'[90] (Of course 'carpet-bomb-
ing' is a euphemism as well: incendiary bombing means the

dropping of incendiaries, nuclear bombing means the dropping of nukes, but carpet bombing does not mean the dropping of textile floor-coverings.) Aum Shinrikyo's nerve-gas attack on the highly crowded Tokyo subway in 1995, meanwhile, managed to kill only twelve people. The phrase 'weapons of mass destruction' conflates very different levels of threat and confuses more than it illuminates, even when not cynically used as a propaganda tool. In July 2005, the Carnegie Endowment for International Peace announced that the newest volume in its twenty-one-year-old series on proliferation would abandon the phrase completely, because it 'confuses officials, befuddles the public, and justifies policies that more precise language and more accurate assessments would not support',[91] in particular obscuring the fact that the gravest danger to the planet was still posed specifically by nuclear weapons.

It is commonly stated that the phrase 'weapons of mass destruction' originated in détente negotiations over the thermonuclear arsenals of the US and the USSR.[92] The phrase was certainly apt in the context of nuclear arms-race concepts such as 'overkill' (how many multiples of the entire population of Earth could be killed if all the nukes were launched) and 'mutually assured destruction', enshrined in history's most apt acronym, MAD. But 'weapons of mass destruction' had actually been coined much earlier, to describe the new, mechanised warfighting vehicles and *matériel* being developed in the 1930s. 'Who can think without horror,' wrote a *Times* editorialist in 1937, 'of what another widespread war would mean, waged as it would be with all the new weapons of mass destruction?'[93] In other words, what are now our ordinary weapons were themselves once feared as WMD. They have been domesticised in our consciousness with the euphemism 'conventional weapons': to fight with them is more socially acceptable because everybody does it: it's conventional. Usefully, a secondary sense of 'conventional', to mean explicitly agreed by convention, is also implied, even though it is argued by many that the use of cluster bombs violates the 1997 UN Convention against landmines.[94] In modern business parlance, however, conventional is boring and unexciting; the virtuous thing is to be unconventional ('think outside the box'). This revolution in commercial affairs, it seemed, had not yet filtered through to weapons-talk. To be unconventional in war is defined as not playing by our rules, which are honest and just: to be unconventional, essentially, is cheating.

In this way there remained a feeling that the chemical and biological weapons lumped together under weapons of mass destruction were incomparably nasty, that fighting with disease or gas, as opposed to rocket-propelled radioactive waste or bombs that spawn hundreds of bomblets, was somehow more underhand. It was just not cricket. Like napalm, it had a powerful 'psychological effect'. It played, perhaps, on age-old fears of the invisible enemy, of silent contagion. It also played on fears of the mad scientist, fears that John Ashcroft was eager to encourage in the following extraordinary statement after the war had been declared won:

> Weapons of mass destruction, including evil chemistry and evil biology, are all matters of great concern, not only to the United States but also to the world community.[95]

Evil chemistry. Evil biology. Picture, if you will, the evil Iraqi researchers in their evil laboratories conducting an evil version of science. This evil science is the dark side. It is not to be confused with the good science that gave birth to the megadeath-inducing Peacekeeper, created the 30,000 tons of chemical weapons stockpiled in the US,[96] and allowed the US Army to be granted, in 2003, the patent for a new type of grenade designed to disperse 'biological agents' and 'chemical agents'.[97] The notion that science itself can be inherently morally inflected recalled the bogus appeals to a notion of 'sound science' in environmental and genetic debates. And 'evil biology' further conjured up useful images of hideously deformed monsters lurking somewhere in Iraq, if not just in

Ashcroft's id. Evil chemistry and evil biology lead to evil only will, as Yoda might say.

After the invasion of Iraq, no WMD were found. True, someone had the parts of a pre-1991 nuclear centrifuge buried in his back yard,[98] but that alone was never going to produce the fantasised mushroom cloud. What to do? The phrase 'weapons of mass destruction-related program activities',[99] enacting a twofold retreat from claims about the actual existence of weapons, was found rather cumbersome by a suddenly sceptical post-war press. Another tack was possible: just redefine 'weapons of mass destruction' to mean whatever happens to be in front of your nose. In April 2005, new Iraqi President Jalal Talabani proved himself agreeably on-message when he wrote, in a letter to Tony Blair: 'Saddam himself was [. . .] Iraq's most dangerous WMD.'[100] In the interim, three Britons were indicted in the US for planning an attack with 'weapons of mass destruction', identified not as nukes, viruses, or evil chemistry, but home-made bombs: 'improvised explosive devices', in the jargon all too familiar from the situation in Iraq. Deputy Attorney General James Comey explained: 'A weapon of mass destruction in our world goes beyond [chemical, biological, or nuclear weapons] and includes improvised explosive devices.'[101] Comey's world, let us hope, is well insulated from the one the rest of us live in, or the contradiction might prove impossible for him to bear. For if a home-made explosive device is a WMD, what is the Mother Of All Bombs?

On the moon

Cheerleading operation names; medical and business metaphors; sanitised names for weapons and killing: they all help us to support a war without having to think about what war is really like. They make war *normal*. They may even make it fun: in April 2004, the Fox News Channel executive John Moody instructed his reporters: 'Let's refer to the US marines we see in the foreground as "sharpshooters" not snipers, which carries a negative connotation.'[102] Indeed: 'sharpshooters' speaks of sporting excellence, as though the soldiers were practising on clay pigeons or competing in the Olympics; it also evokes the golden age of the American Wild West and celebrities such as performing cowgirl Annie Oakley. Any unfortunate negative connotations of long-range killing are to be suppressed.

The ever-increasing levels of abstraction in modern military language are well illustrated in the evolution of one term. The containers in which dead soldiers were returned from Vietnam to the US were called 'body bags', for the Gulf War they were renamed 'human remains pouches', and for the 2003 Iraq war they became 'transfer tubes'.[103] As George W. Bush's mother asked: 'Why should we hear about body bags and deaths [. . .] why should I waste my beautiful mind on something like that?'[104] Why indeed? In this respect it was a brilliant stroke of Donald Rumsfeld's in August 2002 to translate the *mise-en-scène* of the planned Iraq war into the realm of pure science fiction. He preferred to speak of going to war against the moon.

> The construct I would suggest would be, um, what are the benefits – what are the advantages and disadvantages of not acting? And of course, the advantage of not acting – against the moon – would be that no-one could say that you acted. They would say, 'Isn't that good – you didn't do anything against the moon'. The other side of the coin of not acting against the moon, in the event that the moon posed a serious threat, would be that you then suffered a serious loss, and you're sorry after that's over. And in weighing the things, you would have to make a judgement . . . or not . . . do you think you are acting most responsibly by avoiding the threat that could be characterised – X numbers of people dying, innocent people, and it's that kind of a evaluation one would have to make.[105]

War on the moon, we may imagine, would take place in a Kubrickian poetic slow-motion, to a soundtrack of lush Viennese waltzes. No grimy body bags or death. To meditate on such a possibility was the duty of beautiful minds everywhere: they would thereby be insulated from the realities of the 'war on terror'.

6

Terror

Acts of terrorism

In August 2005, John Bolton, America's new ambassador to the UN, attempted to torpedo six months of negotiations by unilaterally submitting a new draft, studded with hundreds of deletions and insertions, of a proposed General Assembly statement on the organisation's aims. The document made fascinating reading, subtly revealing the US stance on many international questions. Here, for instance, is a passage that intended to condemn terrorism. Bolton's deletion is crossed out; his additions are in bold type.

> 65. [. . .] We affirm that the targeting and deliberate killing of civilians and non-combatants **by terrorists** cannot be justified or legitimized by any cause or grievance, and we declare that any **such** action intended to cause death or serious bodily harm to ~~civilians or non-combatants~~ **others**, when the purpose of such an act, by its nature or context, is to intimidate a population or to compel a Government or an international organization to carry out or to abstain from any act cannot be justified on any grounds and constitutes an act of terrorism.[1]

On first sight these might look like trivial changes. Why, for example, did 'by terrorists' need to be inserted in a passage which was ostensibly all about terrorism? To understand what

Bolton was doing, it will help to step back a bit and consider how the term 'terrorism' itself is used. Its meaning has long been debated, because different people start from different ideas of what cases ought to count as terrorism, and then adjust their definitions to fit. Let us, for the sake of argument, start here: terrorism is the threat or use of violence against a civilian population in order to coerce the leaders of that population into a particular political decision.

Coercion works through fear, the essential emotional component of terrorism. The *Oxford English Dictionary* defines 'terrorism' exclusively in these terms: 'A policy intended to strike with terror those against whom it is adopted; the employment of methods of intimidation; the fact of terrorizing or condition of being terrorized.' Contemporary terrorism induces fear by its random choice of victims among the chosen target population. A Palestinian bomb might go off in an Israeli bar or a shopping mall. An Islamist bomb might go off in a Spanish railway station or a Bali nightclub. Sites of civil society that are normally assumed safe are turned into venues for indiscriminate murder. You could be next. A government is supposed to be able to assure the safety of its citizens, so a terrorised population may exert pressure on its rulers to give in to the demands of the perpetrators of terrorism; at least, that is what the latter hope.

So much is uncontroversial. The difficulties arise when people begin to contest specific terms in the definition. For instance, do those targeted really need to be 'civilians'? If they do not, the definition broadens rapidly: then all strikes on military targets could be called terrorism. We should have to call 'terrorism', for example, the attacks on Nazi occupiers by Resistance fighters in France during the Second World War; or the attacks on Soviet occupiers by the Afghan mujahidin during the 1980s. Indeed the term is sometimes used in this way. Princeton professor of international law Richard Falk writes of 'the generally heroic imagery used to describe anti-Nazi terrorism in German-occupied Europe'.[2] British Conservative MP

Julian Amery, recalling his experiences in Britain's Special Operations Executive during the Second World War, said: 'I was a terrorist myself once. One of my duties was the recruitment of people to carry out terrorist actions against the Nazis in Yugoslavia and Albania.'[3]

But then almost every official act of war could also be classed as terrorism. After all, the object of battle is not to obliterate every last man on the enemy side, only to kill enough of them so that the commanders are eventually more afraid of continuing than they are of surrendering. This is coercion through fear by the use of violence to persuade the target group's leaders to make a particular choice. But if we call it 'terrorism', the term becomes so widely applicable as to be useless. So the definition, it might seem, needs to be restricted to non-military victims.

However, here there are difficulties too. During the 1970s and 1980s, the IRA attacked both military and civilian targets in Britain: both army barracks and pubs were bombed. The IRA claimed that their attacks on soldiers were part of their 'war' against the 'occupation' of Northern Ireland by British forces; the British government termed their actions 'terrorism'. In 1982, the IRA set off a bomb in Hyde Park, London, which killed two members of the Horse Guards regiment and seventeen spectators. Inasmuch as it was aimed at a military target, was this an act of terrorism? You might want to say that the Horse Guards, being mainly ceremonial soldiers, were 'noncombatants', a term that is often used in conjunction with 'civilians', as in the UN draft's definition: 'civilians or noncombatants'. But 'noncombatant' is vague: one might be a noncombatant one week and a combatant the next. Attacking a column of infantry who are marching to a battle elsewhere could be said to target 'noncombatants', since they are not actually engaged in fighting at the time of the attack; and yet they are still soldiers.

Furthermore, the category of 'civilian' itself is regularly challenged by those who perpetrate terrorism. Those acting in furtherance of the Palestinian cause often attempt to justify their

killing with a claim that there is no such thing as a 'civilian' in
Israeli society. Thus Hamas leader Aby Shanab: '"Everyone over
seventeen is recruited into the army [. . .] The army occupying
the West Bank is mainly made up of reservists," he added,
claiming that the distinction between soldier and civilian is
blurred in Israel.'[4] Elsewhere, Osama bin Laden has justified
his killing of American civilians by arguing that, since they pay
the taxes that fund US foreign policy, they are culpable for its
actions.[5] Muslim cleric Hani Al-Siba'i, director of London's Al-
Maqreze Centre for Historical Studies, gave his interpretation in
the wake of the July 2005 attacks in London: 'The term "civilians" does not exist in Islamic religious law [. . .] There is no
such term as "civilians" in the modern Western sense. People
are either of Dar Al-Harb or not.'[6] Dar Al-Harb is territory controlled by 'unbelievers', who are thus all, on this view, fair
game. It is interesting that perpetrators of terrorism explain
their actions in this way: they essentially concede that the killing
of innocents is wrong, but go on to claim that those whom they
kill are not innocent.

It might therefore be tempting to adjust our definition of terrorism so that it speaks of 'innocent' victims rather than
'civilian' victims. But to say 'innocent' *tout court*, rather than
'innocent of a particular crime', turns innocence from a legal
into a metaphysical category, and thus one that is even more
contestable than 'civilian'. To speak of 'innocent victims' is to
veer into an area of moralising terminology, to imply good on
one side and hence evil on the other; it is even to idealise the
dead, to sanctify them, perhaps eventually to think of them as
martyrs – just as Islamist suicide bombers are celebrated as martyrs by their fellows. And therein lies the propagandistic power
of terrorism: its twisting of social categories into metaphysical
ones on both sides. Far from all terrorism is religiously motivated, or even religiously described by its perpetrators, but the
phenomenon does in this way evince a quasi-religious concept
of justice, as based on a kind of original sin. Moral culpability is
assigned to one's very existence in a particular polity. And if we

speak of 'innocence' and 'evil' in response, then the perpetrators have won the struggle to define the frame of reference.

The category of terrorism as normally used further implies something about the perpetrators: that they are a small group using limited resources for maximum psychological effect. Just as one might worry that allowing strikes on military targets to be called 'terrorism' stretches the word too far, one might wish to say that 'terrorism' cannot be *committed* by military forces either. We might wish to limit the application of the concept to the traditional examples of perpetrators I have so far mentioned: the IRA, Hamas, Al Qaeda, and so on. But this argument is more difficult to justify.

Remember that people killed by terrorism are not the people the perpetrators wish to persuade. They are exemplars, bargaining chips. There is a disconnect between victims and audience; the violence is a warning to people other than those targeted. (The writer Brian Jenkins has summed up this fact in the catchphrase 'Terrorism is theatre'; a US Army lieutenant colonel went one better, telling a reporter in Baghdad in 2003: 'Terrorism is Grand Theater.'[7]) Unfortunately this, too, is true of many government actions. Consider the nuclear bombing of Nagasaki and Hiroshima in 1945. The US had not identified every citizen in those cities as being an indispensable part of the Japanese war effort. On the contrary, the bombings were designed as an awful demonstration: to instil such fear in the Japanese government that they would surrender. The bomb spoke thus: Give up, or there'll be more where this came from. It also sent a powerful message to a secondary audience: Joseph Stalin. On this measure, Hiroshima and Nagasaki are, by many orders of magnitude, the greatest acts of terrorism in history. (This description, by the way, is separate from an argument about whether they were right or wrong. Some people claim that Hiroshima was justified because it ended the war sooner, saving countless American and Japanese lives, etc. The truth or otherwise of such a claim is not relevant to the fact that in means and intention, it was an act of terrorism.) The Russian invasion of Chechnya in 1994 made no attempt to distinguish 'civilians' from others in its destruction, aiming to terrorise the entire population into submission. Unarmed villagers were summarily shot, indiscriminate vacuum bombs were regularly used, and 25,000 civilians were killed in Grozny alone.[8] The Russians themselves simply termed 'terrorists' anyone bearing arms in the attacked territory, and called their own war of terrorism the 'antiterrorist special operation of the Russian troops'.[9]

States themselves, of course, fiercely resist any characterisation of their actions as terrorism. Richard Falk: 'With the help of the influential media, the state over time has waged and largely won the battle of definitions by exempting its own violence against civilians from being treated and perceived as "terrorism." Instead, such violence was generally discussed as "uses of force," "retaliation," "self-defense" and "security measures."'[10]

So now we can see exactly what John Bolton was doing by adding the seemingly innocent phrase 'by terrorists' to the UN draft. The effect was to exclude any denunciation of the killing of civilians by states, and thus particularly to foreclose any description of US actions as 'terrorism'. It did not seem to worry Bolton that his amended version ended up as question-begging: for if you use the term 'terrorists' within a definition of 'terrorism', you are no further along than when you started. The question remains as to who exactly might count as a 'terrorist' – a problem to which we shall shortly return. Secondly, Bolton's alteration of the description of 'such' acts (again, meaning acts committed by 'terrorists') from targeting 'civilians or non-combatants' to simply 'others', denies that 'terrorism' should apply only to attacks on civilians, and encourages strikes on military targets to be called 'terrorism' as well. As we shall see later, this was a useful terminological strategy to help define the US enemy in Iraq.

Curiously, many internal governmental definitions of terrorism do not explicitly exclude the possibility of its perpetration by states. The FBI defines terrorism as: 'the unlawful use of force or violence against persons or property to intimidate or coerce a government, the civilian population, or any segment thereof, in furtherance of political or social objectives'.[11] A recent US Treasury definition reads: 'the term "terrorism" means an activity that — (i) involves a violent act or an act dangerous to human life, property, or infrastructure; and (ii) appears to be intended — (A) to intimidate or coerce a civilian population; (B) to influence the policy of a government by intimidation or coercion; or (C) to affect the conduct of a government by mass destruction, assassination, kidnapping, or hostage-taking.'[12] The widening of the application of terrorism to attacks on 'property' and not just people in these definitions is notable – presumably, then, the smashing of a McDonald's restaurant window by anti-globalisation protesters could count as terrorism. But these descriptions still do not restrict possible perpetrators to non-state groups. Perhaps because it might be useful to reserve the option of accusing other states of terrorism when necessary – as the US did with Saddam Hussein's Iraq.

On occasion, the fact that states can commit terrorism has been acknowledged by those in responsible positions. During the Second World War, the MP Richard Stokes denounced in Parliament the firebombing of Dresden and other acts, to which he referred as 'terror bombing'.[13] And Winston Churchill himself 'acknowledged in a memo to the Air Ministry that the raid on Dresden and others like it were acts of terror that should be stopped, "even though we call it by another name"'.[14] Meanwhile, in 2003, thirty Israeli helicopter and fighter pilots refused to continue bombing Palestinian cities, and were sacked from the Air Force. The last straw for these men was 'the dropping of the one-tonne bomb [. . .] on the home of a Hamas military leader, Salah Shehade, killing him and 14 of his family, mostly children':

Capt Assaf L, who served as a pilot for 15 years until sacked for signing the letter, had similar doubts. 'You don't have to be a genius to know that the destruction from a one-tonne bomb is

massive, so someone up there made a decision to drop it know-
ing it would destroy buildings,' he said. 'Someone took the
decision to kill innocent people. This is us being terrorists.'[15]

Notably, just as the perpetrators of Palestinian terrorism
challenge the notion of Israeli 'civilians', one rarely hears of a
Palestinian 'civilian' being killed by Israeli forces. Of course the
Palestinians at the time of this writing did not actually have a
civitas, a state, but the refusal to talk of Palestinian 'civilians'
works to entrench an assumption that every Palestinian is a
potential perpetrator of acts of terrorism. It is tempting to slide
from the assumption that there is no such thing as a Palestinian
'civilian' to the assumption that there is no such thing as an
'innocent' Palestinian. Even the Israeli human-rights group
B'tselem, in counting deaths on both sides during the second
Intifada, distinguishes carefully between 'Israeli civilians killed'
and 'Israeli security forces killed' by Palestinians on the one side,
yet refers simply to 'Palestinians killed' on the other.[16] Human
Rights Watch, meanwhile, appears to hedge its bets carefully by
speaking of 'Palestinian civilians not involved in hostilities'.[17]

Terrorism is a method or tactic of violence, and such acts are
terrorism no matter who commits them. Individuals and groups
commit terrorism; so do states. One reason why so many
writers have resisted this obvious conclusion is quite understandable from a psychological point of view. It is that it seems
to open the door to downgrading acts of terrorism that are not
committed by states. Someone might say: yes, Al Qaeda murdered 3000 civilians on 11 September 2001; but the US military
murdered many times more, for example, in South Vietnam.
Unscrupulous thinkers may go on to use the comparison in
order to trivialise non-state terrorism. And this cast of mind
may then segue into a refusal to criticise the Al Qaeda action, or
even an inclination to praise it. But of course you are not compelled into such sordid reasoning simply because you
acknowledge that states can commit terrorism. Any person of
minimal ethical standards simply condemns all murder, except

perhaps on the rare occasions when it can be agreed that a 'just war' is being waged.

There seems to be a natural instinct to imagine that where there is a wrong, there must be a right to balance it. Thus, if we condemn one act, we might feel inclined to praise another that constitutes a kind of counterweight in some global-historical moral scale. In reality there can often just be wrong as far as the eye can see.

Evil folks

In John Le Carré's novel *Absolute Friends* a character remarks: 'A terrorist is someone with a bomb but no airplane.' In the light of 9/11, it might be more accurate to say that a terrorist is someone with a bomb but no airplane, or an airplane but no bomb: either one, but not both. (The notorious shoe-bomber, Richard Reid, did not 'have' his airplane in the sense of being able to direct it over a target.) If you have both a bomb and an airplane, you are a member of a state air force, and so of course you cannot be a 'terrorist'.

Just as the idea of 'terrorism' is politically contested, to name someone a 'terrorist' is also a political act, as is emphasised in this revealing exchange between a reporter and US State Department spokesman Richard Boucher:

> Question: Yes. As a matter of principle, does the U.S. Government consider terrorists those people who are resisting invasion and occupation forces of their own country? For example, Adolf Hitler was calling the brave Polish people who [were] resisting the Nazi forces terrorists during the invasion and occupation of Poland. Could you please clarify the U.S. position on this crucial matter? Otherwise, how do you distinguish the freedom fighter from a terrorist?

> Mr Boucher: We don't.[18]

'Terrorists' was once a proud self-description by those who committed political violence: as Phil Rees remarks in his superb *Dining with Terrorists*, 'The Russian revolutionaries who assassinated Tsar Alexander II and the French anarchists who manned the Paris Commune used the word with pride.'[19] Nowadays, however, the word is a weapon rather than a badge. Its function is to essentialise and delegitimise the target. If his victims are 'innocent', the terrorist is 'evil' – so George W. Bush characterises Al Qaeda as 'these vicious and evil men', 'these evil ones',[20] 'evil people', and even 'evil folks',[21] a phrase that packs a weird combination of homeliness and biblical disapprobation. Now, there is little question that if the word 'evil' means anything it can justly be applied to acts of deliberate murder. Yet there is a difference between calling an act evil and a person evil, just as there is a difference between 'terrorism' and 'terrorist'. To call a person evil is to shut down argument, to deny for ever the possibility of negotiation, to go on the theological offensive. Indeed the imputation of supernatural evil has been part of the word 'terrorist' since it first appeared in the English language, in Edmund Burke's famous denunciation of the French Revolution and 'those Hell-hounds called Terrorists'.[22]

In fact those people called terrorists, rather than just killing for the sheer evil fun of it, almost always have clear and specific political and strategic goals. That is why they commit acts of terrorism: in order to publicise these goals. In some places and at some times, a process begins whereby those goals are recognised as legitimate and desirable, while the tactics (indiscriminate killing) used to further them continue to be condemned, as has happened with the IRA in Northern Ireland and the PLO in Palestine. The unpalatable fact is that some terrorism works. In June 1994, the seizure of a Russian hospital in Budyonnovsk by Chechen forces led to negotiations that ended the first Chechnya war, prompting one commentator to declare the hostage-taking 'the most successful act of terrorism in history'.[23]

The form of terrorism known as suicide bombing is perhaps the most terrifying. Because the attacker intends to die, he cannot be deterred, and so the tactic is highly effective in instilling fear. The Fox News Channel chose to fight the propaganda power of the phenomenon by renaming it, because it was felt that the term 'suicide' gave too much prominence to the sacrifice of the attacker. According to Larry Johnson, former Fox News contributor and once a CIA officer: 'The edict came down apparently to stop referring to suicide bombings in Israel as suicide bombings, to call them "homicide bombings". I thought that was stupid, and I continued to call them suicide bombings, because every bombing that kills someone is a homicide bombing.'[24] Fox was not dissuaded; days after the London bombings of 7 July 2005, its website carried the revelatory headline: 'Evidence Points to Homicide Attacks'. The story referred farcically to the bombings having killed 'at least 52 in what could be the first homicide attacks in Western Europe'.[25]

Suicide bombing, further, is usually explained by secular westerners as having an irreducibly religious component, because, for example, its perpetrators often claim to be going to paradise, and are celebrated as 'martyrs'. This enables us to think of suicide bombers as fanatics, as operating exclusively in an apocalyptic religious dimension and not a rational, political one. So George W. Bush described the Al Qaeda suicide attackers as part of 'a cult of evil'.[26] If, however, we cling to the view that suicide bombers, and indeed all perpetrators of terrorism, are not rational actors, little of a positive nature will result. Robert Pape made a study of all suicide attacks around the world between 1980 and 2003, and found that: 'The data show that there is far less of a connection between suicide terrorism and religious fundamentalism than most people think [. . .] What nearly all suicide terrorist attacks actually have in common is a specific secular and strategic goal: to compel modern democracies to withdraw military forces from territory that the terrorists consider to be their homeland.'[27] The first suicide bombers of modern times, according to sociologist Michael

Mann, were the Hezbollah members who blew up the peace-keeping headquarters in Beirut on 23 October 1983. Mann notes that: 'Hezbollah was more of a Lebanese nationalist than an Islamist movement. In fact, the clerics among its leaders tended to oppose the new tactic, saying Islam could not justify suicide.' Suicide bombing was adopted in 1987 by 'the militants of the secular Tamil Tiger "national liberation" movement in Sri Lanka'.[28] Mann also points out that dead Jewish practitioners of terrorism in Mandate Palestine 'are honored as Israeli martyrs',[29] but this does not change the fact that their aims – the departure of the British and the creation of a Jewish state – were specific and secular.

Osama bin Laden, meanwhile, mixes his geopolitical ambitions of US withdrawal from all Middle Eastern territories and a united Arab caliphate under his reading of Islamic law – ambitions which, however unrealistic, are at least clearly defined – with a call for the extermination of 'Jews and Crusaders'. In 1998, he declared: 'The ruling to kill the Americans and their allies – civilians and military – is an individual duty for every Muslim who can do it in any country in which it is possible to do it, in order to liberate the al-Aqsa Mosque and the holy mosque from their grip, and in order for their armies to move out of all the lands of Islam, defeated and unable to threaten any Muslim.'[30] Since it is hard to imagine any global arrangement in which no American, Jew, or other ally or 'Crusader' is able to threaten any Muslim (long-range bomber aircraft and intercontinental ballistic missiles mean that such a threat would remain possible even if all Americans retreated inside the borders of the continental US, and even if, as seems to be the desire, all Jews were evacuated from the state of Israel to the other side of the world), this incitement to indiscriminate murder seems designed to persist indefinitely.

One might suppose that the fact that bin Laden's tactics of terrorism are in service to an apocalyptic vision of jihad as interminable holy war would render the terrorism itself less effective as a political instrument, albeit highly effective as an instrument of fear. But his sort of rhetoric is not new. Interminable holy war has previously been declared by successful practitioners of terrorism – for example, the 'Stern Gang', aka Lehi (Lohamei Herut Israel, 'Fighters for the Freedom of Israel'), who fought what they considered an illegal British occupation, who freely called their own practice 'terror', and whose Principle I proclaimed: 'An eternal war shall be waged against all those who satanically stand in the way of the realization [of our] aims.'[31] Among the subsequent Prime Ministers of Israel were Stern Gang member Yitzhak Shamir and Irgun member Menachem Begin.[32]

George W. Bush's many references to those defined as Al Qaeda as fuelled by 'hate' of Americans (e.g., 'Why do they hate us?',[33] 'those who hate America'[34]) came under attack for their simplification, their ignorance of the historical roots of animosity. It is true that such considerations were largely ignored in the rhetoric following 11 September 2001, but the ascription of 'hate' is more reasonable than the imputation of evil. For bin Laden and his cohorts do regularly express murderous and indiscriminate hate: they want to kill all and any Americans and Jews, whenever and wherever they can. The message of an audiotape purportedly recorded in May 2005 by bin Laden's alleged associate in Iraq, the Jordanian Abu Musab al-Zarqawi, is similarly open-ended: 'We will sacrifice all that which is dear and precious until God grants victory to his religion and elevates his word or we get killed.'[35] They won't stop until a grandiose metaphysical ambition is realised, but it is difficult to know how we would test whether God really had granted victory to al-Zarqawi's religion or elevated his word. Are we to wait until divine writing appears in the sky?

Bin Laden's loosely knit international gang, then, is engaged in something different from traditional liberationist terrorism: they are not fighting for specific rights of nationhood but for the global dominion of a particular religious worldview. Indeed, the hawkish ex-CIA analyst Michael Scheuer, author of the anonymously published *Imperial Hubris*, calls their official denomination as terrorists 'semantic suicide': he terms them instead 'insurgents', since the training camps in Afghanistan gave instruction for all-round guerrilla warfare rather than just bomb-making, and since, on his view, 'bin Laden and al Qaeda are leading a popular, worldwide, and increasingly powerful Islamic insurgency'[36] (a word we shall return to shortly). Given their dream of endless mass murder, no one seriously recommends that we should negotiate with Al Qaeda rather than trying to kill or imprison its adherents. But for this very reason, their well-publicised existence lends an even stronger totalising charge to the word 'terrorist'. If we have bin Laden's associates in mind whenever we see the word, we are more likely to have an image of a terrorist as an evil maniac. Whatever political grievances or struggle for liberation the person or group involved is trying to draw attention to by their actions is shut out by the absolute condemnation of the word. The terrorist label becomes a means of blanking out nuance and pretending that the problem boils down to individual viciousness. Addressing it as such, of course, is not likely to make the problem go away.

It also makes us more likely to think of a 'terrorist' as a Muslim. The American preacher Pat Robertson, expounding on his view that liberalism is more dangerous than the deliberate murder of civilians, declared: 'Over the course of a hundred years, the gradual erosion of the consensus that's held our country together is probably more serious than a few bearded terrorists who fly into buildings.'[37] In fact, out of the nineteen suspected 9/11 hijackers in photographs released by the FBI, only four had beards, and not flowing bin Laden prophet-style beards but neatly trimmed little goatees or jawline-definers.[38] Robertson thus implied this charming little syllogism: 1) All Muslims have beards; 2) All terrorists are Muslims; therefore 3) All terrorists have beards. Similar views were common:

> [T]here is a disgusting pattern: Not every Muslim is a fascist terrorist, but almost every fascist terrorist is a Muslim. Killers

are not screaming 'Hail Mary' when they machine gun children
in the back, slit the throat of airline stewardesses, or blow preg-
nant women up on buses across the globe.[39]

Either the disgusted author somehow forgot the numerous
acts of terrorism perpetrated in modern times by Catholic
Irishmen, Christian Americans, and Hindu Indians, among
others, or he thought that what he labelled 'fascist terrorism', by
his definition exclusive to Muslims, was *ipso facto* worse than
other kinds. The lines of prejudice were clear. In December 2002,
Armenia was added to the US State Department's list of countries whose citizens were thought to pose an elevated threat in
America. The Armenian ambassador said: 'We are a Christian
country.' Armenia was taken off the list.[40]

Officially, news organisations such as Reuters, the BBC, the
Guardian, and the *Washington Post* recognise all these difficulties
and maintain policies that the organisation itself should never
use the designation 'terrorist' in its own voice, but only when
quoting others who use it. (These rules are not followed with
absolute consistency, however: in February 2005, BBC Radio
carried a story mentioning the decommissioning of the notorious Maze prison, 'which housed hundreds of terrorists at the
height of the Troubles in Northern Ireland'[41]; the BBC website
news story referred only to 'republican hunger-strikers'.) This
has led to what some see as a farcical thesaurus-rush of terms in
general use for those who commit acts of terrorism, such as
'militants', 'gunmen', 'guerrillas', 'extremists', and so on.
Perhaps what remains of the linguistic spectrum when you
abjure the use of 'terrorists' is a bit of an ungoverned mess, but
refusing to use the word is still a good idea. After the July 2005
attacks in London, the BBC changed references to 'terrorists' on
its news website to 'bombers', prompting some controversy.
Columnist Nick Cohen was moved to complain: '"Bomber",
"attacker" and "gunman" allow no distinction between fighters
who assault military targets and fighters who assault civilian
targets.'[42] It is simply false, however, that 'bomber' *allows* no

such distinction: it makes no distinction in itself, but people are not prevented from making whatever distinctions they like thereafter. Rather than being 'castrated language', in Cohen's strange image, 'bombers' is the most accurate, robust, and specific description of the perpetrators of the acts in question; 'killers' would be an appropriate word, too.

A specific example shows how the word 'terrorist' can work as simplistic ideological sleight of hand. After the speedy declaration of victory in Iraq in May 2003, George W. Bush and Tony Blair repeatedly insisted that the continued attacks on US and UK forces were the work of 'terrorists'. Partly this was a rhetorical strategy to entrench the convenient fiction of a link between Saddam Hussein and Al Qaeda; and partly it sought to argue that only 'terrorists' could be violently unhappy about the country's 'liberation'. The truth was that an increasing number of Iraqis were fighting an often brutal military occupation. In April 2004, fifty-two former members of Britain's diplomatic service wrote an open letter to Tony Blair, helpfully explaining why his terminology was inaccurate: 'All those with experience of the area predicted that the occupation of Iraq by the Coalition forces would meet serious and stubborn resistance, as has proved to be the case. To describe the resistance as led by terrorists, fanatics and foreigners is neither convincing nor helpful.' Well, it was helpful in one sense: to bolster in retrospect the justification for war.

But hang on, you might say, isn't the ambassadors' choice of 'resistance' to describe those fighting against the occupation also an ideologically loaded term? It might indeed be read this way. Though 'to resist' is in theory a primarily neutral term, the noun 'resistance' inescapably carries with it heroic overtones of, for example, French action against occupying Nazi forces during the Second World War. (This usage is well understood across the globe: the Arab news service Al Jazeera, for example, calls Palestinian bombers 'resistance fighters'.) Robin Cook, the former Leader of the House of Commons who resigned in protest over the Iraq war, also used the term when he later wrote: 'The nadir of the occupation came at Fallujah when over three weeks in spring US marines attempted to storm a city that was a centre of Sunni resistance.'[43]

The news media made an explicit and considered choice about what to call those who continued to use violence. Recognising on the one hand that the Bush–Blair use of 'terrorists' was propaganda, and that any use of 'resistance' on the other hand could look as though it conveyed approval, almost everyone converged rapidly on the term 'insurgents'. The description 'insurgency' – literally, rising up within – captured the sense of what one reporter on the ground was by the end of 2004 calling 'a genuine and popular insurrection'[44] in Iraq, while at the same time expressing no approval, as it does not with Scheuer's description of Al Qaeda as 'insurgents'. It also chimed with the fact that 'a leaked Foreign Office memo of May 2004 noted that the insurgency had "a reservoir of popular support, at least among the Sunnis".'[45]

US forces in Iraq referred to the insurgents as AIF, for 'anti-Iraqi forces'[46], which was cute, but tended to gloss over the fact that, as of September 2004, the 'anti-Iraqi forces' (comprised principally of Iraqis) had since the end of the war proper killed only half as many Iraqis as had the Americans and their allies: 'Operations by U.S. and multinational forces and Iraqi police are killing twice as many Iraqis – most of them civilians – as attacks by insurgents, according to statistics compiled by the Iraqi Health Ministry.'[47] Soldiers in Iraq, as well as reporters, agreed that the problem was far broader than a few 'determined killers and terrorists', as US Secretary of State Condoleezza Rice characterised it.[48] Christopher Hitchens argued against the use of the word 'insurgents', suggesting that, instead, 'Baathist or Bin Ladenist or jihadist would all do'[49]. The problem was that although some of the perpetrators of violence in Iraq did fit into one of those categories, not all of them did. And in many cases it was impossible to know whether they did or not. In June 2005, the overall commander of the forces in Iraq, Lt. Gen. John R. Vines, stated categorically that, as well as former

Ba'athists and Al-Qaeda-inspired fighters, the 'insurgency' included a 'broader group' of Iraqis who 'want[ed] to see all foreign forces leave the country'.[50] Indeed, this category of fighters was referred to internally by the military with the unambiguous phrase POI – 'pissed-off Iraqis'.[51] So a general term such as 'insurgents' seemed useful. In July 2004, intelligence officer Major Thomas Neemeyer, with the US First Infantry Division in Iraq, had summed up the problem vividly: 'The only way to stomp out the insurgency of the mind would be to kill the entire population.'[52]

To resist the use of 'terrorists' in this case, and to insist on the word 'insurgents', was not to express approval of car-bombings that killed civilians, or even of the killing of soldiers. It was equally important to refuse to talk of a 'resistance'. The media's adoption of the most politically neutral terminology may even have caused some at the top to adopt the prevailing language: in September 2004, US Secretary of Defense Donald Rumsfeld was referring to 'the assassins and the terrorists'[53] in Iraq; eight months later, he referred to the 'insurgency'.[54] The case of the 'insurgents' was a small triumph of journalistic resistance to propagandistic terminology.

Terrorist suspects

Such small triumphs, however, go hand in hand with a continuing carelessness even in closely related contexts. In the debate about how to combat the threat of terrorism in Britain and the US, one highly loaded phrase that has so far slipped the net is the very common 'terrorist suspects', which has become the norm to describe those who attract police interest. It is used freely both by those who defend detention without trial and by those who argue for the conservation of civil liberties. It appears in apparently innocuously neutral contexts such as the following newspaper report: 'The Metropolitan Police Commissioner, Sir Ian Blair, will also urge further debate on the use of ID cards to track terrorist suspects during an interview on BBC's Breakfast with Frost programme.'[55] Even though newspapers claim that they do not use the word 'terrorist' in the supposedly objective authorial voice, they freely use 'terrorist suspects'. But the choice of this phrase subtly poisons the argument and contributes to a climate of fear.

What's wrong with it? Well, it's easy to see if you substitute the alleged crime. To call somebody not yet convicted of any offence a 'rapist suspect' or a 'murderer suspect' is already to assume the guilt of the person in question, by attaching to them the descriptive label reserved for those whose crimes have been proven in court. In the same way, to use the phrase 'terrorist suspect' commits a pre-emptive essentialism: the person is first defined as a terrorist – and remember, a terrorist is a person who is inherently evil – and only then is it grudgingly acknowledged that the basis for such a categorisation is as yet untested. Actually it need never be tested according to the normal standards of criminal prosecution: the whole point of designating someone a 'terrorist suspect' is to be able to lock them up without trial. You can be a terrorist without ever having committed an act of terrorism.

You might still think it desirable that anyone accused of a crime should be presumed innocent until proven guilty. The widespread usage of the phrase 'terrorist suspects', on the contrary, goes a long way towards indicating guilt. It derives from, and feeds back into, an assumption that the lamentably old-fashioned ideal of presumed innocence is no longer appropriate to modern times. It is at one with the fine contemporary tradition of contempt for the courts evinced by Labour Home Secretaries in Britain. In April 2005, at the end of the notorious 'ricin plot' trial, Kamal Bourgass, who was already serving life in prison for the murder of a policeman, was convicted of conspiring to cause a public nuisance by planning to smear home-made ricin on doorknobs and cars in north London. His four co-defendants were unanimously acquitted, and a further prosecution collapsed. In response, Home Secretary Charles

Clarke said: 'We will obviously keep a very close eye on the eight men being freed today, and consider exactly what to do in the light of this decision.'[56] Once you are a 'terrorist suspect', it seems, not even acquittal will help you. You are for ever guilty of having once been a suspect.

The assumption contained within the phrase 'terrorist suspects' may also make it more comfortable to order torture and indefinite imprisonment without trial, or to export victims to regimes where it is known they will be tortured, a practice known in the US by the euphemism 'rendition' and publically condemned in April 2005 by Human Rights Watch (of which more in Chapter Seven). After all, if we already know they're guilty, then we don't feel so morally squeamish about applying any possible sanction. 'Terrorist suspects' can easily come to mean just 'terrorists', with the second word added as a verbal sop to bleeding-heart liberals but not taken seriously in a judicial process.

The phrase 'terrorist suspects' (or its singular) does not appear a single time in the archives of the *Guardian* and *Observer* for the whole of the year 1998. During 1999 and 2000, the construction appears nine and eleven times, respectively, in almost all cases involving alleged members of the IRA. Then something happens: the phrase gets hip. There follows an implacable crescendo: 79 uses in 2001, growing to 127 in 2004, and 94 up until the beginning of September 2005. But 'terrorist suspects' was not suddenly invented in 1999; it was already in use from the mid-1930s, as a British description of detained Jews in Palestine, or later as an Israeli description of detained Palestinians, or a British description of detained Irish persons, allegedly members of the IRA. The archives of the *New York Times* show the phrase 'terrorist suspects' occurring on average five times a year in that newspaper since 1934. Having bobbed along in single figures for decades, however, it suddenly leaps to 54 uses in 2001, 45 in 2002, and 73 in 2003. Clearly the modern preponderance of the phrase has something to do with the growth of 'war on terror' rhetoric in recent years.

The phrase is now enshrined in British law; but it has not always been so. Consider the evolution of language in British anti-terrorism legislation. The government passed three Prevention of Terrorism Acts that were designed to deal with the IRA. The first, the Prevention of Terrorism (Temporary Provisons) Act of 1974, does not even use the word 'terrorist', let alone 'terrorist suspect', but talks coolly (by modern standards) of 'terrorism' and 'acts of terrorism'. Next came the Prevention of Terrorism (Temporary Provisions) Act of 1984 (you already see the comedy in this repeated use of the word 'temporary': governments are always loath to give up new powers, even if they were only meant to last a short while). Here, too, the talk is of 'acts of terrorism', or 'terrorism' alone, but still never of a 'terrorist' or a 'terrorist suspect'.

The word 'terrorist' arrives with the Prevention of Terrorism (Temporary Provisions) Act of 1989,[57] but only as an adjective, in combination with other words. So we read of 'terrorist funds', 'terrorist activities', and 'terrorist investigations'. (Happily, the context makes it clear that the legislators mean funds belonging to terrorists, rather than money that throws bombs; and investigations of terrorism, rather than investigations which kill people.) There is still no example of 'terrorist' being used to denote a specific individual.

By 1994, though, things have changed. The Criminal Justice and Public Order Act of that year suddenly uses the phrase 'terrorist suspects', not in the main body of the text but almost as an afterthought in a technical section dealing with how the Act revises previous law. In Schedule 10, Consequential Amendments, the descriptive heading of paragraph 62 reads: 'Samples: application to terrorist suspects'. The prejudicial concept has been smuggled into law by the back door.

The Terrorism Act 2000 was designed to replace the Prevention of Terrorism legislation. In December 1999, when the bill was before Parliament, the then Home Secretary Jack Straw explained its aims in the *Guardian*, and used our weasel phrase 'terrorist suspects': 'The PTA allowed ministers – not judges –

to decide whether a terrorist suspect should be detained by the police for longer than 48 hours.'[58] As we have seen, in fact no version of the Prevention of Terrorism Act specifically used the phrase 'terrorist suspect'; and the Terrorism Act 2000 itself uses the less loaded phrase 'suspected terrorists', almost as though the use of 'terrorist suspects' in the 1994 Criminal Justice Act had been an injudicious mistake. Yet a public servant is freely disseminating the phrase to the public. And the Act itself is already more prejudicial than those preceding it, according to barrister Helena Kennedy: 'The presumption of guilt permeates the Terrorism Act 2000. It enshrines a reversal of the burden of proof, with accused persons having to show beyond reasonable doubt that they did not have items for terrorist purposes.'[59]

'Terrorist suspect' becomes cemented in the legal language in the Anti-terrorism, Crime & Security Act of 2001. Passed on 14 December 2001, in the wake of the attacks on America in September, this legislation is notable in that it immediately starts using more fizzy, populist language. Instead of 'terrorist funds', for example, it talks about 'terrorist cash'. (Probably because 'funds' is a term of respectable financial institutions, while 'cash' conjures up black-market, underhand dealings.) For those under suspicion, the Act continues to use the traditional 'suspected terrorists' and 'suspected international terrorists', but finally gives in to the old temptation at paragraph 89, whose heading is 'Fingerprinting of terrorist suspects'.

In America, meanwhile, the phrase 'terrorist suspects' as a public legislative concept first appears in a Congress resolution 'Regarding American victims of terrorism'[60] that was referred to the Senate Foreign Affairs Committee in 1998. The 'terrorist suspects' in question are Palestinians, said by the Israeli authorities to have been involved in the killing of US citizens in Israel or the occupied territories; the resolution calls for them to be prosecuted in the US. This matter, and the phrase 'terrorist suspects' itself, eventually pass into US public law in an Act passed on 29 November 1999 – just two weeks, coincidentally, before Jack Straw uses the phrase in his *Guardian* article on the other side of the Atlantic. The phrase appears in Section 805, 'Report on Terrorist Activity in Which United States Citizens were Killed and Related Matters', and commissions a State Department report on 'The policy of the Department of State with respect to offering rewards for information on terrorist suspects', a list of requests by the US 'for the transfer of terrorist suspects from the Palestinian Authority and Israel', and 'A list of any terrorist suspects in these cases who are members of Palestinian police or security forces, the Palestine Liberation Organization, or any Palestinian governing body.'[61]

Thereafter the phrase 'terrorist suspects' is liberally used in bills presented to the House and Senate, and after 11 September 2001, it is used in many official White House press releases and news briefings: for example, in a section-heading of a news briefing, 'Gun purchases/terrorist suspects';[62] in a factsheet about how the FBI is 'Monitoring Terrorist Suspects';[63] and in a triumphant report about 'the successful apprehension of several dangerous terrorist suspects'[64]. Notice how the prejudicial nature of the phrase is particularly useful in the last case: the arrest of a suspect is only a victory in counter-terrorism if the suspect is in fact a terrorist. Don't worry: these guys are not just 'terrorist suspects', they're *dangerous* 'terrorist suspects'. One would have thought that a person could only be described as 'dangerous' in this context once a court finds that he has committed, or was conspiring to commit, an act of terrorism. But the language launches a pre-emptive strike on the legal process. The case is effectively closed before it begins.

In contrast, the Council of Europe's 2002 'Guidelines on human rights and the fight against terrorism' noticeably refrains ever from using the word 'terrorist' to describe a person, real or hypothetical. Instead there are 'acts of terrorism', or 'terrorist acts', or 'terrorist activities'. And instead of the egregious phrase 'terrorist suspect', the Council goes out of its way to use the phrase 'a person suspected of terrorist activities'[65]. That might be a mouthful, but at least it displays a cool, forensic accuracy, quite the opposite of the public language in the Anglosphere.

So what have we found? That the phrase 'terrorist suspects' begins to crop up in official legislative language in the US and UK between 1994 and 2001. Since 2001, it has gained ever-wider currency in the press. Does this prove that politicians cunningly engineered the phrase to serve their own illiberal purposes and were then helped to disseminate it by deliberately complicit journalists? No. But it's clear that the introduction of 'terrorist suspects' in official discourse created an atmosphere in which it increasingly seemed to others that that was an appropriate phrase to use – or rather that, now it was there, they saw no reason *not* to use it: precious few people noticed its prejudicial quality. It is an example of what you might term unconscious collaboration.

It is not as though there are not more accurate descriptions available to politicians and reporters: to say 'suspected terrorist' or 'terrorism suspect', or even the headline-friendly 'terror suspect', does not carry the same prejudicial charge. But 'terrorist suspect' sounds sexier, more arresting; it gets the buzzword 'terrorist' into the mind first. It may look difficult to pronounce quickly, until you realise you don't have to pronounce the 't' in the middle but can elide it into a long hiss of disapproval: 'terrorissssssuspect'. Furthermore it has, out of any of the alternatives, the most musically satisfying rhythm, as you trip through the troika of 'terrorist' and land with two satisfying hammer-blows on 'suspect'. In a lighter mood, you could even sing it to the tune of 'Eleanor Rigby'.

We can even sometimes see all the alternatives used within a single article. In a brilliant discussion of the US practice of 'rendition',[66] the writer Jane Mayer uses 'suspected terrorist(s)' (twice), 'terrorism suspects' (three times), and 'terror suspects' (once), but she also uses the phrase 'terrorist suspects' no fewer than six times, which is as many as the rest combined. And yet 'terrorist suspects' contains the attitude – we know they're guilty, so it's fine to torture them – that this author deplores. Perhaps out of an understandable writer's desire for elegant variation (she did not respond to a request for comment), Mayer thus, in a small but significant way, reinforces the justification for the phenomenon she is exposing. The article well illustrates the extent to which we have to be on our guard in adopting language that justifies a certain point of view. At other times, its use just becomes absurd, as when it was reported in the *Guardian* that Jean Charles de Menezes, the Brazilian shot by British police, had 'emerged from a block of flats police believed housed terrorist suspects'.[67] Did the police *believe* the block housed 'terrorists', or did they *know* that it housed certain people whom they *suspected* of terrorism? Using the term 'terrorist suspects' in this way, vaguely ascribed to police 'beliefs', the paper's own account of who was culpable or suspected of what was muddied beyond repair.

To resist the use of this kind of irresponsible language does not imply that one does not also recognise the real difficulties of the issue. Clearly, you cannot wait until someone kills hundreds of people before taking any action at all. But to accept the sly assumption of the phrase 'terrorist suspects' is to assume the infallibility of police and intelligence services, in the face of notorious recent evidence that they can be very fallible indeed. 'Terrorist suspect' Jean Charles de Menezes, as we have seen, was presumed guilty and shot to death. Journalists have a responsibility to recognise prejudicial language for what it is. Any notion of fair and accurate reporting should require that the phrase 'terrorist suspects' be erased from the lexicon.

Another problem with the word 'terrorist' as a noun, rather than an adjective, is that it becomes merely a generalised word of abuse, much like 'fascist' has done. He is a fascist because he wants to stop me from smoking, or hunting foxes, or driving fast; she is a terrorist because, well, she just disagrees with me in one way or another. The infantile American TV and radio host Bill O'Reilly, who regularly screams 'Shut up!' at his invited guests, has called the American Civil Liberties Union 'terrorists'[68] (and, for good measure, 'fascists').[69] According to author Rebecca Hagelin, MTV, sex education in schools, and internet pornography all combine in one terrifying phenomenon of 'cultural terrorism'.[70] And on a TV chat show, Richard Perle, who at the time was chairman of the Pentagon's Defense Policy Board, described the investigative journalist Seymour Hersh as 'the closest thing American journalism has to a terrorist'.[71] When pressed on this choice of abusive terminology, Perle said: 'Because he sets out to do damage and he will do it by whatever innuendo, whatever distortion he can.' This is alarming: if 'innuendo' and 'distortion' now make you a terrorist, then people who make sexual jokes or turn up their guitar amplifiers are terrorists, too.

Perle equates Hersh's speech with terrorism; Osama bin Laden, in a 1998 television interview, equated terrorism with speech: 'They kill and murder our brothers. They compromise our honour and our dignity and dare we utter a single word of protest against the injustice, we are called terrorists.'[72] This is a whine of epic disingenuousness. The destruction of buildings and mass killing is something more than uttering a single word. (Unless, perhaps, it is the word of God.) Those who deplore murder – and Perle is presumably to be included among their number – ought to insist on that distinction rather than trying to elide it.

Just as deflationary of the currency of 'terrorist' is the extent to which the word has actually become, especially in cultural discussion, a word of approval, signalling an edgy willingness to shock complacent audiences, to disrupt commercial structures, or just to be rude. People from John Lydon to Bill Drummond and Damien Hirst have been called 'art terrorists', even though the last is the most establishment of modern artists, and a man called AK47, who steals bits of British public sculpture, applies the label proudly to himself.[73] Perhaps it's time to retire the word 'terrorist' for good. Or wait, maybe we could start a war against it.

War on terror

It was a phrase exquisitely engineered for public consumption. Revealingly, they didn't use it themselves: within the US military and intelligence world, it was known as GWOT, for Global War On Terrorism, which at least made for a more satisfying acronym. The public, however, needed something with fewer syllables, something snappier. So 'war on terror' it was, and so George W. Bush announced it, on 20 September 2001.

The US had not declared war on fear itself, since Hollywood still made slasher movies and funfair ghost trains did not become illegal. Rather, the war was supposed to be against terrorism. In fact, a 'war against international terrorism' had already been declared in March 1981 by Reagan's Secretary of State, Alexander Haig. (Aptly, John Arbuthnot wrote two centuries earlier that there were some 'Political Lies' which, 'like your Insects, die and revive again in a different Form'.)[74] But the idea made no more sense back then either. Wars are things you have against nation states. Terrorism is a tactic of violence. The idea of a war against a tactic is blatantly absurd: it is like declaring war against sniping, or war against high-altitude bombing. As former US National Security Advisor Zbigniew Brzezinski writes: 'No one, for instance, would have declared at the outset of the Second World War that the war was being fought against "blitzkrieg".'[75] Sir Harold Walker, the UK's former Ambassador to Iraq and one of the fifty-two who signed the letter to Tony Blair, says that 'war on terror' 'is a very prejudicial and ill-chosen phrase, because it's impossible to have a war on a technique. Terrorism is a technique, it's not a state or a building or a soldier, it's a technique, so logically it's rather difficult to have a war on terrorism. You can have a war on certain terrorists, certain people who use terrorist techniques.'[76]

So much is clear, and must have been clear to the person who coined the phrase 'war on terror'. The interesting question is why it was nevertheless thought useful. When Bush announced it, he said: 'Americans should not expect one battle, but a lengthy campaign unlike any other we have ever seen.'[77] Campaign was the *mot juste*: as in advertising campaign, or propaganda campaign, or even, perhaps, campaign for re-election. The 'war on terror' prepares the public for a potentially indefinite state of emergency. In March 2002, the US Department of Homeland Security unveiled a new colour-coded 'Advisory System', indicating the current threat of terrorism. It has five possible settings, but the lowest two have never been used: the nationwide threat level has been at either yellow ('Significant Risk of Terrorist Attacks') or orange ('High Risk of Terrorist Attacks') ever since.[78] 'Raising the threat condition has economic, physical, and psychological effects on the nation,' comments the Advisory System's internet page.[79] Maybe it is precisely those 'psychological effects' that are desired. The first Secretary of Homeland Security, Tom Ridge, has stated that 'some people' often insisted on raising the threat level against his wishes:

> Ridge said he wanted to 'debunk the myth' that his agency was responsible for repeatedly raising the alert under a color-coded system he unveiled in 2002. 'More often than not we were the least inclined to raise it,' Ridge told reporters. 'Sometimes we disagreed with the intelligence assessment. Sometimes we thought even if the intelligence was good, you don't necessarily put the country on (alert). . . . There were times when some people were really aggressive about raising it, and we said, "For that?"'[80]

One might suppose that the repeated use of the blunt substantives 'war on terror', along with official threat alerts that according to the nation's security chief were not warranted, is simply part of a strategy not to dispel fear but actually to induce it. Consider the language of an official leaflet about the threat of terrorism which was distributed to the British public in 2004: under the heading 'Possible signs of terrorism', it says: 'Terrorists need [. . .] A place to live: Are you suspicious about

any tenants or guests?'[81] Being suspicious of neighbours had
always been a great British pastime; now apparently it was
grounds for denouncing them as terrorists.

Why would it be useful to induce fear in a population?
Perhaps because a frightened population is more docile. You
could then get away with passing laws that repeal their freedoms
(in the name, of course, of protecting freedom). Harold Walker
commented: 'It's amazing to me, given that the United States is a
very active sort of democracy, that because of the war on terrorism, the way the reaction to 9/11 was worked out, the Americans
have allowed an astonishing array of potential infringements –
well, not to mention actual infringements – of their liberties
under Homeland Security measures.' Presumably, indeed, the
perpetrators of terrorism have then won, given that they were
said to be assaulting liberty in the first place ('our very freedom
came under attack'[82]). More to the point, they have also won if
governments deliberately collude in the strategy of instilling fear
in their populations. Lord Steyn, the British law lord, decried
'the public fear whipped up by the governments of the United
States and the United Kingdom since September 11 2001 and
their determination to bend established international law to
their will and to undermine its essential structures'.[83] The London
Underground bombings of July 2005 were taken by some commentators to have disproven the idea that official concentration
on the threat of terrorism amounted to fearmongering. But it
is of course possible for governments to inflate a real threat's
magnitude to the detriment of taking concerted action against
other threats, such as the New Orleans hurricane, or pandemics
of infectious disease, or the European heatwave of summer 2003,
which killed 35,000 people, and about half of whose intensity has
been attributed to global warming.[84]

The idea of the 'war on terror' also provided an overarching
narrative for unrelated military adventures across the globe, a
sort of rhetorical glue. The authors of the 9/11 Commission
Report complained: 'The enemy is not just "terrorism," some
generic evil. This vagueness blurs the strategy. [. . .] It is the

threat posed by *Islamist* terrorism – especially the al Qaeda network, its affiliates, and its ideology.'[85] But to blur the strategy was precisely the intention. The vagueness of the phrase was deliberate, because it was not meant to apply just to a fight with Al Qaeda. The writer Mark Massing watched Fox News for several months at the end of 2004, and noticed: 'Whenever news about Iraq came on, the urgent words "War on Terror" appeared on the screen, thus helping to frame the war exactly as the President did.'[86] The choice of 'terror' in the slogan rather than 'terrorism', as in the Reagan administration's previous version of it, was useful as it enabled its users to elide any distinction between suicide bombers and repressive dictators. Bush, Rumsfeld, *et al.* made repeated references to Saddam Hussein's Iraq as both a 'terror regime' and a 'terrorist regime', so that the invasion could be more easily filed under the rubric of the 'war on terror' (so states *can* commit terrorism after all); meanwhile, the weapon of Al Qaeda was said to be both 'terrorism' and 'terror'. There was for a time a useful distinction available between 'terror', understood as the violent actions of a state against its own population (as in *La Terreur* in revolutionary France), and terrorism, understood as a violent act against civilians intended to coerce a government. The 'war on terror' deliberately erased such differences.

It was not just conservative cable news channels that mirrored the language of 'war on terror'. The Democrats' 2004 Presidential candidate, John Kerry, did too. Instead of attacking the assumptions contained within the phrase 'war on terror', he parroted it himself, and just limply promised that he would 'do a better job of waging' it.[87] But clearly Bush was already doing an excellent job of waging it, since there had been no more attacks on American soil, despite the years of flashing yellow and orange lights on the Terrorist Threat Advisory System – which confluence of facts indicated, it would be logical to assume, that countless terrorist plots had been brilliantly foiled. Perhaps some had; and yet for some reason it was never thought appropriate to lower the threat level to 'Guarded' ('General Risk of Terrorist Attacks'), let alone 'Low'.

More widely, the media in general, along with Tony Blair, adopted the phrase 'war on terror' and repeated it uncritically as though it made sense, so contributing to the President's unending campaign. A few resisted: the BBC *Newsnight* presenter Jeremy Paxman tended to say, with a customary sneer, 'the so-called "war on terror"',[88] while BBC World Service presenter Kirsty Lang, when presented with a script using the phrase, would change it herself: 'I'm always very careful to use the phrase "President Bush's war on terror".'[89]

Of course, if you have a war, it must be logically possible to win it. As Harold Walker notes: 'The phrase "war on terrorism" suggests you can defeat terrorism – whatever that is – by military means alone. And that's largely what I think the Bush administration seemed to think when they started off. And of course, as the poor old British with their long colonial history know, it's a load of rubbish! You can't defeat insurgency or terrorists by military means alone. Of course you have to have military means, you have to have police means, but you also have to go for the root causes.'

There is in fact an official explanation of what victory in the war on terror would look like. It came very early on, from Donald Rumsfeld:

> Now, what is victory? I say that victory is persuading the American people and the rest of the world that this is not a quick matter that's going to be over in a month or a year or even five years. It is something that we need to do so that we can continue to live in a world with powerful weapons and with people who are willing to use those powerful weapons. And we can do that as a country. And that would be a victory, in my view.[90]

It is worth pausing to admire the awesome rhetorical invention on display here. Like a bebop saxophonist, Rumsfeld takes a theme, crawls into it, turns it inside out, and rebuilds it at crazy angles. Translated into simple declarative English, he is saying that the war on terror will be won when everyone is convinced that the war on terror cannot be won in any foreseeable future. Victory is defined as persuading us that victory is impossible. This persuasion appeared to have worked when a Fox News poll in September 2005 found that 62 per cent of Americans thought that they would not see the end of the 'war on terror' in their lifetimes.[91]

'War on terror' was also a politically useful phrase in that any action that was said to be a part of it could not properly be called a war itself. After all, wars are not made up of wars; they are made up of battles. We could see this rhetorical strategy in operation in the following remarks made in 2005 by Dr Paula J. Dobriansky, the US Under Secretary of State for Global Affairs:

> Democracies are inherently more peaceful than other forms of government. If you look at major, modern conflicts, you will find that none took place between democracies with universal suffrage. In wars between democracies and non-democracies, it is invariably the latter that is the aggressor.[92]

Hold that thought: invariably, it is non-democracies who attack democracies. But in 2003, the US and Britain, exemplars of modern democracy, entered Iraq with a lot of tanks, helicopters, and so on, having not actually been attacked by that country. How to reconcile these two facts? At first one might think that Dr Dobriansky is in the vanguard of an interesting sociolinguistic change. Perhaps the word 'invariably' was always a hostage to fortune: the all-too-potent idea of 'variable' is in the process of drowning out that pernickety little negative prefix 'in-'. Maybe we have come to think of 'in-' as a bland intensifier, on analogy with the curious fact that 'invaluable', which originally meant 'incapable of being valued' and so was used to mean either 'of the utmost value' or 'worthless', now means simply the same as 'valuable'. Thus 'invariably' comes to mean 'quite often', or 'some of the time', or 'whenever I say so'.

But the true message is that the war in Iraq was not actually a war. It was a conflict or a liberation, but not a war. According to Dobriansky elsewhere in her speech, what happened was two things: 'the coalition forces destroyed Saddam Hussein's regime and liberated Iraq'. No mention of a war there. Who said 'war'? Nothing to see here; move along. Helpfully, if what happened in Iraq was not a war, it doesn't count as disproof of her historical theory.

In fact democracies these days call their own proactive military action by any name other than war. That simply follows the process established when the US Department of War was rolled into the Department of Defense in 1949, and the British War Office swallowed up by the Ministry of Defence in 1964. After all, how could you ever start a war if you're called 'Defence'? Indeed, the US Congress has not officially declared war since 1941, though the American military has not quite been idle since; and Parliament has not declared war since 1942.

Refusing to call the actions in Afghanistan or Iraq 'wars' had another use. As Parliamentary researcher Andrew Blick pointed out, the constitutions of both Japan and Italy, drawn up after the Second World War, unambiguously renounce the practice of war. 'Aspiring to an international peace based on justice and order, the Japanese people forever renounce war as a sovereign right of the nation and the threat or use of force as means of settling international disputes'; 'Italy repudiates war as an instrument offending the liberty of the peoples and as a means for settling international disputes.' Even so, 'both Italy and Japan managed to participate in the allied operation in Iraq from 2003',[93] although Japanese soldiers did not join offensive operations. There was no contradiction as long as you are careful never to say that what happened in Iraq was a war.

But of course we still do hear the word 'war' a lot these days. It's simply that war is declared exclusively on abstract nouns or inanimate objects. Terror, drugs, fat, drunk-driving, weeds, the forces of conservatism . . . Even the *reductio ad absurdum* of such paradoxical formulations, 'war on war', has been a slogan for, among others, V. I. Lenin and Karl Popper. War on Want, the charity whose name was invented by Harold Wilson in 1952, may be to blame for the contemporary popularity of the 'war on' trope, though there are even older precedents: in 1918, it was reported that 'the Government is making war on the cattle tick'.[94] One may wearily join in the plea of Ezra Pound's Count Pitigliano: 'wd. you not stop making war on / insensible objects'?[95]

Dr Dobriansky continued this trope with a new name for US foreign policy: the 'war on tyranny'. Coincidentally enough, a war on tyranny was also what Osama bin Laden said he was conducting. In the 1998 document announcing the formation of the World Islamic Front, he wrote:

> There is no doubt that every state and every civilization and culture has had to resort to terrorism under certain circumstances for the purposes of abolishing tyranny and corruption . . . The terrorism we practise is of the commendable kind for it is directed at the tyrants, the traitors who commit acts of treason against their own countries and against their own faith and their own prophet and their own nation. Terrorizing those are necessary measures to straighten things and make them right.[96]

It is striking the extent to which the protagonists in the 'war on terror' mirror each other's rhetoric. Of course here bin Laden was attempting to reclaim the idea of terrorism, which for Bush represented unnegotiable evil: he was harking back to the positive use of 'terrorism' by French and Russian revolutionaries to describe their own activities. Yet there is no way in which the attacks of 11 September 2001 can be said to have been 'directed at the tyrants', since the tyrants in question are Arab rulers, none of whom, so far as it is known, kept offices in the World Trade Center. Nonetheless, bin Laden's talk of 'terrorising' tyrants found its exact analogue in the 2003 American announcement of a 'Shock and Awe' campaign against Saddam Hussein and the Republican Guard: this too was an attempt to terrorise a tyrant.

Iraqi shock and awe were supposed to be the results of the massive aerial bombardment of Baghdad that opened the 2003 war; in fact the real psychological campaign was represented by the repeated public announcements of 'shock and awe' that preceded the actual dropping of bombs, attempting to provoke mass desertion among the Iraqi military. Inasmuch as its targets were at the time not fighting, and as it hoped to provoke a political decision through instilling fear, 'shock and awe' was an act of terrorism itself.

Moreover, the phrase, describing as existing in reality what it only hoped to provoke, worked beautifully in propagandistic terms. Nearly two years later, historian John Lewis Gaddis was able to refer complacently to 'The shock and awe that accompanied the invasions of Afghanistan and Iraq',[97] thus translating a PR description into an established historical fact. Nevertheless, the targets of 'shock and awe' did not in fact appear to be much deterred. As Fred Halliday puts it: 'Shock and Awe. US military term, much heard in 2001–3, for the use of overwhelming military force against an enemy, in this case Iraq. Rather underestimated compliance of target population.'[98] However, there was one set of people for whom 'shock and awe' might have been quite an accurate description of their response: that is, the global television audience who were able to watch, on CNN and the BBC, live pictures in ghostly green nightvision of bombs exploding in Baghdad. Perhaps indeed it was television spectators who were the primary intended targets of 'shock and awe' all along, in which case it might be accounted rather a success.

The phrase 'war on terror' itself had a similar use, too: it energised the imagination. It sounded awesome, evoking a picture of an apocalyptic fight of good against evil. 'Terror' was reified as an impacable, chthonic force infecting the globe. This theological application was explicitly illustrated when George W. Bush announced: 'Our war is against evil.'[99]

In many ways, then, 'war on terror' obeys faithfully the principles set out in another eighteenth-century satirical pamphlet. *Peri Bathous, or Martinus Scriblerus his Treatise of the Art of Sinking in Poetry*, was published in 1727 and is attributed to John Arbuthnot and Alexander Pope. To write the worst possible verse, they advised: 'The *Expression* is adequate, when it is proportionably low to the Profundity of the Thought. It must not be always *Grammatical*, lest it appear pedantic and ungentlemanly; nor too *clear*, for fear it become vulgar; for Obscurity bestows a Cast of the Wonderful, and throws an oracular Dignity upon a Piece which hath no meaning.'[100]

Mark well: not too *clear*. Obediently, 'war on terror', this flexibly potent phrase, also enabled a fog of constructive ambiguity to arise around the status of the enemy. The war on terror was a war when the US wanted it to be and something else when it didn't – for example when it wished to recruit as allies countries that had renounced war. But who was it fighting?

Just as they have sought to muddy the use of the term 'civilian' for their targets, those called terrorists have historically always seen themselves as soldiers fighting a war, as can be seen, for instance, in the name of the Irish Republican Army, or in the radical Islamist interpretation of the concept of jihad as holy war. To acknowledge one's opponents as soldiers, however – even as 'guerrillas', or irregular soldiers, from the Spanish diminutive of *guerra*, war – is already to accord them a kind of legitimacy, so the usual response of governments is to refuse to use that terminology. Such an argument was explicitly joined in South Africa in the 1970s, with one newspaper commentator protesting: 'The Minister cannot expect journalists to do violence to the English language [. . .] by describing guerrilla warfare as terrorism at all times and in all circumstances.'[101] For the same reasons, the French never used the word 'war' for their actions in Algeria between 1954 and 1962.[102] Similarly, Margaret Thatcher resisted the notion that her government was engaged in a 'war' against the IRA, and 'insisted that Britain was fighting terrorists'.[103] The IRA appeared to have the last word when they announced in July 2005 that the 'war' was over.

It might seem trickier, though, to do this once you have actually announced a 'war on terror'. Surely if a war is being fought, both sides consist of soldiers? On the one hand this makes things easier: for during a war you do not try to arrest the enemy, but merely shoot him. 'It is not a metaphorical war,' insisted Air Force Brigadier General Thomas Hemingway.[104] But it would surely be annoying to have to treat captured terrorists, or 'terrorist suspects', according to their rights of protection under the Geneva Convention. And so for these purposes, the war on terror was not really a war after all but a 'conflict'. On 7 February 2002, George W. Bush signed the following statement: 'I . . . determine that none of the provisions of Geneva apply to our conflict with Al Qaeda in Afghanistan or elsewhere throughout the world.'[105] No mention there of a 'war'. The 'war on terror' is only for public consumption. In careful legal terms, the use of 'war' would imply that the provisions of Geneva did in fact apply. And thus it's only a 'conflict'.

'Asymmetric warfare' is the term employed by the US military for fighting people who don't line up properly to be shot at: on the one side you have battalions of American infantry, marines, tanks, and aircraft; and on the other you have terrorists, or guerrillas, or militants, or insurgents. But the more revealing asymmetry lies in the giving of names in the 'war on terror'. We are soldiers; you are terrorists. Asymmetric warfare means: we are fighting a war; but you are not. And so when we capture you, do not expect to be a prisoner of war. You will be a terrorist suspect, an illegal combatant, a ghost detainee. And so the deliberate blurring of categories in the phrase 'war on terror' led straight to Abu Ghraib.

7

Abuse

Repetitive adminstration

In December 2002, two prisoners at the US base in Bagram, Afghanistan, died after trauma to their legs of such severity that the coroners compared it to the results of being run over by a bus. The subsequent official investigation was nothing if not creative. The death of one was explained in this way:

> 'No one blow could be determined to have caused the death,' the former senior staff lawyer at Bagram, Col. David L. Hayden, said he had been told by the Army's lead investigator. 'It was reasonable to conclude at the time that repetitive administration of legitimate force resulted in all the injuries we saw.'[1]

The logic of this is startling. You may compare it in some ways to the Chinese method of execution, used until 1905, known as 'death by a thousand cuts'. Since no one cut can be determined to cause death, no one is responsible for the killing. Similar is the principle behind the firing squad: everyone fires at the same time and one soldier has a blank, so no one soldier can be sure that he killed his comrade. But at least in these two cases the intention is avowedly to cause death. To use the argument as an excuse for 'accidental' extrajudicial killing is different. It is perhaps more like a sophistic application of

Zeno's paradox of motion. Since at every place in the flight of an arrow it can be considered at rest, an infinite number of such points of rest cannot possibly add up to travel, so the arrow does not actually move and can never reach its target. Similarly, no number of 'legitimate' things can ever add up to something that is illegitimate. It's just one of those unfortunate things.

But this is deliberate linguistic misdirection. The insertion of the word 'legitimate' before 'force' aims exactly to pre-empt the question of legitimacy. Even if one allows that some force might be legitimate, one is dissuaded from wondering whether a repetitive sequence of legitimate blows can be illegitimate. That principle is common in other areas of law: repetitively playing your music too loud can add up to a disturbance of the peace. 'Legitimate' force also implies that the victim had been found guilty of a crime deserving of violent punishment; but the dead prisoners had never had a trial.

The argument is weak on a more physical level, too. If I tap you lightly on the head a hundred times, you may become very annoyed, but this will not add up to crushing your skull. Equally, repeated light blows to the thighs will not add up to crushing them as though you had been run over by a bus. The 'legitimate force' in these blows must in truth be fierce. And so the whole defence does nothing but beg the question of legitimacy itself.

In fact the blows to the legs were not mild slaps but 'peroneal strikes', a deliberately disabling strike to the side of the leg, just above the knee, which targets the peroneal nerve. One of the former police officers who trained the guards in this technique said that it would 'tear up' a prisoner's legs if used repeatedly. A military policeman at the base, Specialist Jones, testified as to how entertaining it was to brutalise a detainee in this way and hear him cry out to his god: 'It became a kind of running joke, and people kept showing up to give this detainee a common peroneal strike just to hear him scream out "Allah," he said. 'It went on over a 24-hour period, and I would think that it was over 100 strikes.'

Inflicting pain for its comic value might not be many people's idea of 'legitimate force'. By the time the man who so amused the military police died, most interrogators at the base had concluded that he was an innocent taxi driver.

The word 'administration', meanwhile, is another example of the bureaucratisation of the language of violence. Medicine is administered; civil government is administration. Punishment is administered only after due process. To call the beating of an unconvicted prisoner the 'administration' of force is already to approve of it, by describing it in the language of official sanction. The very phrase 'repetitive administration' is designed to coat the mind in grey cotton-wool, to conjure vistas of endless similar days in fluorescent-lit offices, and thus to mask the reality of brutal violence inflicted for sadistic enjoyment. In the end, the best translation of Colonel Hayden's words is: 'Yes, we beat these men to death, but we have determined that we had the right to do so.'

Abuse; or, the torture word

This case was reported in the *New York Times* under the heading of 'Detainee Abuse'. 'Abuse' is the usual word for the physical and psychological violence inflicted upon prisoners captured in the 'war on terror' and held at Bagram, Abu Ghraib, Guantánamo Bay, and elsewhere. It is an administrative euphemism that has been widely adopted by a media cravenly hedging its bets. Indeed, 'abuse' is a productively vague term. As a noun, 'abuse' implies a lamentable exception to normal rules, which, as we shall see shortly, is used to displace blame. As a verb, to 'abuse' an inanimate object is 'to use improperly, to misuse'.[2] The idea of 'abusing' a person, then, is a distasteful metaphor, implying as it does that human beings are tools with more or less correct uses, rather than, as Immanuel Kant argued, being ends in themselves. It is nonetheless understood in specific constructions such as 'child abuse' that the mistreatment involved is of a very serious nature. On the other hand, simply to 'abuse' a person can mean calling him an idiot. Or, apparently, torturing him to death.

It is rather helpful to have recourse to such a term, because it does not necessarily imply criminality; rather, it names a wide spectrum of activity, some of which is criminal (beating) and some of which isn't (name-calling). When asked a question about 'torture' in the wake of the public dissemination of the Abu Ghraib photos, Donald Rumsfeld responded thus:

> I think that – I'm not a lawyer. My impression is that what has been charged thus far is abuse, which I believe technically is different from torture. Just a minute. [. . .] I don't know if the – it is correct to say what you just said, that torture has taken place, or that there's been a conviction for torture. And there-fore I'm not going to address the torture word.[3]

Rumsfeld claims that 'abuse' is 'technically' different from torture; however, there is no 'technical' definition of 'abuse' in general at all: that is precisely why the term was chosen, because in its generosity of scope it obscures the particulars of violent acts. Rumsfeld feels obliged to remind his audience that he is not a lawyer, as though the Secretary of Defense must not be expected to have any understanding of international law, whether it relates to torture or anything else. And finally, he refuses to 'address the torture word'. Not the matter of torture, not the physical facts of torture; just the 'word' itself. The very word makes him squeamish: in slamming the dictionary shut on it, he acknowledges its power.

A series of US government memoranda in 2002 showed no such unwillingness to 'address the torture word'; indeed they addressed it so enthusiastically that they have become known as the 'Torture Memos'. Among the most notorious passages from these documents is the following, from Assistant Attorney General Jay S. Bybee:

> Physical pain amounting to torture must be equivalent in
> intensity to the pain accompanying serious physical injury,
> such as organ failure, impairment of bodily function, or even
> death. [4]

This is a much more restrictive definition than any previous
concept of 'torture' delineated in US or international law. The
UN Convention Against Torture and Other Cruel, Inhuman or
Degrading Treatment or Punishment (CAT), which entered into
force in 1987, defines torture thus:

> [T]he term 'torture' means any act by which severe pain or suf-
> fering, whether physical or mental, is intentionally inflicted on
> a person for such purposes as obtaining from him or a third
> person information or a confession, punishing him for an act he
> or a third person has committed or is suspected of having com-
> mitted, or intimidating or coercing him or a third person, or for
> any reason based on discrimination of any kind, when such
> pain or suffering is inflicted by or at the instigation of or with
> the consent or acquiescence of a public official or other person
> acting in an official capacity.

So the CAT's 'severe pain or suffering' has been creatively
glossed by Bybee as 'the pain accompanying serious physical
injury, such as organ failure, impairment of bodily function, or
even death', a far narrower description. How to get round this
obvious incompatibility? The trick is to argue that the United
States is not in fact strictly bound by the Convention's terms. On
the same day that Bybee redefined 'the torture word', Deputy
Assistant Attorney General John C. Yoo wrote a memo helpfully explaining that the US had entered a 'reservation' with its
ratification of the Convention to the effect that it would be
bound only by its own definition of torture and not the one set
out in the Convention itself. According to international lawyer
Philippe Sands, however, this was not actually true: 'Yoo has
misunderstood what the US did in ratifying the Convention. It

did not enter a "reservation" redefining torture and setting the bar at a higher level; it entered an "understanding". This is an entirely different thing. Whilst a reservation can change the international legal obligation, an "understanding" cannot.'[5] Throughout his memo, Yoo incontinently switches between the terms 'reservation' and 'understanding', climaxing with this marvellous logical circle: 'under international law we consider it [the 'understanding'] to be a reservation if it indeed modifies the Torture Convention standard.'[6] That is like saying we consider a wildebeest to be a fish, if it indeed can breathe underwater.

What was the effect of changing the definition of torture? According to Bybee, the result was that 'there is a significant range of acts that though they might constitute cruel, inhuman or degrading treatment or punishment fail to rise to the level of torture'. What kind of work is the phrase 'significant range' doing here? If it is a significant range, rather than just a range, presumably the author wants to draw attention to it, and to its rich possibilities for action. He is perhaps offering it as a menu. Go ahead and pick, this sentence says: we might get embroiled in some annoying arguments about 'cruel, inhuman or degrading treatment or punishment', but you can be sure these acts do not constitute torture, since I have just redefined torture explicitly so as to exclude them. Let's see what he has in mind. Bybee refers to a case where a victim was made to kneel, and then kicked in the stomach with military boots. 'We would disagree,' he writes coolly, that this 'rose to the level of "severe pain or suffering".'[7] Note the repetition of the image of violent acts failing to 'rise to the level' of torture, as though torture were a pinnacle of human endeavour, rather than its nadir. The clear implication is that US interrogators have a legal green light to kick prisoners in the stomach.

After this flurry of sophistry over the word 'torture', US military personnel entered a series of official requests for approval of certain interrogation techniques. In an October 2002 memo from Guantánamo's Lt. Col. Jerald Phifer entitled 'Request for

Approval of Counter-Resistance Strategies', one technique for which authorisation was sought was: 'The use of stress positions (like standing), for a maximum of four hours.'[8] In agreeing to this, Donald Rumsfeld scrawled the following at the bottom of the memo: 'However, I stand for 8–10 hours a day. Why is standing limited to 4 hours?'[9] This is a beautiful illustration of plausible deniability. The language of 'stress positions (like standing)' is innocuous, and it is easy to imagine an incurious Secretary of Defense idly picturing a prisoner remaining on his feet but able to wander around, talk on the telephone, drink coffee, and so on. The reality of 'stress positions' is not quite like that, as Adam Hochschild explains:

> What is a stress position? Mike Xego, a former political prisoner in South Africa, once demonstrated one for me. He bent down and clasped his hands in front of him as if they were handcuffed, and then, using a rolled-up newspaper, showed me how apartheid-era police officers would pin his elbows behind his knees with a stick, forcing him into a permanent crouch. 'You'd be passed from one hand to another. Kicked. Tipped over,' he explained. 'The blood stops moving. You scream and scream and scream until there is no voice.'[10]

Another form of 'stress position' is that in which a prisoner's wrists are shackled behind his back, and he is then suspended by them from the ceiling. This form of torture was mechanised by the medieval strappado; nowadays it is often called 'Palestinian hanging', owing to its alleged use by the Israeli military on Palestinian prisoners. In November 2003, a man named Manadel al-Jamadi was hung up in this way in a shower room at Abu Ghraib during questioning by the CIA: he died after half an hour. One guard told investigators that he was surprised al-Jamadi's arms 'didn't pop out of their sockets'.[11] US soldiers were subsequently photographed alongside al-Jamadi's corpse, grinning and giving thumbs-up signs.

The phrase 'stress positions (like standing)' first implies that

all stress positions are merely standing, but even 'merely standing' is not as harmless as it may sound: one of the most feared
methods of torture in North Korea, according to the US's own
Committee for Human Rights report, is to be made 'to stand
perfectly still for hours at a time'.[12] But secondly, the phrase
that Rumsfeld signed off on deliberately leaves an undefined
range of other actions unspoken, hidden behind the bland
euphemism of 'stress', as though being strung up from your
wrists amounts to no more than a stressful day in the office (a
day marked, perhaps, by 'repetitive administration'). 'Stress' is
a word like 'abuse': it conceals a multitude of sins. In refusing to
address the stress word, Rumsfeld turned a blind eye to the
reality of what he was sanctioning. An FBI email of May 2004
clarifies the matter, referring to an 'Executive Order signed by
President Bush' that authorised the use of '"stress positions"
such as half squats'.[13] The US Army's own set of rules for interrogators, Field Manual No. 34-52 on 'Intelligence Interrogation',
states: 'Examples of physical torture include – [. . .] Forcing an
individual to stand, sit, or kneel in abnormal positions for prolonged periods of time.'[14]

Jerald Phifer's memo also sought, but did not on this occasion obtain, permission for the 'Use of a wet towel and dripping
water to induce the misperception of suffocation.'[15] The dainti-
ness of the language here is impressive. Phifer talks of the 'use'
of a wet towel rather than, as would seem logical, 'abuse' – in
the sense of *mis*use – since few would argue that near-suffoca-
tion was the correct application for wet towels the world over.
Clearly 'abuse' is a term for public consumption; between
friendly soldiers, calmly discussing the means of inflicting suffering, there is no such thing as 'abuse', only strategies that are
more or less functional. Wet towels were not the only quotidian
objects that interrogators wanted to abuse. A method of beating
used at Abu Ghraib involved putting the subject into a sleeping
bag and then rolling him around on the floor. A US Army interrogator, defending this practice as 'appropriate', explained: '[A]
sleeping bag is not inherently a weapon.'[16] Indeed it is not; nor

is a wet towel. Nor is a pencil, though that will hardly be any comfort if I stab you in the eye with it. Just as terrorism seeks to erase the notion of a safe place in its target population by bombing bars and railway stations, the systematic exploitation of towels or sleeping bags to inflict pain erases the notion of a safe object.

Moreover, Phifer's choice of the word 'misperception' in explaining that the wet towel will 'induce the misperception of suffocation', rather than simply the 'perception' of suffocation, is a subtle example of pre-emptive justification. It's OK, that little 'mis-' says, the subject might *think* he's suffocating, but he won't actually be, so no harm is done. Any distress caused must be the victim's fault for failing to interpret the situation correctly. In fact, the wet towel, which is placed over the subject's face, is a variety of what is ordinarily called 'water torture'. Another species of this torture, given the fun action-sports name 'water-boarding', consists of strapping the subject to a horizontal board and then tipping his head into water until he is on the point of drowning, a method reportedly practised by the CIA on alleged Al Qaeda operatives.[17] Such techniques induce physical suffering, but also psychological damage. In a Guantánamo memo entitled 'Legal Review of Aggressive Interrogation Techniques', Lt. Col. Diane E. Beaver advised that the wet-towel technique would be 'permissible', although 'caution should be exercised' with it, 'as foreign courts have already advised about the potential mental harm that this method may cause'.[18]

As the UN Convention Against Torture makes clear in the phrase 'severe pain or suffering, whether physical or mental', what Beaver calls 'mental harm' can count as torture even if no physical pain is inflicted. An example of this kind of torture, sometimes called 'psychological torture', is mock execution. (After public release of the first batch of Abu Ghraib photographs, the US Army destroyed pictures of soldiers in Afghanistan posing with their guns held to prisoners' heads.)[19] The deliberately made imminent threat of violence or death is in itself torture. The notorious photograph from Abu Ghraib of a hooded man standing on a box with wires attached to his out-stretched hands shows a man being tortured: he was told that he would be electrocuted if he stepped off the box. The prosecution in Specialist Sabrina Harman's court martial for this case stated that the man 'was trembling, shaking, afraid he was going to be electrocuted'; the defence responded that the episode was 'a joking type of thing'.[20] It is interesting how often the claim of 'joking' arises as a defence, as though inflicting suffering for giggles is somehow an extenuating circumstance. It may not be irrelevant that it is the opposite of the 'just following orders' defence: in other words, to say that you were torturing for the sick fun of it lets your superiors off the hook.

The fact that such mental suffering in the absence of directly inflicted physical pain is still torture posed a problem for memorandist Jay S. Bybee. He rose to the occasion, however, with the following definition:

> For purely mental pain or suffering to amount to torture [. . .] it must result in significant psychological harm of significant duration, e.g., lasting for months or even years.[21]

Here Bybee pays ingenious homage to Zhou Enlai, the Chinese Prime Minister who, when asked in 1968 for his opinion on the historical impact of the French Revolution, famously replied: 'It is too soon to tell.' Likewise, on Bybee's definition, for months or even years after mental harm has been inflicted on a prisoner, it will still be too soon to tell whether it was actually torture; presumably the further hope is that after a few years the problem will have gone away. The definition thereby effectively pre-empts any accusation of psychological torture at the time it was committed, or for an indefinite period thereafter.

Nonetheless, in a May 2005 report, the group Physicians for Human Rights concluded: '[P]sychological torture [. . .] was at the center of the treatment and interrogation of detainees in US custody in Afghanistan, Guantánamo and Iraq since 2002.'[22]

The level of mental health of Guantánamo prisoners during 2003 may be measured by the fact that in that year, according to a US Army spokesman, 'there were 350 acts of self-harm' among the population, including '120 "hanging gestures"'.[23] Though 'gestures' conjures an image of melancholic mime artists, what is meant here is attempted suicide. Another FBI observer recorded the following:

> On a couple of occasions, I entered interview rooms to find a detainee chained hand and foot in a fetal position to the floor, with no chair, food or water. Most times they urinated or defecated on themselves, and had been left there for 18–24 hours or more. On one occasion, the air conditioning had been turned down so far and the temperature was so cold in the room, that the barefooted detainee was shaking with cold [. . .] On another occasion, the [air conditioner] had been turned off, making the temperature in the unventilated room well over 100 degrees. The detainee was almost unconscious on the floor, with a pile of hair next to him. He had apparently been literally pulling his hair out throughout the night.[24]

Among other documented practices defined as 'psychological torture' by the report writers were sensory deprivation and sleep deprivation. The use of such techniques is corroborated by the previously cited FBI email of May 2004, which after referring bluntly to 'sleep deprivation' as one of the techniques used at Guantánamo, acknowledges the usual bureaucratic euphemism for this form of torture with ironical scare quotes, in referring to the phrase 'sleep "management"'[25]. Of course, 'management' usually means the correct handling of affairs, whereas enforced sleep deprivation induces severe cognitive impairment; a truer description would be 'sleep mismanagement'. If we turn again to the US Army's interrogation manual, FM 34-52, we find that 'abnormal sleep deprivation' is defined, along with mock executions, as 'mental torture'.[26]

The FBI agent who wrote the May 2004 email was concerned,

too, with the problem of what exactly constituted 'abuse'. He had been ordered that FBI observers at Guantánamo should report any instances they witnessed of 'abuse', and responded thus:

> This instruction begs the question of what constitutes 'abuse.' We assume this does not include lawful interrogation techniques authorized by Executive Order. We are aware that prior to a revision in policy last week, an Executive Order signed by President Bush authorized the following techniques among others[:] sleep 'management,' use of MWDs (military working dogs), 'stress positions' such as half squats, 'environmental manipulation' such as the use of loud music, sensory deprivation through the use of hoods, etc. We assume the OGC [Office of General Counsel] instruction does not include the reporting of these authorized interrogation techniques, and that the use of these techniques does not constitute 'abuse' [. . .] there may be a problem if OGC does not clearly define 'abuse' and if OGC does not draw a clear line between conduct that is clearly abusive and conduct that, while seemingly harsh, is permissible under applicable Executive Orders and other laws.[27]

This agent clearly knows what is going on; and it is understandable for him to attempt to reduce the level of cognitive dissonance by suggesting the interpretive course he elaborates: that, by definition, anything authorised by the President cannot be 'abuse'. The President, like the Pope or Emperor Hirohito, is morally infallible. Since this memo also reveals that 'abuse' had not been 'clearly define[d]', moreover, Donald Rumsfeld's claim that the violence at Abu Ghraib was 'technically' 'abuse' is shown to be an empty appeal to a non-existent technic.

This brings us to what is arguably the most important function, in propaganda terms, of our terribly useful term of Unspeak, 'abuse'. Particularly when used as a plural noun, 'abuses', it performs the function of claiming that all the many documented examples of torture at US prisons are not to be thought of as collectively authorised, but instead constitute only a series of individual exceptions. The implication is that the administration has an iron rule against torture, and the torture that did in fact occur was the regrettable result of a 'few bad apples' disobeying the rules. By definition, 'abuses' are those things that are not authorised. This point of view is attractive to some journalists: one was able to write in 2005 that 'multiple probes and courts martial have found no evidence that the U.S. condones or encourages torture'.[28] There are two ways in which it is possible to arrive at such an opinion: either one simply declines to examine the evidence, or one silently accepts the Bybee definition of 'torture' as covering only the most egregious imaginable acts. However, the record shows that the US government did authorise a range of acts that its own military establishment defines as torture. In December 2003, another FBI observer referred flatly to what he had witnessed at Guantánamo as 'torture techniques' practised by Department of Defense interrogators pretending to be FBI agents.[29] If the sanctioning of torture was not the government's intention, it is difficult to imagine a plausible alternative explanation for the existence of a series of memos that were in such a hurry to redefine the torture word. Difficult, too, to think of an alternative explanation as to why, even by November 2005, Dick Cheney should have been vigorously seeking an exemption from new Senate anti-torture legislation for the CIA, which continued to operate a network of secret prisons for the interrogation of 'terrorist suspects' in Eastern Europe and Asia.[30]

Enemy combatants

Who were the people being tortured? They were 'like dogs'.[31] (And so threatening to attack them with dogs seemed quite appropriate.) They were the raw material for 'Human Exploitation Teams'.[32] (They were 'human resources' to be 'exploited'.) They were 'enemy combatants'.

Another series of declassified US government memos
shows the amount of legal creativity that went into denying
suspected members of Al Qaeda or Taliban fighters the pro-
tections of the Geneva Convention on the treatment of
prisoners of war (GPW). The reason why people held in
Guantánamo, Abu Ghraib, and elsewhere were referred to by
the administration and a compliant media as 'detainees' rather
than the normal 'prisoners' may indeed specifically have been
to avoid associations with the concept of 'prisoner of war'.
Just as the war on terror is not a war when it suits the government, those captured during it are not PoWs. Instead a new
legal category was dreamed up: that of 'enemy combatant'.
When challenged publically about torture in 2004, George W.
Bush responded:

> The instructions went out to our people to adhere to law. That
> ought to comfort you. We're a nation of law. We adhere to laws.
> We have laws on the books. You might look at these laws. And
> that might provide comfort for you. And those were the
> instructions from me to the government.[33]

Officers of the government did indeed 'look at these laws'
that were 'on the books' regarding the treatment of prisoners,
but the 'comfort' they intended to provide in so doing was comfort to politicians: reassurance that in doing what they planned
to do they would not be prosecuted for war crimes. According
to Alberto Gonzales in his memo of January 2002, one of the reasons why it would be a good idea to decide that Geneva did not
apply was that such a determination 'Substantially reduces the
threat of domestic criminal prosecution under the War Crimes
Act [. . .] "War crime" for these purposes is defined to include
any grave breach of GPW or any violation of common Article 3
thereof (such as "outrages against personal dignity").'[34] Were
the government not desirous of committing – or, more likely,
already committing – actions that at the very least constituted
'outrages against personal dignity' against its prisoners, it is

hard to see why this should be worth mentioning. On the debit side, Gonzales conceded, 'Concluding that the Geneva Convention does not apply may encourage other countries to look for technical "loopholes" in future conflicts to conclude that they are not bound by GPW either.' Gonzales here acknowledged that what he was himself proposing was a 'loophole'.

Rather than being a 'comfort', then, laws were an irritation to be circumvented whenever possible. That is precisely what the lawyers advised. On 1 February 2002, John Ashcroft wrote: 'We expect substantial and ongoing legal challenges to follow the Presidential resolution of these issues. These challenges will be resolved more quickly and easily if they are foreclosed from judicial review [. . .] by a Presidential determination that the Geneva Convention III on prisoners of war does not apply.'[35] The tiresome workings of the legal system, such as judicial review, were held in contempt by the Attorney General. They just got in the way. The case with which legal thinkers decide that law is an expendable luxury was subsequently visible in the dissenting opinion of Antonin Scalia in the 2004 case of *Rasul v. Bush*, when the Supreme Court eventually ruled that the federal courts could hear appeals from people entombed indefinitely in Guantánamo Bay. The location of Guantánamo had been specifically chosen because the US was able to argue that Cuba had sovereignty there, thus circumventing domestic law about what it was able to do on its own territory. Scalia wrote testily: 'The Commander in Chief and his subordinates had every reason to expect that the internment of combatants at Guantanamo Bay would not have the consequence of bringing the cumbersome machinery of our domestic courts into military affairs.'[36]

Ashcroft's fantasy of resolving issues 'quickly and easily', and Scalia's sneer at the 'cumbersome machinery' of the law: the issue is clearly one of expediency rather than of justice. This was reflected in the language of the President's decision, early on in the 'war on terror', that he could imprison suspects without any formal presentation of evidence of their guilt: 'I find [. . .] that it is not practicable to apply in military commissions under this order the principles of law and the rules of evidence generally recognised in the trial of criminal cases in the United States district courts.'[37] 'Not practicable': this does not mean 'unnecessary' or 'not required by law'; it just means inconvenient. Meanwhile, other memos chipped in with suggestions that the President could even explicitly authorise torture if he wanted to, because in a state of war he is simply above the law. As Bybee wrote to Gonzales: 'Congress may no more regulate the President's ability to detain and interrogate enemy combatants than it may regulate his ability to direct troop movements on the battlefield.'[38] There is a certain impatience evident here: tired, perhaps, of all this legal legerdemain, Bybee in the end comes to the happy conclusion that the laws, and the books in which they are written, can simply be thrown out with the garbage. Yale Law School dean Harold Koh called Bybee's memo 'the worst piece of legal analysis from the Justice Department he had ever seen'.[39]

On 7 February 2002, the President officially decided that Geneva would not apply to suspected members of Al Qaeda or the Taliban. Nonetheless, he wrote: 'The United States Armed Forces shall continue to treat detainees humanely and, to the extent appropriate and consistent with military necessity, in a manner consistent with the principles of Geneva.'[40] The appeal to 'military necessity', of course, instantly undermines the rest of the sentence. The point of principles is that they are governing rules: you cannot decide when to adhere to them and when to ignore them. The UN Convention Against Torture explicitly refuses to recognise any possible 'necessity' defence to the crime: '[n]o exceptional circumstance whatsoever, whether a state of war or a threat of war, internal political instability or any other public emergency may be invoked as a justification of torture'. In the same memorandum, Bush claimed that there are people who 'are not legally entitled' to 'humane treatment'.[41] In fact the UN Convention Against Torture leaves no person in the world unprotected from inhumane treatment. Even Jay S.

Bybee had felt compelled to point this fact out, though he did his best to divert attention from it by burying it in a footnote: 'We note that Section 2340A [of the US criminal code] and CAT protect any individual from torture.'[42]

Furthermore, the President's memorandum opened with the grandiose statement that what is required is 'new thinking in the law of war'. Let us dwell on this idea for a moment. First, the phrase appeals to the idea that 'new thinking' will always be better than old thinking: a notion whose merit may be tested by comparing the ideas of, for example, contemporary British ex-footballer David Icke, who believes that the world is run by a race of alien reptiles (among whose number is film actor and singer Kris Kristofferson), with the ideas of any randomly selected eighteenth-century British philosopher, such as David Hume. Next, the 'law of war' is a set of international instruments governing armed conflict, negotiated between the countries of the world. If one party to these agreements, such as the United States, decides unilaterally to indulge in some 'new thinking' on the topic, it must mean that it has decided that the old rules no longer apply to it, and that it will henceforth play by some new rules. As an individual, I am not at liberty to perform some new thinking in the law of murder so as to enable me to kill someone with impunity. And so it is with states. In plain language, 'new thinking in the law of war' means breaking the law of war. The President thus demonstrated that he should be taken very seriously when he says: 'I don't know what you're talking about by international law.'[43]

Bush's February 2002 statement had designated Al Qaeda and Taliban prisoners 'unlawful combatants': a term that does not appear in the Geneva conventions, but has been customarily used to denote people who are deemed not to be protected by their provisions for prisoners of war. Geneva says that 'a spy or saboteur' would fall into this non-PoW category, but must nonetheless be 'treated with humanity'.[44] However, the generalised language of 'unlawful combatant' could be seen to apply more widely than desired. For example, since Iraq had been invaded without the authorisation of the UN Security Council, it would be possible to argue that all US forces in that country were 'unlawful combatants' themselves. So the administration subsequently described its prisoners by using 'unlawful combatants' interchangeably with 'enemy combatants' and 'illegal enemy combatants'. Clearly, the last two phrases do some extra work. By definition, 'we' are not 'enemy'. And like 'terrorist suspect', the phrase 'enemy combatant' prejudges the question of the subject's guilt. The prisoner is automatically categorised not just as one of the enemy, but one of the enemy who was fighting at the time of his capture. If we are thus assured of their guilt, we might be less squeamish about whatever interrogation techniques are used on them down at Guantánamo.

This is how it went, for example, with the writer Christopher Hitchens. In 2001, Hitchens published *The Trial of Henry Kissinger*, a meticulous examination of the ways in which one US politician flouted international law. As his epigraph, Hitchens quoted approvingly Kurt Vonnegut's denunciation of Kissinger as a man who 'made war gladly'. But Hitchens's respect for the rule of law, and his disapproval of glad warmakers ('I'm a war president,' smiled George W. Bush),[45] did not long survive the instigation of the 'war on terror'. In 2005, he wrote a column explaining why the outcry over Guantánamo was unjustified. This article is worth examining in some detail, since it collects in one place a number of characteristic rhetorical strategies employed by uncritical pundits.

Members of 'al-Qaida and its surrogate organizations', Hitchens began by explaining, do not wear uniforms and do not fight on behalf of a recognised authority with which negotiations may be conducted; 'They are more like pirates, hijackers, or torturers – three categories of people who have in the past been declared outside the protection of any law.'[46] Of course, many foolish things had been declared 'in the past'. In the past, for instance, it was declared by various authorities that accused witches who failed to drown were guilty, that the sun revolved around the earth, and that Jews were subhuman. In 2005, by contrast, it was not difficult to find out that no person on earth was 'outside the protection' of such legal instruments as the UN Convention Against Torture or the Universal Declaration of Human Rights. But why should Hitchens try to insinuate that some people were? We must follow carefully each link in his unspoken chain of logic.

Hitchens was sure that everyone in Guantánamo deserved to be there. They were, he assumed, all members of Al Qaeda, or 'foreign sadists taken in arms in Afghanistan'. On what basis he had decided that they were all 'sadists', specifically, is an interesting question. Official uses of the term are to be found rather in descriptions of the actions of US soldiers at Abu Ghraib, where General Antonio M. Taguba wrote of 'numerous incidents of sadistic, blatant and wanton criminal abuses'[47]; while James R. Schlesinger described 'acts of brutality and purposeless sadism'[48] (although it was purposive rather than purposeless, since the 'abusers' were responding energetically to a directive to set 'favorable conditions' for interviews[49]).

Regardless of what secret information Hitchens may have possessed as to the sexual predilections of Taliban soldiers, his larger assumption was that no one imprisoned at Guantánamo was there through accident or error. The administration routinely referred to its prisoners as 'killers', 'terrorists'[50], 'bad people', and 'suicide bombers'.[51] They were 'picked up on the battlefield in the war on terrorism',[52] a claim that sounds persuasive – what were they doing on the battlefield if they were innocent? – until you realise that the 'battlefield' of the war on terror is planet Earth. General Richard Myers stated that the Guantánamo prisoners were 'the same folks' who 'took four airplanes and drove them into three buildings on September 11th',[53] even though the 'folks' who committed those attacks were all quite deceased. Hitchens, it seemed, simply trusted such pronouncements, evincing a degree of faith in the extrajudicial determinations of government that he had not in his previous writings seen fit to extend to any other state. The record in the current matter, however, was not spotless. Among people eventually released from Guantánamo were a fifteen-year-old unemployed Afghan farmer (after fourteen months' imprisonment),[54] shepherds, cobblers, bakers, and taxi drivers. Perhaps perfect accuracy was ensured by the mere passage of time: perhaps, in May 2005, it was simply unthinkable that there could be anyone left in Guantánamo Bay whose guilt was not self-evident.

Indeed, Hitchens opined: 'I think it is fairly safe to say that not one detainee in Guantanamo is there because of an expression of opinion.' We may be happy that Hitchens considered himself safe to express his own opinion. But he was merely guessing, because any evidence for the guilt of the vast majority of Guantánamo prisoners was kept secret. Often it was kept secret from the accused men themselves, a state of affairs which resulted in the following tribunal scene.

The Recorder (not a member of the tribunal) read out the allegation that: 'While living in Bosnia, the detainee associated with a known Al Qaida operative':

Detainee: Give me his name.

Tribunal President: I do not know.

Detainee: How can I respond to this?

Tribunal President: Did you know of anybody that was a member of Al Qaida?

Detainee: No, no.

Tribunal President: I'm sorry, what was your response?

Detainee: No.

Tribunal President: No?

Detainee: No. This is something the interrogators told me a long while ago. I asked the interrogators to tell me who this person was. Then I could tell you if I might have known this person, but not if this person is a terrorist. Maybe I knew this person as a friend. Maybe it was a person that worked with me. Maybe it was a person that was on my team. But I do not know if this person is Bosnian, Indian or whatever. If you tell me the name, then I can respond and defend myself against this accusation.

Tribunal President: We are asking you the questions and we need you to respond to what is on the unclassified summary.

Subsequently, the Recorder read out the allegation that Mustafa Ait Idir had been arrested because of his involvement in a plan to bomb the US Embassy in Sarajevo. The detainee asked to see the evidence against him. He said that in the absence of such evidence, 'to tell me I planned to bomb, I can only tell you that I did not plan'. He continued: 'I was hoping you have evidence that you can give me. If I was in your place – and I apologise in advance for these words – but if a supervisor came to me and showed me accusations like these, I would take these accusations and I would hit him in the face with them. Sorry about that.'

The transcript reveals that 'everyone in the Tribunal room laughs', after which the Tribunal President said to Mustafa Ait Idir: 'We had to laugh, but it is okay.' The detainee continued: 'Why? Because these are accusations that I can't even answer. I am not able to answer them. You tell me I am from Al Qaida, but I am not an Al Qaida. I don't have any proof to give you except ask you to catch Bin Laden and ask him if I am a part of Al Qaida. To tell me what I thought, I'll just tell you that I did not. I don't have proof regarding this. What should be done is you should give me evidence regarding these accusations because I am not able to give you any evidence. I can just tell you no, and that is it.'

On 20 October 2004, the CSRT [Combatant Status Review Tribunal] determined that Mustafa Ait Idir was an 'enemy combatant'.[55]

Laughter in the dark: the 'enemy combatant' often found himself in the position, whether in the courtroom or in the torture chamber, of being the only one who didn't get the joke.

Let us return to Christopher Hitchens, serenely convinced that Mustafa Ait Idir and everyone else at Guantánamo were bad guys. He wrote: 'The man whose story of rough interrogation has just been published in *Time* had planned to board a United Airlines flight and crash it into a skyscraper. I want to know who his friends and contacts were, and so do you, hypocrite lecteur.'[56] This referred to the case of 'Detainee 063', Mohammed al-Qahtani, who, the *Time* article in question reported, was 'believed by many to be the so-called 20th hijacker'.[57] Notice how *Time*'s 'believed by many' turned into Hitchens's bald statement as fact, 'had planned'. However, since al-Qahtani had actually said he was a follower of Osama bin Laden, the case was a useful one for Hitchens to cite: it could be offered as representative of hundreds of others, such as Idir's, where there was no evidence of culpability available at all. What is known of the 'rough interrogation' – 'rough' being another handily vague term, like 'abuse' – included enforced sleep deprivation while the prisoner was under medical supervision for severe dehydration. But Hitchens was impatient with such details; he was simply hungry for information about al-Qahtani's 'friends and contacts'.

The flourish of 'hypocrite lecteur', reminding the reader that Hitchens had read Baudelaire, could not distract from the crudity of this sentiment. What did 'I want to know' mean, precisely? Did it mean: 'I want to know, and I don't care how you get the information'? Or did it even mean: 'I want to know: go ahead and torture him so I can know'? Hitchens elaborated in the next paragraph, with the rhetorical question: 'Is al-Qaida itself to be considered a "ticking bomb" or not?' The phrase 'ticking bomb' is shorthand for the classic defence of torture. We imagine a hypothetical situation in which a man is captured, and his bomb is set to go off in one hour. In order to save the lives of many who would be blown up, it is considered acceptable to torture the bomber in order to get him to disclose the bomb's location.

Hitchens asked whether Al Qaeda should be considered a '"ticking bomb" or not?'. Note that the specific phrasing – 'or not?' – expresses impatience, entertaining if not positively demanding an answer in the affirmative. In this way, Hitchens was doing something remarkable for a writer who was admired by many for his previous denunciations of human-rights violations in Latin America and elsewhere. It seemed that he was actually justifying torture. Refusing to say so explicitly, however, he resorted to coded language and insinuation: that prisoners were unprotected from any law; that he 'want[ed] to know' what they knew; and that they constituted a 'ticking bomb'. To such degraded, underhand modes of discussion does the use of Unspeak lead.

One may have more respect for a politician or writer who has the courage to conduct such an argument in clear terms, away from the murky shadow-world of Unspeak. 'We think we should torture these people,' such an argument might run, 'and here is why.' As it happens, the dividing lines in such arguments are quite clearly drawn: those who propose torture are those with little experience of interrogation who fantasise about 'ticking bomb' scenarios; while among those who oppose torture are the majority of military personnel with concrete experiences of interrogation, who tell us simply that torture doesn't work. Among the latter may be counted Napoleon Bonaparte, a man who knew a thing or two about the exigencies of war. Napoleon wrote in 1798:

> The barbarous custom of having men beaten who are suspected of having important secrets to reveal must be abolished. It has always been recognised that this way of interrogating men, by putting them to torture, produces nothing worthwhile. The poor wretches say anything that comes into their mind and what they think the interrogator wishes to know.[58]

Napoleon's opinion is echoed closely in the US Army's interrogation manual: 'Use of torture and other illegal methods is a poor technique that yields unreliable results, may damage subsequent collection efforts, and can induce the source to say what

he thinks the interrogator wants to hear.'[59] Individual soldiers
concur. Retired Air Force Colonel John Rothrock, who led a
combat interrogation team in Vietnam and who questioned cap-
tives in numerous real 'ticking bomb scenarios', told Anne
Applebaum: 'If I take a Bunsen burner to the guy's genitals,
he's going to tell you just about anything', and added that he
didn't know 'any professional intelligence officers of my generation' who thought that torture was 'a good idea'; interrogator
Colonel Stuart Herrington, whose experience ranged from
Vietnam to Panama and the first Gulf War, added that torture
was just 'not a good way to get information'.[60] Meanwhile, the
FBI noted in December 2003 that the 'torture techniques' used at
Guantánamo Bay had resulted in 'no intelligence of a threat
neutralization nature to date'.[61]

George W. Bush had justified the continuing incarceration of
suspects at Guantánamo on the grounds that they could provide 'information that might not only protect us, but protect
citizens in Europe'.[62] Three weeks later, it became clear that the
torture regime had notably failed to avert the London bombings
of 7 July 2005. Instead, this event provided Bush with an opportunity to reassure the world that 'The war on terrorism goes
on.'[63] In the end, the argument from futility is the most fatal to
the pro-torture camp, because a state's decision to use torture in
the first place is always born from impatience, the hope of a
shortcut: the desire that things should be resolved, in John
Ashcroft's phrase, 'quickly and easily'.

Even if torture does not work, however, we are protected
from becoming too upset on behalf of its victims once we have
accepted the dehumanisation evident in the language used
to talk about them: 'dogs', 'sadists', 'killers', and so forth. The
euphemism for the US practice of exporting certain 'enemy
combatants' to countries where it was known they would be
tortured was 'extraordinary rendition', a practice described by a
former CIA officer as 'an abomination'.[64] Suspects were said to
have been 'rendered', a verb that is also used in the language of
industrial meat-processing. According to the US Environmental

Protection Agency: 'Meat rendering plants process animal by-product materials for the production of tallow, grease, and high-protein meat and bone meal.'[65] In these 'animal rendering processes', the 'raw material' of animals is converted into useful products. Similarly, suspects who are 'rendered' to foreign torturers are pieces of anonymous meat to be converted into useful information by any means necessary. In the view of the renderers, this is their use, not their 'abuse'. 'People are fungible,' Donald Rumsfeld once said of his own soldiers.[66] Fungible means replaceable, or convertible into other currencies. If the human beings of US forces are thus considered in a purely instrumental way, how much more so are 'enemy combatants'. The fungibility of a 'rendered' person denies his individuality, denies his presumed innocence, in the service of a dark fantasy of transubstantiation in which the flesh is made word.

The CIA also had an extraordinary name for those prisoners whose existence was officially denied, who were illegally kept off prisoner lists given to the Red Cross. They were called 'ghost detainees'.[67] This did not imagine the men killed at Bagram persisting as phantoms to haunt their tormentors; it was just another way of dehumanising subjects. It worked in the same way as the term 'debriding' pictured the guerrillas of Fallujah as necrotic tissue, flesh that was already dead. Manadel al-Jamadi, the man who died after being strung up in a shower room at Abu Ghraib, was one such 'ghost'.[68] But it mattered little what you did to 'ghost detainees' – after all, they were not alive to begin with.

Though it had been introduced in 2002, the term 'enemy combatant' was not formally defined until two years later, in an order of US Deputy Secretary of Defense Paul Wolfowitz: then, it was said to denote 'an individual who was part of or supporting Taliban or al Qaeda forces, or associated forces that are engaged in hostilities against the United States or its coalition partners. This includes any person who has committed a belligerent act or has directly supported hostilities in aid of enemy armed forces.'[69] In Judge Joyce H. Green's January 2005 opinion

regarding the legality of denying hearings to Guantánamo prisoners, she pointed out that the use of the word 'includes' in
this definition leaves open an unspecified range of other persons who might qualify. Green recounted how, unsatisfied with
this definition, she had directly quizzed the government on
some hypothetical cases. The response was that the government
considered it had the right to imprison indefinitely without trial
'"a little old lady in Switzerland who writes checks to what she
thinks is a charity that helps orphans in Afghanistan but [that]
really is a front to finance al-Qaeda activities"; "a person who
teaches English to the son of an al-Qaeda member"; "and a journalist who knows the location of Osama Bin Laden, but refuses
to disclose it to protect her source"'.[70] The deliberate abuse of
both words in the phrase 'enemy combatant' was illuminated
for all to see. An elderly woman of charitable sentiments, who
was not an 'enemy' nor a 'combatant', could nonetheless be
defined by fiat as an 'enemy combatant', and therefore a candidate for torture.

A sophisticated concept

Just like terrorism, torture has the effect of perverting categories.
Torture is 'abuse', or 'repetitive administration', a tedious day at
the office; towels and sleeping bags are weapons; little old ladies
are 'combatants'. At Guantánamo Bay, military doctors assisted
in 'coercive interrogations of detainees, including providing
advice on how to increase stress levels and exploit fears',[71] a
practice condemned by the Red Cross as a 'flagrant violation of
medical ethics'.[72] The Pentagon justified this practice with a
claim of ingenious simplicity. According to Dr David Tornberg,
Deputy Assistant Secretary of Defense for Health Affairs, when
a physician assists in interrogation, 'he's not functioning as a
physician', and so the obligations of the Hippocratic oath can
be jettisoned.[73] In other words: if you think that this is an
inappropriate thing for doctors to do, we will just say that the

doctors are not doctors. And so the problem goes away. Meanwhile, the practice of keeping 'high-value' prisoners in 'sealed white climate-controlled cells' was named not 'isolation' but 'segregation', as though the point were merely to prevent prisoners from socialising – perhaps because they would then constitute a 'nuisance' – rather than to inflict psychological suffering.[74]

In a society that authorises routine torture, then, we are in a world beyond the looking glass, where, as Humpty Dumpty said: 'When *I* use a word, it means just what I choose it to mean – neither more nor less.'[75] US Senator Lindsey Graham, while deploring the violence at Abu Ghraib, claimed that the interrogation system at Guantánamo was 'a sophisticated concept',[76] which seems to mean: a) that it was admirable; b) that if you disapprove of it, you don't understand it; and c) that any gap between the official expression of this 'concept' and the practice (as authorised by classified memos and documented by the FBI) could be dismissed as 'abuse'. Or perhaps Graham was hinting that Guantánamo was not what it seemed at all: that it cared nothing about 'information', but existed in the realm of theatrical terrorism. On this scheme, the enemies of the US would see TV clips of shackled men in orange jumpsuits and know that the 'war on terror' meant business. The Pentagon, meanwhile, insisted that Guantánamo was a 'professional operation',[77] appealing to the inherent moral good of all bureaucratic organisation. The prisoners there had nothing to complain about, said Vice President Dick Cheney, because they were 'living in the tropics'.[78]

Such a world of inverted and abused meanings makes possible the further inference that beating people to death is a necessary device for the promulgation of an 'ideology of compassion'.[79] The ends justify any means. It is no longer a paradox to say that we must torture our way to freedom.

8

Freedom

On the march

The 'war on terror' would be depressing if it were only defined negatively, as against something. Can't it have a positive aspect too? Let us say, then, that it is also a war for freedom. On Memorial Day 2005 in the United States, George W. Bush gave a speech at Arlington National Cemetery. He took advantage of the occasion to drive home the propaganda message:

> Because of the sacrifices of our men and women in uniform, two terror regimes are gone forever, freedom is on the march, and America is more secure.[1]

The hastiness of this shorthand, cramming three precision-tooled sound bites into a single sentence when purportedly commemorating soldiers who have died as a result of one's policies, looks almost insulting. But the catchphrases are useful. We have dealt with 'terror regimes'; here let us consider 'Freedom is on the march'. At first blush it looks like an oxymoron. To be 'on the march' means to be unfree, insofar as one is subject to military discipline. So freedom is not actually perfectly free. Now, it is true that this apparently contradictory idea has a pedigree. Hegel thought that liberty consisted in one's right to obey the police.[2] ('Freedom' and 'liberty' are used essentially interchangeably in English,[3] and will be so treated in this chapter. French, for example, has only one word: *liberté*.) Less paradoxically, Rousseau, in *The Social Contract*, offered the following pert observation:

> At Genoa, the word Liberty may be read over the front of the prisons and on the chains of the galley-slaves. This application of the device is good and just. It is indeed only malefactors of all estates who prevent the citizen from being free. In the country in which all such men were in the galleys, the most perfect liberty would be enjoyed.

It has long been agreed that freedom depends on law. The law demands that in exercising your freedom, you do not unduly reduce that of others. We do not think anyone should be free to murder people. John Locke made the point with aphoristic precision: 'Where there is no law, there is no freedom.'[4] The noted human-rights professor Michael Ignatieff had somehow forgotten this maxim when in 2004 he wrote: 'Sticking too firmly to the rule of law simply allows terrorists too much leeway to exploit our freedoms.'[5] Of course, the 'freedoms' he is so concerned to protect from 'exploitation' can only be guaranteed by sticking firmly to the rule of law. Ignatieff's glib claim that one can stick to the law 'too firmly' implies greater and lesser degrees of firmness, and so opens up a grey zone of wiggle room in obedience to the law – just the kind of grey zone that the Bush administration enthusiastically exploited to authorise torture. Meanwhile, when Donald Rumsfeld responded facetiously to reports of widespread looting and disorder in Iraq following the 2003 invasion by saying 'Freedom's untidy', he meant not freedom but anarchy.

So freedom depends on law, and law in the end will be enforced, if necessary, through violence. But this is still a long way from the idea that freedom itself could be 'on the march'. One way in which the idea of being on the march is useful is that it is similar to the concept of a 'road map' for peace in Israel/Palestine: one does not claim to be at any specific destination. And so, should a curmudgeon have complained at the time of Bush's speech that the US was noticeably failing to condemn the violent repression of democratic revolt in Uzbekistan, perhaps because of that country's oil and gas reserves and its special status as a favoured franchisee for out-sourced torture or 'rendition', he could have been told that freedom cannot march everywhere at once, but it was on its way there too.

When it got there, what would happen? Would freedom just hold a big party to celebrate itself? One may be forgiven for supposing that to be 'on the march' means to be in a belligerent attitude. Metaphoric uses of 'on the march', applied to non-human entities, generally have a threatening tone: thus, if the land is drying out, 'deserts are on the march'; or ants are seen to be 'on the march' through the rainforest.[6] Things that are 'on the march' are on the attack, like Imperial stormtroopers, or Martian tripods. To be 'on the march' is to be on the way to battle. Now, the point of battle is to coerce one's enemy through violent means to do what one wants. So we must picture bat-talions of the unfree (soldiers, insofar as they are under orders), marching in step so as to curtail the freedom of the command-ers of other equally unfree battalions. Out of all this unfreedom we can happily derive an image of overarching freedom by the Rousseauldian method.

One cannot of course be completely confident that Bush and his speechwriters were making ironical reference to a philoso-pher, long dead, who lived in France. And it happens that there is an alternative explanation for 'freedom on the march', one to which you could recruit Rousseau only with the greatest diffi-culty. The key is provided by Bush's 2004 Inaugural Address, according to which there is a person known as the 'Author of Liberty', who not only invented freedom but controls world affairs: 'History also has a visible direction, set by liberty and the Author of Liberty.'[7] Interestingly, US Secretary of State Condoleezza Rice reused this phrase in 2005, when she called Thomas Jefferson the 'author of liberty' (even though, as a

slave-owner, he was 'imperfect in his beliefs in liberty').[8] This
looks like a deliberate ruse, albeit historically dubious, to secu-
larise the notion. For it is clear that when Bush spoke of the
'Author of Liberty' he meant the Christian God. The official
White House transcript reverently capitalises the words
'Author of Liberty'; and the phrase is also a deliberate echo of
George Washington's First Inaugural Address, that spoke of
God as 'the Great Author of every public and private good'.
Bush had expressed a similar concept when he told the UN in
2001: 'We're confident [. . .] that history has an author who fills
time and eternity with his purpose.'[9] In claiming that God
authors not just liberty but history itself, Bush was also casting
himself – as an actor in history – as God's instrument.

If freedom was on the march, and the person who 'authored'
freedom was God, what Bush seemed to envisage was the
global hegemony of a specifically Christian army. This became
even clearer in June 2005, when Bush stated: 'There is no higher
calling than service in our Armed Forces.'[10] This is explicitly
theological language: a 'higher calling' is normally understood
to be the vocation of priesthood, just as Bush famously said he
appealed to a 'higher father' than his biological parent in conducting his foreign policy.[11] The word 'crusade' may have been
hastily removed from the President's public lexicon after he
used it in the wake of 9/11, but the concept was going strong.

Freedom had already been declared to be on the march by
Bush's predecessors, but what they meant was different. In
1987, President Reagan announced: 'America is at peace tonight,
and freedom is on the march.'[12] In other words, the war
machines were, for the time being, silent; *only* freedom was on
the march, and that kind of march could coexist with 'peace'.
Meanwhile, campaigning for the 1992 election, Bill Clinton said:
'In a world where freedom, not tyranny, is on the march, the
cynical calculus of pure power politics simply does not com-
pute. It is ill-suited to a new era.'[13] Thus freedom's march was
defined in contrast to the operations of 'pure power politics'.
But when George W. Bush dusted off the phrase, he made it

new, by using it to equate the march of freedom with two military invasions. 'Overgrown military establishments,' George Washington had declared in his Farewell Address, 'are inauspicious to liberty.' In the twenty-first century, by contrast, an overgrown military establishment simply *was* liberty.

Alternatively one could posit that freedom was not quite the same thing as the army, and that it was theoretically able to march by itself, but it needed the help of bombs and bullets to clear for it a route through the thickets of unfreedom. As when Condoleezza Rice declared: 'Ladies and gentlemen, America must open a path to the march of freedom across the entire world.'[14] The metaphor of 'opening a path' was reassuring. Like 'paving the way', it implied the bringing of order and civilisation to a chaotic world, much as the Roman Empire built excellent roads. Coincidentally, the American missile that killed sixty-two people in a street market in Baghdad in March 2003 was either a 'Harm' or a 'Paveway'.[15] It may be hoped that freedom encountered no major obstacles on its subsequent march along the way paved by a laser-guided bomb.

The abuse of the term 'freedom' as denoting a military entity was also transferred to the idea of 'democracy'. Condoleezza Rice said: 'We know that when democracy is on the march that America is safer, and when democracy is in retreat Americans are more vulnerable.'[16] If the only two postures available to democracy are to be either 'on the march' or 'in retreat', then democracy is an army and nothing else. This sort of image, deliberately conflating war with peace, may be patently absurd, but it is tried and tested. In 1923, Bertrand Russell noted that the First World War had been called a 'war for democracy', and diagnosed the rhetoric thus: 'Its sole purpose is to make the reader feel that the hatred stirred up in him is righteous indignation, and may be indulged with benefit to mankind.'[17]

Indeed, it was only around this time, following Woodrow Wilson's famous call to make the world safe for democracy, that the term 'democracy' had begun to exude the wholly positive connotations it has for the West today. In 1956, a Unesco commission published the results of its inquiries into the meaning of democracy. It concluded:

> [T]he term 'democracy' has h[e]ld and still holds a rather exceptional position in political terminologies of very different kinds. It is scarcely possible to discover any large political group in any country where the term is used in a derogatory way – at least officially. [. . .] The occurrence of a word having such a status is almost unique in the history of the human languages. It has most probably never happened before that the same political term, which for a very long time has been used in eulogistic, derogatory and neutral ways, has been almost unanimously accepted as the main political slogan of nearly all political parties.[18]

For most of the twentieth century, then, it seemed that 'democracy' meant all things to all people. It was used simply as a synonym for virtue. Totalitarian states such as the Soviet Union and communist China used it and associated concepts, calling themselves 'People's Republics', as propaganda tools, arguing that only their political systems accorded real power to the people. (It was Stalin who, in a radio broadcast of July 1941, was the first Allied leader to name 'democracy' as one of the things for which the Second World War was being fought.)[19] However, the stage at which everyone agreed that democracy, whatever it was, was a good thing seemed to have passed by the early years of the twenty-first century. The scholar of Muslim society Gilles Keppel wrote that, as a result of US foreign policy:

> [T]oday, the word 'democracy,' preceded by the adjective 'Western,' has negative connotations for a large swathe of the educated Muslim middle class – although that class was the potential beneficiary of democratization. The Arabic word *damakrata*, which designates the democratization process, is frequently used pejoratively, signifying a change imposed from without.'[20]

That the 'march of freedom' had caused such a shift in meaning of the term 'democracy' among the very people it promised to help must be accounted a serious propaganda failure. By June 2005, such disillusionment with US rhetoric had even begun to take hold among hawks, when Republican congressman Walter Jones, the man responsible for rechristening French fries 'freedom fries' after France's refusal to sign up for an invasion, called for American troops to withdraw from Iraq.[21]

The etymology of the word 'democracy' – from the Greek *demos*, people, and *kratein*, to rule – makes it clear that democracy means people governing themselves. The devil is in the detail: how exactly are they to govern themselves? The history of democratic thinking is too vast and subtle a subject to attempt to précis here. But it may be said that in part, it is the history of attempts to limit the power of the people. For the people are volatile, whimsical, easily swayed by momentary passions: they cannot be relied upon to make the right decisions. And so it has seemed a good idea to limit the franchise to those of the right sort of qualifications. In the newly wrought American democracy, the right to vote was bought by money: the precepts of the Constitution were such that 'the only democratic organ it was intended the government should possess was the House, based on a suffrage highly limited by property qualifications'.[22] At that time democracy was rather a dirty word: Thomas Jefferson and his allies generally called themselves Republicans, 'and were only called "democrats" when the Federalists wanted to discredit them'.[23] The vote of a black person, notoriously, was considered to be worth only three-fifths of a white vote. Things have improved in that regard, at least. In the bonus second round of voting for the 2000 US Presidential election, the vote of Supreme Court Justice Clarence Thomas, like that of each of his benchfellows, was worth the combined votes of about seventeen million ordinary citizens.

In the twentieth century the implication that 'democracy' meant power to the people troubled the philosopher F. A.

Hayek to such an extent that he recommended changing the word altogether, because it was an example of a lamentable 'confusion of language'. His argument shows well the extent to which the term 'democracy' can be seen to imply a whole unspoken worldview. Hayek distinguished between what he called the 'opinion' of the people – their view of general principles – and the 'will' of the people – their view on what should actually be done in any concrete situation.[24] (Thus our contemporary phrase 'public opinion', usually meaning the results of polls on particular matters, would translate into Hayek's 'will'.) Hayek then argued that the people's 'opinion' should be sovereign, but their 'will' should not ever determine the actions of the state. Therefore, he went so far as to suggest that the term 'democracy' itself should be abandoned in favour of 'demarchy'. The Greek verb *kratein* meant 'to rule' in the fine-grained sense of taking actual decisions, which he did not want the people to do; while *archein* meant to rule in a more general sense of a governing principle.

Yet, one might argue now, 'will' and 'opinion' are not always so easily divorced. Even if one assumes that the massive popular demonstrations against a war in Iraq in March 2003 expressed a majority view of the British people, Hayek might have agreed that Tony Blair was within his rights to ignore them, because they simply expressed the people's 'will' on a singular matter. But whence did this 'will' derive? It surely grew logically from an 'opinion' about what, in general, justifies or fails to justify a war. And such an 'opinion', on Hayek's view, ought to be the 'highest authority'.

Blair had perhaps armed himself against such barbs with his repeated statements over the years that Britain should be, or was already, a 'meritocracy'. If we compare 'meritocracy' with 'democracy', we see a marked change in who is doing the ruling. It is no longer the dull mass of 'people', but those with 'merit'. The word 'meritocracy' does a lot of Unspeak work. It could be read as saying, for example, that those currently at the top of society must deserve to be there, and that the poor and downtrodden have only themselves to blame. And yet it is usefully silent on what appears to be the crucial matter of how 'merit' itself is measured: money, education, athletic ability, a discriminating palate for wine? In fact the word 'meritocracy' was coined for satirical purposes, in the title of a 1958 novel called *The Rise of the Meritocracy*. It was written by Michael Young, one of the drafters of Labour's 1945 election manifesto. His novel was meant to show that a concentration on 'merit', defined as the acquisition of official degrees and diplomas, to the exclusion of other qualities that did not submit to measurement, would result in an elite ruling minority and a large 'underclass': exactly what had since happened to Britain, Young argued in 2001, deploring the official misappropriation of his word.[25]

Democracy, meritocracy, or something else? Sir Harold Walker, former UK Ambassador to Iraq, comments: 'The Iraq war has shown up the truth of the phrase "Britain is ruled by an elective dictatorship". As long as the Prime Minister can keep his party voting for him in Parliament, he can do anything he likes.'[26] Rousseau had expressed the idea thus: 'The people of England regards itself as free; but it is grossly mistaken; it is free only during the election of members of parliament. As soon as they are elected, slavery overtakes it, and it is nothing.' In modern democracies, the electorate exerts its democratic right to choose its leader every four or five years; in the interim, it appears, the people may safely be ignored. This has led many theorists to relabel current western political systems as 'thin democracy',[27] 'pseudo-democracy',[28] or 'low-intensity democracy',[29] a nicely ironic nod to the military concept of 'low-intensity warfare'.

And yet we are not slaves. Harold Walker goes so far as to say that 'Parliamentary democracy, with all its warts, is the best political system yet invented'. This can be true, however, only if democracy is something more than just rare elections. Democracy is theorised by contemporary political scientists as a complicated interlinked process – one involving elections, institutions, law, the protection of minorities, 'a government which grants freedom of press and of speech to all',[30] and so on – the kind of system that does obtain, though it functions imperfectly, in the industrialised West. Yet this poses problems for those who wish to argue that they are spreading democracy to more benighted countries. First, the complexity of any democratic system worth the name makes it hard to take a quick look at a society and say 'Yes, we have democracy here': there is no easy test. Second, in a modern culture where news is disseminated visually, it is impossible to film the whole tedious process of democracy in a thirty-second report, and thereby prove in images that democracy is happening. As a consequence, television news adopts a kind of shorthand: the shot of people standing in line to vote has become the standard means of showing 'democracy'. The danger of such visual telescoping is that it will come to imply that voting is all there is to the concept: that democracy is nothing but elections.

Such a deliberate confusion of the part for the whole may have its propagandistic uses. When eight million people voted in the Iraq elections of January 2005, this was held up as proof that the project of bringing democracy to that country had succeeded. 'Democracy takes hold in Iraq,' announced George W. Bush.[31] But, Harold Walker argues: 'The elections deserved a huge hurrah, but in terms of democracy that's just an election of one man, one vote, which is really at most one third of any democracy that's worth having at all. You must have one man one vote, but you must also have human rights and the rule of law.' The election itself was not immaculate: Sunnis had boycotted it completely, and it was subsequently alleged that there had been a covert US programme to rig the vote in favour of its preferred candidate, former Ba'athist and CIA asset Iyad Allawi, the interim Prime Minister, who polled at 3 or 4 per cent throughout 2004 and then garnered nearly 14 per cent of the vote.[32] One UN official told Seymour Hersh: 'The election was not an election but a referendum on ethnic and religious identity.'[33]

Neither had US forces successfully ensured that all the institutions of democracy were in place for the election. A week
before the vote, Baghdad bus driver Ali Hatem glossed the term
as he saw it: 'Right now in Iraq democracy means you can do
anything you want, including killing people in the street.'[34] The
US, moreover, had shown itself actively hostile to the idea of a
free press, as was evidenced by their habit of 'accidentally'
bombing the offices of Arab news station Al Jazeera (in both
Afghanistan and Iraq) and closing down newspapers whose
propaganda contradicted their own. Still, the election was a
great publicity coup. George W. Bush had claimed that his own
re-election as President in 2004 had constituted his 'accountability moment',[35] thus implying that he had felt accountable to
no one during his first term, and would not during his second.
Similarly, the precipitate christening of the Iraq elections as
'democracy' reduced the complex notion of democracy to the
idea of a 'democratic moment'.

It was also, we were told, a 'vote for freedom'.[36] In 1917, Sir
Mark Sykes of the British Foreign Office had made the following statement to the people of Baghdad: 'Our armies have not
come into your cities and lands as conquerors or enemies but as
liberators.'[37] In 2003, Paul Wolfowitz said that the Iraqi people
'view us as their hoped-for liberator'.[38] Having been liberated
again, Iraqis in 2005 were certainly voting for freedom, but their
conception of freedom did not necessarily coincide with the
American one. Harold Walker argues: 'To us, at the particular
stage we are in our political development, freedom on the
whole means freedom against the government of the day. But to
an Iraqi, freedom from the Americans, or freedom from the
Ottomans or the French or the British, is more important, relatively, than freedom from his own government. [. . .] When the
Americans went into Iraq, they talked of Iraqis who would
automatically want freedom from Saddam, and embrace western democracy – well, they wanted freedom from Saddam,
certainly, 90 per cent of them, but then they didn't want bloody
foreigners in their country either.' One Marine who was in Iraq

summed up the matter succinctly: 'After seven months patrolling Ramadi, I know that most Iraqis are ambivalent towards the American presence in Iraq. They are happy we removed Hussein, but frustrated we are still there. They are also angry that we haven't provided them everything we promised: peace and safety, or even water and electricity.'[39]

Once it was the case that 'liberation' meant ridding a country of a foreign occupying power: thus one talked of the liberation of France from Nazi occupation in the Second World War, and it would have sounded mighty strange to sell that war's aim, at the beginning, as the liberation of the German people from their own government. Things have changed. The 'liberation' of Iraq in 2003 turned instantly into an occupation by the same forces. This fact was inconvenient to Paul Wolfowitz, who saw the accurate description of it as bad PR. 'Once we accepted the label of being an occupation authority, it hurt us,' Wolfowitz complained. 'It was debated among the lawyers, and ultimately we were told this was the international legal framework. I didn't like it. Just the word "occupation," I think, has allowed al-Jazeera to draw a parallel with the Israeli occupation of Palestinian territories.'[40] Wolfowitz acknowledged that, according to international law, the US was in fact engaged in 'occupation', but still argued that they shouldn't have 'accepted the label'. In other words, he seemed to think that if they had simply called it something else – perhaps a mass sleepover – then no one would have noticed that the occupation was actually an occupation. This shows a very strong faith in the power of language to pull the wool over people's eyes: a remarkable commitment, indeed, to the principles of Unspeak.

Nonetheless, the people of occupied Iraq did turn out to vote in great numbers, despite dangerous and violent conditions. And on our television screens there was a curious visual rhyme between the Iraqi citizens at polling stations lining up two and three abreast, and columns of soldiers. Maybe freedom and democracy really were on the march after all.

Real tangible benefits

Why should the global march of freedom and democracy be considered desirable for the participants in the 'war on terror'? Is it because, as Paula Dobriansky tried to argue, democracies don't start wars, or, as George W. Bush recast the notion in a mathematical formula: 'Democracies equal peace'?[41] Hardly. Is it instead because terrorism cannot emerge in democracies? Ask the victims of Oklahoma bomber Timothy McVeigh, or Basque group ETA, or Japanese cult Aum Shinrikyo. An alternative reason for the championing of freedom and democracy is suggested by a revealing form of language that sometimes slips out into official pronouncements. This is Bush's account of how he told Vladimir Putin why Russia should become more democratic:

> I told him it was very important that capital see a rule of law, that there be stability, there not be a doubt about whether or not somebody invests or whether or not the laws change.[42]

'Capital' is here anthropomorphised as a needy person, on whose behalf the President of the US has been sent to negotiate with the President of Russia. Stephen Krasner, head of policy planning at the State Department, said: 'What we want is a world of democratic, market-oriented countries.'[43] The second term glosses the first. 'In the 1980s,' according to Richard Falk, 'the Reagan Doctrine identified adherence to a market economy as the crucial defining feature of a democratic polity.'[44] It proved to be a durable doctrine.

Condoleezza Rice's 2005 trip to Latin America brought further illumination as to the meaning of democracy: 'The success of democracy in Latin America,' she explained afterwards, 'depends on the continued openness of our hemisphere, openness to new ideas and to new people, and especially to new trade.'[45] Trade is mentioned last in this list, almost as an afterthought; but the use of 'especially' means it is valued above all the rest. Politely, Rice paid lip-service to vague, feel-good concepts of 'openness', 'new ideas', and 'new people', before coming to the real business at hand: trade. State Department spokesman Adam Ereli explained further: 'Talk,' he instructed the assembled journalists, 'about things like economic reform, development of entrepreneurship, good governance, transparency, anti-corruption [. . .] programs that translate principles of political participation, principles of emancipation, principles of tolerance and opportunity into real tangible benefits.'[46] High-flown principles are just so much waffle; they can only be 'translated' into 'real tangible benefits' by the operation of western-model capitalism. Ereli's view that principles are useless in themselves seemed to be confirmed by the foreign adventures of one famous US corporation. In June 2005, users of Microsoft's newly launched Chinese weblog service were banned from using words and phrases such as 'democracy' or 'democratic movement': attempts to type these terms invoked an error message that read: 'This item contains forbidden speech.'[47] The 'principles of emancipation' had got lost in translation; but 'real tangible benefits' were no doubt accruing to someone.

And yet trade is, on some people's views, the perfect democratic instrument. Indeed, if we are happy to redefine 'democracy' to mean only that moment at which elections are held, it is possible to consider capitalism as the ideal form of democracy, consisting of a grand procession of innumerable little electoral moments, when 'consumer choice' is exercised in the supermarket or the cinema or the car showroom. Now, a company can only succeed if it attracts the monetary 'votes' of customers. Branches of Starbuck's could not have ramified across the western world, in what is sometimes regarded as a lamentable example of 'globalisation', had people in their vast multitudes not actually walked through its doors and paid remarkable sums of money for its tasty lattes. So it is tempting to suppose that the most successful companies must be the best at giving people what they want. Then one might conclude that profit is a measure of democratic efficiency, and even virtue.

You might then even criticise existing forms of democracy on the basis that they do not adequately recreate capitalist models, as Matthew Taylor of Britain's Institute for Public Policy Research did: 'Would you choose the same supermarket for four years?' he asked. 'Nobody would tell an elector that they could not go to Sainsbury's because they made a four-year contract with Tesco.'[48]

As a universal analysis, the idea of capitalism as ideal democracy might be challenged by the existence of monopolies (such as Microsoft) that limit people's real options, and businesses (such as Halliburton) that do not sell directly to the people but to government agencies, in a feedback loop whereby executives move back and forth between corporate and public positions. (As of May 2004, more than a hundred officials in the Bush administration were involved in regulating businesses for which they had previously worked 'as lobbyists, lawyers or company advocates'.[49]) Yet the view that commercial success equals pure moral good is one that businesspeople have used Unspeak to advocate for many hundreds of years.

Historian Quentin Skinner has shown that the newly emerging business class in sixteenth- and seventeenth-century England made deliberate raids on the language of virtue in order to render their own operations respectable. There was, as Skinner explains, 'a certain element of structural similarity – which they eagerly exploited – between the specifically Protestant ideal of individual service and devotion (to God) and the alleged commercial ideals of service (to one's customers) and dedication (to one's work).'[50] Thus, for example, commercialists tried to apply the word 'religious' to their ideals of strict observance of timekeeping and administrative competence. However, Skinner argues, since ordinary people did not accept that the normal criteria for using the word 'religious' actually obtained in commercial operations, the attempt to cloak trade in godly virtue was a failure. The result was simply to create a new, weak meaning of 'religious', as in 'I attend the meetings of my Department religiously.'[51] Similarly with the claims of modern businesses to have a 'philosophy', which is set out in their 'literature': we understand that these are watered-down metaphorical applications, rather than viewing the companies as sharing the rich and complex virtues of real philosophy and real literature.[52]

On the other hand, a successful revolution was made in the application of the term 'commodity', which had been first borrowed by the capitalist classes as a term of Unspeak:

> Before the advent of commercial society, to speak of something as a commodity was to praise it, and in particular to affirm that it answered to one's desires, and could thus be seen as beneficial, convenient, a source of advantage. Later an attempt was made to suggest that an article produced for sale ought to be seen as a source of benefit or advantage to its purchaser, and ought in consequence to be described and commended as a commodity. [. . .] [E]ventually the original applications withered away, leaving us with nothing more than the current and purely descriptive meaning of commodity as an object of trade.[53]

Other terms of commerce appear to have followed a similar pattern, without being quite as successful in annihilating previous meanings. Consider the language of lending money. 'Credit', which means credibility, trustworthiness, or moral praiseworthiness (from Latin *credere*, to believe), was hijacked to mean either lending money to your bank – if your cheque account is 'in credit' you are therefore virtuous – or being allowed access to the bank's money via a plastic card. 'Interest', meanwhile, which originally meant either intellectual curiosity or a legal or moral claim to something, became the mechanism by which money breeds more money. (We may suppose that this use was promoted by those who found money inherently *interesting*.)

The term 'economy', too, underwent a notable shift. Spelled 'oeconomy', it originally denoted the management of a domestic household, from the Greek word usually applied to a steward. It subsequently came to be applied to the management of a nation's finances, first by Thomas Hobbes in *Leviathan* and more systematically with the invention of the phrase 'political economy' in the late eighteenth century.[54] It was perhaps hoped that the connotations of domestic virtue contained in the original usage would pass over into its new use in theories of capitalism. Yet this was not to everyone's taste: in the twentieth century, Hayek argued that this use of 'economy' was another instance of the confusion of language, because it might imply that an economy had to be directed and managed. Since he was, on the contrary, in favour not of direction but of 'spontaneous order', he proposed the term's wholesale replacement with 'catallaxy'. This term, he explained, 'derived from the Greek verb *katallatein* (or *katallassein*) which significantly means not only "to exchange" but also "to receive into the community" and "to turn from enemy into friend"'.[55] Hayek's novel philological proposal, sadly, met with limited success, but the notion that trade turned enemies into friends persisted, as we shall see later.

Most radical of all the attempts by business to insinuate itself into pre-existing civil vocabularies was the borrowing of the term 'corporation'. It originally meant a political grouping of people united along local-government, religious, or other lines. Its first use in a commercial sense came in the US, noted by Charles Dickens in 1842.[56] The word literally means embodiment. By the process of 'incorporation', the company becomes flesh, and is understood in law to be a person. Conversely, the rhetorical attitude of corporations to their workers took a dehumanising turn: remember how the phrase 'human resources' implies that people are undifferentiable assets that can be used up and replaced. Thus, by means of Unspeak, businesses became people, and people became fungible matter.

Having borrowed terms from the vocabularies of civil virtue and domestic life, commerce in the twentieth century rendered itself more exciting by opening a new front on the language of war. A businessperson could already be described, for example, as a 'captain of industry'. The naval metaphor may be intended peacefully, as though industry were merely a flotilla of luxury yachts, sailing lazily down the river; but a 'captain' was originally the director of a warship. Meanwhile, businesspeople conducted corporate 'raids', and engaged in 'battles' in the boardroom and price 'wars' with competitors. Commercial products were 'launched', like rockets from an artillery tube. Employees were 'fired', as though they were mere cannon fodder. Such warrior vocabulary combines with the use of business metaphors in war – military interrogators at Guantánamo are just another kind of 'professional'; while missiles and bombs are 'delivered', like courier packages – to blur the rhetorical lines between the two pursuits. Any shift in the tenor of public language from war to peace and back again is usefully minimised. War is business as usual.

The exploitation by business of two apparently opposed lexicons, one of peace and one of war, may be traced simultaneously in the word 'executive'. From the mid-seventeenth century, it had denoted the part of government – the 'executive branch' – concerned with carrying out the law. The application of the word to employees of businesses, dating only from the early twentieth century, might thus have been an attempt to cloak commerce in a halo of associations with justice, law, and proper government.[57] As businesspeople and politicians developed ever more symbiotic relationships, the use of one word to cover them all perhaps seemed appropriate. But to 'execute', of course, had also long meant 'to put to death', and a bloody tang of power still clung to the idea of 'executives' conducting their business according to martial metaphors, as well as to Executive Orders that authorised torture. Also exploiting the latent authority of the term, Islamist radicals who murdered people by beheading or other means claimed, in messages to the West, to 'execute' them – a word that, merely because it sounded exciting, was often adopted by the western press to describe those very actions. 'EXECUTED,' ran the one-word headline describing the May 2004 murder of Nick Berg in Iraq in London's *Evening Standard* newspaper. Of course, for a killing to be described as an 'execution', it must be preceded by a legitimate judicial process. To describe slaughter-as-PR as an 'execution' was therefore to be complicit with the murderers' own justifications.

Meanwhile, a US Navy admiral said that Al Qaeda had gone from being 'an IBM-type of organisation' to being 'like McDonald's'.[58] This was meant to explain how Al Qaeda operated more as a franchise than as a centralised command structure. But it also illustrated how in all matters, from democracy to terrorism, business was now the prevailing frame of reference.

Trading in freedom

The idea that everything is now subordinate to what 'capital' wants to 'see' is not merely an *idée fixe* of paranoid anti-globalisation protesters, but stated clearly in public by those who minister officially to capital's desires. Back in the US, George W. Bush declared: 'We need to reform our legal systems so the people, on the one hand, can get justice; on the other hand, the justice system doesn't affect the flows of capital.'[59] First a hasty sop to liberals – acknowledging that, sure, people should still be able to 'get' justice, just as they pop down to the store to get a can of soda – and then the remarkable notion that justice, on the other hand, should never interfere with the operations of money. So justice is a subeconomy within the larger one (you can 'get' justice), but it has no right to interfere with overarching systems of profit. Justice is subordinate to and dependent on capitalism, as is even 'the strength of our families', according to Canadian Prime Minister Paul Martin.[60]

To argue, in the same fashion, that 'freedom' was dependent on the oil business would sound like another conspiracy theory had it, too, not been officially stated. In May 2005, US Secretary of Energy Samuel Bodman celebrated the opening of an

Azerbaijan pipeline that would carry crude from the Caspian Sea to the US while avoiding Russia and Iran. Bodman said: 'As Azerbaijan deepens its democratic and market economic reforms, this pipeline can help generate balanced economic growth, and provide a foundation for a prosperous and just society that advances the cause of freedom.'[61] That is an awful lot for one pipeline to do: not content with carrying oil, it also provided the foundation for the advance of freedom. It was truly the little pipeline that could.

The order of priorities in western 'freedom' and 'democracy' was again evident in the spiritually ascendant language of another Bush pronouncement: 'In every region, free markets and free trade and free societies are proving their power to lift lives.'[62] It seemed the commercialists had finally got their way: markets were indeed acknowledged to be quasi-divine autonomous systems raising all to heaven. Why, then, if they were so free, could they not be left alone to function in their utopian way? Bush was not just compelled to tell Vladimir Putin how to change his country in order to clear a path for the march of free markets. The mollycoddling was necessary domestically as well: 'It's important for the markets to see that we've got enough discipline in Washington, D.C. to make hard decisions with the people's money,' Bush said in 2004.[63] This speech was reported the next day in the *New York Times* under the headline 'Bush Says Social Security Plan Would Reassure Markets',[64] as though 'markets' were frightened children.

How protean, indeed, these markets were. On the one hand, they dispensed God's justice, free from any interference by merely human justice; yet on the other hand, when the rhetorical occasion demanded, the markets were vulnerable little flowers, in desperate need of 'reassurance'. It is true that markets, being essentially consensual hallucinations, depend on confidence, but calls to 'reassure' them on one point or another are often made for unstated ideological reasons, if not to disguise a simple motive of private profit. Similar kid gloves were apparent in former UK Trade Secretary Margaret Beckett's announcement that 'Britain's businesses need to be able to trade throughout the world's markets as easily as they can in home markets without facing high tariffs, discriminatory regulations or unnecessarily burdensome procedures'.[65] Businesses may indeed *want* these things, but for Beckett to say that they 'needed' them, presumably in order to flourish maximally, was to endorse their wants without weighing them against the wants of others.

After her trip to Latin America, Condoleezza Rice had gone on to declare: 'A region that trades in freedom benefits everyone.'[66] She did not mean, we can assume, trading in freedom like trading in textiles or precious metals: I will sell you this much freedom for so many bananas. Celebrating the signing of the Central American Free Trade Agreement, Rice was invoking again the concept of 'free trade', under the auspices of which, as British Chancellor Gordon Brown once explained, poor countries have 'obligations' to 'create the conditions for new investment'.[67]

The freedom granted by 'free trade' was not quite symmetrical. Among the 'obligations' of poor countries under World Bank and International Monetary Fund deals have been, for example, the obligation to import food from the heavily subsidised US and EU agricultural industries, thereby driving local producers out of business; the rich countries kept high tariffs on imports such as clothing and leather goods, thus preventing the poor countries from competing freely.[68] Meanwhile, 'creating the conditions for new investment' meant, for example, allowing western companies to take over indigenous public services and run them for profit. Water privatisation in Manila and electricity privatisation in India have resulted in price increases of up to 80 per cent; in sub-Saharan Africa, according to the Organization for Economic Co-Operation and Development, 'profit-maximising behaviour has led privatised companies to keep investments below the necessary levels, with the result that rural communities and the urban poor were further marginalised in terms of access to electric power and water supply'.[69] Tens of millions of pounds of the UK's aid budget were given to 'privatisation consultants' at big accountancy firms, the acceptance of whose advice was made a condition of aid to poor countries.[70] To render the enlargement of such 'free trade' more palatable to an increasingly informed and concerned public, the IMF, in a transparent coup of Unspeak, had simply changed the name of its 'structural adjustment programmes' to 'poverty reduction and growth programmes'.[71] No one would be so churlish as to disagree that 'poverty reduction' was a fine idea, yet there was no new evidence that the same old policy, thus relabelled, would actually achieve it.

One meaning of bringing freedom to Iraq, in particular, was clear in George W. Bush's May 2004 explanation of why things were going so well in that country:

> [A] growing private economy is taking shape. A new currency has been introduced. Iraq's Governing Council approved a new law that opens the country to foreign investment for the first time in decades. Iraq has liberalized its trade policy, and today an Iraqi observer attends meetings of the World Trade Organization.

International lawyer Philippe Sands explains that Coalition Provisional Authority Order Number 39 had 'opened much of Iraq's economy to foreign ownership [and] . . . stretched the limits of what an occupying power was entitled to do under long-established rules of international law'.[72] Note that what Bush acclaims as 'foreign investment', implying generosity, Sands translates bluntly as 'foreign ownership'. The order, in fact, made possible total foreign ownership of industries in all sectors except that of 'natural resources', defined closely as oil and gas;[73] in a subsequent interview, trade minister Ali Allawi did not rule out future foreign ownership in those industries either.[74] Business and income taxes for 'investors' would be capped at 15 per cent. The Iraq economy was thus obliged to be much more 'free' than, say, the US itself, which has laws governing foreign ownership of media companies, among others, and whose politicians worked hard in the summer of 2005 to ensure that a Chinese takeover bid for its oil company Unocal would fail.[75] Bush's implication that the Governing Council was the source of the Iraq ruling, meanwhile, hid the fact that the Council was essentially obliged to rubber-stamp ('approved') the US order. Of course, these agreements were not simply a one-way street, and Iraq enjoyed some quid pro quos. In July 2005, for example, it was announced that the US would reduce to zero its import tariffs on Iraqi dates.[76]

The US Congress had voted to spend $18.4 billion of taxpayers' money to reconstruct post-war Iraq. By the end of June 2004, Paul Bremer's Coalition Provisional Authority had spent only $300 million of this sum. Instead, up to $20 billion of the Iraqi people's own money, kept in the Development Fund for Iraq and meant by the UN to be used 'in a transparent manner to meet the humanitarian needs of the Iraqi people [. . .] and for other purposes benefiting the people of Iraq',[77] had been handed out, most in no-bid contracts to American corporations such as Halliburton and its subsidiary Kellogg, Brown & Root, and in ways that were poorly accounted for.[78] It was later alleged by Henry Waxman and the House Committee on Government Reform that in one such contract, Restore Iraqi Oil, Halliburton had overbilled by 'more than $177 million', charged to the Iraqi people.[79] (In logistical contracts paid by the Defense Department, Halliburton charged $100 to clean a bag of laundry, and hundreds of millions for meals that were never served to troops.)[80] In September 2004, the $18.4 billion of US money meant for reconstruction was reassigned to counter-insurgency warfare. For Iraqis, it seemed, freedom came at a rather hefty price.

Meanwhile, George W. Bush had quietly signed an order granting blanket immunity from criminal prosecution or civil lawsuits in the US to any American company or individual working in any industry related to the Iraqi oil business.[81] Perhaps that was what he meant when he scrawled, on a note from Condoleezza Rice informing him that 'Iraq is sovereign' in June 2004, the possibly rehearsed reply: 'Let freedom reign!'[82]

All kinds of liberties

If Rice had meant not 'free trade' but trading in freedom like trading in bananas, it would have sat well with another current in thinking about freedom. Just as the world of 'commodities' is one of many various individual things, so it makes sense to some people to break 'freedom' itself down into lots of little freedoms. In his ecstatically gloomy book on democracy, historian John Lukacs moaned:

> If 'liberalism' means the extension of all kinds of liberties to all kinds of individuals, mostly as a consequence of the abolition of restrictions on all kinds of people, these have now been institutionalised and accomplished in formerly unexpected and even astonishing varieties of ways. (And with not a few fateful and, yes, deplorable consequences, such as laws approving abortions, mercy killing, cloning, sexual 'freedoms,' permissiveness, pornography . . . a list almost endless.)[83]

It is curious that a list containing just six items should cause Lukacs such emotional anguish that he sees it as 'almost endless'. (A thing is either endless or it isn't; this one patently isn't.) In putting scare quotes around 'freedoms' in the phrase 'sexual "freedoms"', Lukacs is clearly not objecting to the plural use, since he is happy to say 'liberties'. Rather, he seems to be saying (without saying why) that this kind of freedom is not really a freedom at all – and since freedoms are plural and separable, this one ought just to be abandoned, for the moral good of society. This contrasts with the classical liberal view of freedom as one thing, hedged around by law but homogeneous, in terms both of the set of 'rights' it affords individuals, and the relationship of each individual to everyone else, so that unjustly to

curtail one person's freedom is an insult to all. The growth of
civil rights – or, if you prefer, the march of freedom – thus consists not in adding extra discrete freedoms to those we already
have, but in approaching ever more closely to the ideal of this
one big freedom, defined by Thomas Paine simply as 'the
power of doing whatever does not injure another'.[84]

Robin Cook, discussing in 2005 the British government's
plans for house arrest of 'terrorist suspects', summed up this
view in the phrase: 'Liberty is indivisible.'[85] However, to com-
plicate matters, that same phrase has also been used by those
who think that the ultimate good is 'free markets'. In this tradition were the remarkably named Young Americans For
Freedom, a group of ninety conservative-minded college students who in 1960 set out their principles: 'That liberty is
indivisible, and that political freedom cannot long exist without
economic freedom [. . .] That when government interferes with
the work of the market economy, it tends to reduce the moral
and physical strength of the nation.'[86] Here again we find the
age-old hard sell, that the operations of markets are actually a
source of 'moral strength'. Yet these Young Americans ('Do you
remember your President Nixon?' David Bowie was to ask
them some years later) were also somewhat confused on the
indivisibility or otherwise of freedom, since their same manifesto also refers to 'liberties' in the plural.

Yet if freedom is really fungible (just as people are, according
to Donald Rumsfeld), then the resulting 'freedoms' can be
thought of as just another symbol of exchange, a currency. I will
decide that you can have these freedoms but not those others.
And she can have these freedoms, but he can't. If other social
systems, such as justice, are declared publically by officials such
as George W. Bush to be subordinate to capital, it might be that
the exchange of freedom is too. John Lukacs writes: 'People
throughout the world are now customers (I write "customers"
rather than "beneficiaries," since many of those "benefices" are
indeed questionable), of "freedoms" of which less than a century ago even the most radical liberals would not have

dreamed.'[87] Deplorable, isn't it, having to watch people go about their lives enjoying such pseudo-'freedoms'? What is interesting is that by writing 'customers', Lukacs assumes that the economic metaphor of 'freedoms' as commodities is appropriate. He would perhaps be surprised to find that in this, though for evidently different reasons, he coincides with Noam Chomsky, who writes:

> In a well-functioning capitalist society, everything becomes a commodity, including freedom; one can have as much as one can buy, and those who can buy a lot have every reason to preserve an ample supply.[88]

Remember that 'commodity' used to denote something inherently good; now, everything inherently good, such as freedom, may be viewed as a commodity. Tony Blair bought into this worldview when he declared that: 'Security is life's most precious commodity.'[89] This will doubtless have cheered locksmiths, manufacturers of burglar alarms, and architects of 'gated communities' everywhere. For they were selling 'security', which means protection from assaults on one's liberty. In other words, they were trading in freedom.

The objects of war

When contemporary American and British politicians talk of 'freedom' and 'democracy', then, they have quite specific meanings in mind. Freedom is the freedom of capital, which if unhindered by the obstructions of justice may in turn grant 'freedoms' to individuals. Democracy, meanwhile, is represented by a brief moment at the ballot box, and otherwise denotes the minimal state of affairs that enables capital to go about its business. Probably we are unnecessarily bamboozled by what we might suppose are the more complex and valuable meanings of freedom and democracy. We should stop worrying and trust that the new versions of them, inexorably on the march as they are, will indeed lead to global calm and happiness.

That is, indeed, a modern article of faith, an assumption made even by such writers as LSE professor of international relations Fred Halliday. Rebutting the idea that the West 'needs' an enemy, Halliday writes: 'The logic of capitalism is, rather, that a peaceful world in which countries trade and peacefully compete with each other is the most desirable.'[90] It is perhaps more correct to say that capitalism doesn't care where the profits come from, and to remember that, in certain countries, the military industry accounts for no insignificant proportion of capitalism. In 1970, the US Department of Defense owned '10 per cent of the assets of the entire American economy'.[91] In the second financial quarter of 2003, military spending accounted for 60 per cent of the growth rate of US gross domestic product.[92] It has long been observed that the running-up of deficits with enormous increases in military spending can fuel short-term growth, a phenomenon that economists have christened 'military Keynesianism': evidently, this worked for the Iraq invasion. By 2004, one out of every 27 working people in the US was employed either directly by the Pentagon or by the 'defence industry',[93] much of whose profits depend on selling weapons overseas. As Ezra Pound remarked: 'gun sales lead to more gun sales / they do not clutter the market for gunnery / there is no saturation.'[94]

It is also true, of course, that the 'defense industry' has contributed many useful things to the modern world, such as computers, the internet, and microwave ovens.[95] But that is not its only function. And capitalism can be peaceful, as witness, for example, the number of countries invaded recently by Sweden; but it is not evident that it must be. Capitalism is not inherently evil; nor is it inherently good. It is agnostic on matters of good and evil. It is not immoral, it is amoral. (Which is why, despite the rhetoric of 'free trade', western capitalist democracies protect themselves with vast edifices of law and regulation.) And once you are agnostic about the rights or wrongs of war, you may be intensely relaxed about the fact that war can be very good for business.

We may contrast Halliday's view of the 'logic of capitalism' as inherently pacific with the following bravura passage by American politician and financier Alexander Hamilton, author of most of what are known as the Federalist Papers. His political views would today be described as conservative rather than liberal, yet he did not view capital as a panacea for the world's ills. In 1787, he wrote:

The genius of republics, say they, is pacific; the spirit of commerce has a tendency to soften the manners of men, and to extinguish those inflammable humours which have so often kindled into wars. Commercial republics, like ours, will never be disposed to waste themselves in ruinous contentions with each other. They will be governed by mutual interest, and will cultivate a spirit of mutual amity and concord. We may ask these projectors in politics, whether it is not the true interest of all nations to cultivate the same benevolent and philosophic spirit? If this be their true interest, have they in fact pursued it? Has it not, on the contrary, invariably been found, that momentary passions, and immediate interests, have a more active and imperious control over human conduct, than general or remote considerations of policy, utility, or justice? Have republics in practice been less addicted to war than monarchies? Are not the former administered by men as well as the latter? Are there not aversions, predilections, rivalships, and desires of unjust acquisition, that affect nations, as well as kings? Are not popular assemblies frequently subject to the impulses of rage, resentment, jealousy, avarice, and of other irregular and violent propensities? Is it not well known, that their determinations are often governed by a few individuals in whom they place confidence, and that they are of course liable to be tinctured by the passions and views of those individuals? Has commerce hitherto done anything more than change the objects of war? Is

not the love of wealth as domineering and enterprising a passion as that of power or glory? Have there not been as many
wars founded upon commercial motives, since that has become
the prevailing system of nations, as were before occasioned by
the cupidity of territory or dominion? Has not the spirit of
commerce, in many instances, administered new incentives to
the appetite both for the one and for the other? Let experience,
the least fallible guide of human opinions, be appealed to for
an answer to these inquiries.[96]

At the time of this writing, experience had still not given an
answer compatible with the rhetoric of western leaders.
Perhaps, then, it was time to change the labels once more.

9

Extremism

Extreme

Nearly four years after the 'war on terror' was first declared, the US administration appeared to decide that the slogan had been counterproductive in publicity terms. What America was engaged in now, it announced, was a 'Global Struggle Against Violent Extremism'.[1] The differences between this shiny new catchphrase and the old, much-maligned one were several. A 'war on' something sounds rather bellicose and unilateral, but a 'struggle' has a sense of built-in righteousness. It does not boast of physical superiority, but of moral superiority. One struggles against illness, or misfortune, or poverty. To struggle connotes a kind of heroism. The word also has a history in the language of communism, as in the 'class struggle': Lenin wrote of 'the struggle of the proletariat';[2] 'struggle meetings' were held in revolutionary China for people to demand the removal of officials from office.[3] The new US catchphrase might even have been designed with that sense also in mind, in a heartwarming attempt to reconcile socialists to the cause. A struggle, moreover, is not conducted only with bombs: General Richard Myers emphasised this implication of the change in language by saying that the new Global Struggle would be 'more diplomatic, more economic, more political than it is military'.[4] Better late than never, perhaps.

Thus the Global Struggle Against Violent Extremism was one

in which all right-thinking people would wish to share. For 'violent extremism', furthermore, seemed to be a bad thing. But it was also rather a vague thing. To be sure that struggling against it was a good idea, we should know more about what it is. Yet 'extremism' itself is a rather slippery term of Unspeak. Let us trace its roots.

The base word, 'extreme', comes from the Latin *extremus*, the superlative form of *exterus*, outward (hence the English 'exterior'). So 'extreme' began its life meaning 'outermost': at the limit of something. It is in this sense that the Catholic Church uses 'extreme unction': it is the last sacrament given to a dying person. But the strictly superlative usage, to mean right at the outer limit, was not honoured for long. Shakespeare, for one, thought that something could be more or less extreme (he uses the constructions 'not so extreme' and 'extremest'), a usage that Samuel Johnson later mocked for its illogicality in his *Dictionary*. In its new comparative use, the word was able to pass from a purely descriptive term to one expressing a form of moral disapproval. There was a spectrum of possible behaviour in any context, and acts near one end or the other would be denounced as 'extreme'. Too much physical exercise was 'extreme', argued Bishop Joseph Hall in 1614, while William Cowper by 1734 was denouncing the 'extreme' dress of your average avaricious parson.[5]

The words 'extremism' and 'extremist' were invented only in the second half of the nineteenth century, but they carried a similar freight of rhetorical disapprobation. It works like this: first we imagine a spectrum of all possible ideas, then we say that anything near one end or the other constitutes 'extremism'. But those 'extreme' ideas are only near the end of the spectrum because of the way we have drawn it in the first place. Those accused of extremism may wish to draw very different spectra, with their own views in the middle. For instance, one person may consider 'extremism' the views of an animal-rights activist who breaks into laboratories to free monkeys or cats and insists that everyone has a moral duty to become a vegan. The activist, for her part, would consider acceptance of the mass cruelty of animal experimentation and factory farming to be the 'extreme' position: she would say that her own view was the only reasonable one to take after due moral consideration. Indeed, as George Lakoff noted, members of animal-rights organisation People for the Ethical Treatment of Animals had already been denoted 'terrorists' for releasing minks; it would do just as well henceforth to call them 'extremists', a term that had already been applied to environmental activists.[6] In 2005, even people peacefully signing petitions to ban the shooting of doves in the US were labelled 'anti-hunting extremists' by the National Rifle Association.[7] An alternative view might consider the desire to fire bullets at birds to be the extreme position.

To call someone an 'extremist' is to denounce him merely for his position on our imaginary spectrum of ideas, rather than to engage with what he is actually saying. An extremist is someone whose opinions differ markedly from ours. He will not listen to argument, and so we should not listen to him. It is perhaps for this reason that, by 2005, 'extremist' seemed to have replaced the old standby 'fundamentalist', particularly for referring to violent Islamism. Not only is 'extremist' much more flexible in its application, it also gets around the possible problem that to call someone a 'fundamentalist' is to acknowledge that he has some kind of *foundation*, which is to say that his actions do not just derive from some arbitrary evil. Especially if he goes on to claim that his foundation is a holy book, it becomes difficult to denounce him other than by saying that your holy book is better than his. 'Extremism' replaces incommensurable factions of different religions with simple geometry: it is thus much more obvious that what it denotes must be bad.

One of the earliest systematic campaigns that employed the new concept of 'extremism' was the British war of words against Indian nationalism in the first decade of the twentieth century. One faction in the Indian National Congress, represented by Aurobindo Ghose, wanted the British colonial rulers to leave immediately and let India rule itself: the ideal as he expressed it was 'a free national government unhampered even in the least by foreign control'.[8] Aghast at such boldness, the British press and politicians immediately dubbed his group the Extremists, an appellation that has passed into normal historical parlance, where they are contrasted with the so-called Moderates, who wished only that their British rulers might allow them a little more freedom to self-govern.

There were links between the so-called 'Extremists' and the perpetrators of acts of terrorism in Bengal from 1908 onwards, but the former had already been labelled as beneath serious debate because of their views. They were 'extremists' in mind, not merely in deed. For Ghose and his fellows, any desire to be free of imperial rule was automatically categorised as extremism, and therefore dismissed politically. The British could not conceive that there might be a sincere fight for national liberation going on – and so they termed the Bengali bombings 'anarchism', quite missing the point.[9]

To label the Indian revolutionaries 'Extremists', then, was simply to say that they had no right to ask for what they wanted. The label has a further useful function: to imply that such a person cannot possibly be thought reasonable on any matter at all. An 'extremist', it is easy to suppose, does not hold just one opinion with which we disagree, but is habitually, *essentially* extreme: impossible to talk to, impossible to welcome into civilisation. In that respect the appellation 'extremist' works much like 'terrorist', conflating many kinds of motivation and action under one all-purpose bogey-word. Vladimir Putin's violent suppression of Chechen rebellion became 'partnership' in the 'war on terror'; it would equally easily become part of the struggle against violent extremism. Just like the 'war on terror', the new struggle was defined so as to outflank and outlive any mere fight with Al Qaeda.

The interdependency of terms in this phrase 'violent extremism' is quite complex. It would seem that violent extremism is considered the natural kind of extremism. To speak of 'peaceful extremism' would sound plain weird. The metaphorical violence done to respectable thinking implied by the holding of an 'extreme' view always has the potential, in the view of those denouncing the extremists, to transmute into physical violence: it is only a matter of time before an extremist bombs or kills. In this way, the appellation 'extremist' works deliberately to blur the distinction between opinion and behaviour. And the potential violence, concomitantly, is rendered all the more horrible because it is extremist – there is an associative sense of 'extreme violence' as compared to other kinds. After all, it would not do to argue that perhaps all violence constitutes an 'extreme' approach to a situation, even if one supposes that, *in extremis*, it may be justified.

Yet another sense of 'struggle', by the way, is that it better conveys the sense of indefinite, even permanent conflict that Donald Rumsfeld had to twist himself into crazy jazz locutions to justify in the previous linguistic context of a 'war'. Struggle does not imply certain victory. The sense of a never-ending crusade was reassuringly intact. A Global Struggle Against Violent Extremism was, then, a righteous, permanent, planetary fight against, in principle, anyone whose views differed greatly from ours. And there was one more thing: the new catchphrase had an attractive acronym. Could it have been coincidence that Global Struggle Against Violent Extremism telescoped into the snappy G-SAVE? G for God, or GI, or G-Man, the implacable FBI agent of national-security lore. And SAVE for, well, *save*. Save the world. Save civilisation. Who could not feel inspired to sign up to that?

Not two weeks later, however, G-SAVE turned out to be a botched product launch. Former CIA officer Larry Johnson reported that George W. Bush had complained 'No one checked with me', and insisted it was still a war.[10] Bush rammed the new old message home in a speech where the repeated syllables of 'war on terror' rang out like anvil-blows:

Make no mistake about it, we are at war. We're at war with an enemy that attacked us on September 11th, 2001. We're at war against an enemy that, since that day, has continued to kill. [. . .] To win this war on terror, we will use all elements of national power. [. . .] Part of winning this war on terror is to remind others of what's at stake, and to work diplomatically to get people to keep pressure on the enemy. [. . .] Iraq is the latest battlefield in the war on terror [. . .] Our men and women who have lost their lives in Iraq and Afghanistan and in this war on terror have died in a noble cause, in a selfless cause. [. . .] We got a big task in Washington, D.C., and that's to remember the stakes of the war on terror, and to do our duty, and to be true to the principles of the greatest nation on the face of the Earth.[11]

Perhaps Bush worried that the change to 'struggle' implied potential failure; and so the return to 'war' worked to erase that admission. Even the improvising soloist Rumsfeld fell into line after this, going back to 'war on terror'; yet he could not help but spice it up with the blue note of 'extremism' while he was at it: 'This war of ideas is at the heart of the war on terror; a conflict between a totalitarian ideology of the extremists, and the now-tested vision of free societies.'[12]

And so a kind of compromise seemed to have been reached. It was still a 'war on terror', but the enemy was now comprised of 'extremists' of all possible types. The effect was that the war's scope was wider than ever. And happily, unlike the dismayingly long and unwieldy GLOBAL STRUGGLE AGAINST VIOLENT EXTREMISM, the phrase WAR ON TERROR would still fit perfectly on a television news graphic.

Moderation

The inherent evil of 'extremism' is commonly contrasted with the supposed opposites of 'moderation' or 'balance'. To call one-self a 'moderate' is to appeal to virtues of sobriety and impartiality, but it is just as much a trick of drawing the appropriate spectrum as the denunciation of extremism is. Someone might call himself a 'moderate' on judicial punishment, for example, if he thinks people should be executed by the state, but only for heinous premeditated murders. He may describe this as a 'moderate' position by appealing to one extreme of people who call for the execution of petty thieves, on the one hand, and an opposing extreme of people who want to offer killers nothing but warm baths and PlayStations. Note that it doesn't matter if no such people of either kind exist: the very naming of a possible strand of opinion, regardless of whether anyone holds it, is sufficient to draw the spectrum of ideas that places one's own view in an admirable position. Of course for some people, all life is sacred and killing is never justified, so for them a 'moderate' approach to punishment would necessarily be drawn between different points. Thus 'moderate' means nothing until you define the context. This was well illustrated by a group of Iranian students, who in summer 2005 wrote an open letter to the G8 summit:

> During the past two weeks, the theocratic regime in Iran held its elections for the successor to Mohammad Khatami, which according to the mafia theocratic Regime resulted in a run-off between Ali-Akbar Hashemi-Rafsanjani, a 'moderate' and Mahmoud Ahmadinejad, a 'hardliner.' In reality, these terms of 'moderate' and 'hardliner' mean little. Both of these men, as well as all those who ran for any office in Iran, did so only upon the approval of the Guardian Council. While the Islamic Republic Regime decides who is allowed to run for office, we Iranians are only allowed to pick our political leaders and representatives from a field of supporters of the oligarchic Regime.[13]

It should not be surprising, either, that the label 'moderate' has in recent years been applied to each of Howard Dean,[14] Colin Powell,[15] and Dick Cheney,[16] although the views of those men are rather divergent. The neofascist British National Party, meanwhile, was criticised as being 'too moderate' by the father of its own leader.[17] 'Moderate' is clearly an eminently movable feast.

Ideas of 'moderation' also threaten to debase substantive arguments by implying that thoroughly different factors should be accorded the same respect. A 'moderate' stance on the environment, for example, might hold that yes, on the one hand, global warming is a huge threat to the planet; but on the other hand 'economic growth' is very important, so we must not make too many onerous impositions on polluting businesses. One can better appreciate the erroneous logic of such 'moderation' by exaggerating the scenario somewhat. Say that a massive asteroid is hurtling towards Earth, threatening billions of deaths. Some people call for the mustering of all means possible to divert the rock so that it passes by harmlessly. Others say yes, well, this is obviously a problem, but it would cost a lot of money and effort to make absolutely sure we divert it; why don't we adopt a 'moderate' solution and just knock it slightly off course so that it hits, say, Africa? Clearly there are some issues on which to be 'moderate', to compromise, is wrong.

The media has its own special analogue of 'moderation', called 'balance'. Radio and television have a fetish for the duel. In what is called a 'three-way', the presenter will chair an argument between two people holding diametrically opposed views. Here again we see the three-points-on-a-line picture. Indeed, the presenter is said to 'moderate' the discussion, supposedly adopting a neutral middle ground. Maybe someone once dreamt that, as in the famous Hegelian formula thesis + antithesis = synthesis, such 'debates' would illuminate an issue. Mostly they are fatuous shouting matches. Worse, this model of 'balance' often leads to a distorted and untruthful view of the facts. Remember the story of the global-warming 'sceptic' in such a discussion on the BBC: he turned out to be paid by an oil company. But even if he hadn't been merely an industry shill, the very fact of putting one person in front of a microphone to say that global warming is a threat, and another person in front of the opposing microphone to say that it is a phantom menace, implies that the debate at large is similarly 'balanced', with about half of experts agreeing with each guest. In the case of global warming, as with evolution versus 'intelligent design', this is patently false.

Even if one's coverage is heavily politically biased, one can still easily claim 'balance', by the familiar method of shifting the spectrum's endpoints. Hence the brilliance of the Fox News Channel's slogan, 'Fair and Balanced'. This heavily conservative US media outlet, which, as you will remember, hosts Bill O'Reilly's denunciations of civil libertarians as 'terrorists', refuses to call US Marines 'snipers' because it sounds too violent, and reported that the 2005 London Undergound bombings were the first ever 'homicide attacks' to have taken place in Western Europe, is certainly not 'balanced' in the sense of giving equal time to Republican and Democrat viewpoints, for instance. Yet perhaps it thought of its spectrum as merely stretching from one side of the White House to the other. Seeking illumination, I wrote to Fox's Senior Vice-President in charge of News Editorial, John Moody. Perhaps, my email wondered, Fox considered itself 'balanced' in a wider sense, as a corrective to some perceived 'liberal bias' in the media? Moody replied thus: 'Your project sounds interesting. I believe, however, there is no need for me to explain the idea of balance.'[18]

Indeed there was not. It was obvious that Fox's claim to 'balance' was a glowingly blatant untruth, but one could not help admiring the power of its insistence. When a graphic screaming 'Fair and Balanced' interrupts coverage every few minutes, the claim somehow passes beyond the stage where it might be interpreted as protesting too much, and rockets the channel into a realm where the meaning of words like 'fair' and 'balanced' is entirely obliterated. They become phatic speech: designed to make the viewer feel good, but not to convey any particular idea to the mind. The void of sincerity in the appeal to 'balance' was ably demonstrated by another Fox character. In the wake of the attacks on the US of 11 September 2001, conservatives had criticised certain news stations as 'unpatriotic' for, among other things, reporting the toll of civilian casualties in the Afghanistan war. Fox anchor Brit Hume expressed the sentiment like this: 'Look, neutrality as a general principle is an appropriate concept for journalists who are covering institutions of some comparable quality. This is a conflict between the United States and murdering barbarians.'[19]

Hume was at least right in that, in the version of the English language that most people spoke outside the Fox network, 'balance' did imply a studied neutrality, a refusal to criticise one side more than another – even if the existence of one 'side' was more or less fictional. When reporting controversies, newspapers often interpret this idea of neutrality by refusing to do any more than simply relay what is said to them by each party. This results in an abrogation of their duty to inform the public, particularly when cynical politicians eagerly exploit this structural feature simply by telling lies.

In the wake of the hurricane that destroyed New Orleans in August 2005, the *Washington Post* reported that a 'senior Bush official' had said that Louisiana governor Kathleen Blanco 'had not declared a state of emergency' as of 3 September.[20] In fact, as would have been easily verifiable had the newspaper checked, the source's claim was false. Blanco had declared an emergency on 26 August, as the *Post*'s subsequent correction acknowledged. Such cynical official briefing exemplifies contempt for the 'reality-based community'. It derives from a tactical low cunning: the idea is simply to buy time, to muddy the waters, in the hope that by the time the falsehood is exposed it will be old news.

A special case of this phenomenon occurs when politicians claim to be 'clarifying' what they have previously said. In January 2005, Senator Joe Lieberman, on being asked about 'social-security reform', said: 'If we can figure out a way to help people through private accounts or something else, great.'[21] Two months later, the *New York Times* reported:

Mr. Lieberman this week clarified his position on Social Security, telling his hometown paper, The New Haven Register, that he was 'totally unconvinced' by the idea of creating private accounts, calling it 'a very risky thing to do.'[22]

It is not clear in this instance even whether Lieberman used the term 'clarified' himself; if he had not, the report demonstrated an unseemly eagerness to assist in the rhetorical massage of his volte-face. A more blatant 'clarification' taught readers about Arnold Schwarzenegger's concern for the environment:

Mr. Schwarzenegger has long been a booster of the gas-guzzling Hummer, the S.U.V. that groups like the Sierra Club love to hate. On one campaign stop, he made an offhand remark suggesting that the state should abolish its E.P.A [Environmental Protection Agency]. Mr. Schwarzenegger's advisers later clarified the remark and said he supported the E.P.A.[23]

In Unspeak, then, 'clarification' means simple denial or lying. Politicians and their spokespeople may claim to 'clarify'; newspapers that uncritically adopt that weasel word collude in public deception and grant their imprimatur to official dishonesty.

Forward, not back

The idea of a linear spectrum of ideas, and so a virtuous kind of 'moderation' in the middle, is hard to get rid of since it is inherent in the ordinary language used to describe political views: 'right wing' and 'left wing'. To use these phrases implies all too easily that there are only ever two sides to every question, and that the Conservative and Labour, or Republican and Democrat, positions on every conceivable issue by themselves exhaust the entire repertoire of possible thought about the subject. Blair and Clinton's boast, in the late 1990s, of a 'Third Way' was a clever propaganda strategy exploiting this very idea, turning the somewhat tepid position of 'moderation' into one of thrusting dynamism. Yet, like 'moderation', a Third Way can mean just about anything depending on how you draw the spectrum, which explains why Third Ways had previously been declared by Hitler and Mussolini, as well as by French Communists in the 1970s. By the end of Tony Blair's second term in government, however, Labour no longer talked of a third way. The newly fashionable mode of rhetoric was a resurrected old favourite: the false dichotomy.

A false dichotomy proposes only two alternatives when there are actually many. This is evident in the simple sloganeering of Labour's 2005 election campaign, whose catchphrase was 'Forward, not back'. According to this image, we ride a single axis of history; a groove or rail or world-spirit-teleology points in only one possible direction towards the utopian horizon. Anyone who would prefer another bearing must be a retrograde philosopher, because the only other possible direction is backwards. The only vehicle in which you can go either forward or back, and in no other direction, is a train. But whereas an ordinary train has a destination, where it stops, the train of progress can never stop. It is a perpetual train. Moreover, so as to avoid any disagreeable notion of circularity, of getting back to where you started, we must imagine that this train makes its epic journey on a boundless flat Earth. 'Forward, not back' is a quasi-totalitarian view – the leader maps out the only possible future and invites merely our monologic assent – mingled with an Italian-Futurist notion of the erotics of speed and machinery.

Another use of the false dichotomy is to invent a position opposed to your own that is patently absurd, so as to encourage the view that your own opinion is the only reasonable one. Thus, George W. Bush's chief strategist, Karl Rove, said in 2005:

'Conservatives saw the savagery of 9/11 in the attacks and prepared for war; liberals saw the savagery of the 9/11 attacks and wanted to prepare indictments and offer therapy and understanding for our attackers.'[24] The fact that this was just a fantasy was irrelevant. Simply invoking the absurdity of one imaginary 'extreme' worked to bolster the apparent rationality of what 'conservatives' did, and buried any debate over what kind of 'war' it was appropriate to prepare for, and how it and its sequels should or should not be conducted. One could, if one wished, read Rove's proposition as an appeal to 'moderation' by imagining the symmetrically opposing 'extreme': say, a bellicose recommendation to shower all the 'Axis of Evil' countries with Peacekeepers – the nuclear, rather than the UN sort. Then one would be led to the happy conclusion that everything the government subsequently did was correct, by virtue simply of falling in the middle of two ridiculous alternatives that no one actually proposed.

Regime change

Zealously offering up false dichotomies already debases thought in political adverts or rabble-rousing speeches; but when they are used to frame arguments over large strategic decisions, they become positively dangerous. This is what happened during the run-up to the 2003 war in Iraq. It can be traced in the use of one phrase of Unspeak: 'regime change'.

To begin with, 'regime' in our time is already a term that connotes disapproval of what it describes. Whereas it used to mean any system of government, a neutral sense that persists in non-political usages such as 'exercise regime', to call a government a 'regime' nowadays is to say that it is somehow illegitimate, whether it be headed by a genocidal dictator or just not 'democratic' in the special sense of being friendly to privatisation by western companies. One hears of the 'regime' in Iran, North Korea, and Cuba, but not often of the Bush regime or even the Berlusconi regime. So to call a government a 'regime' is already to say that it would be nice to change it. This point was made with ironic force by anti-Bush bumper stickers that appeared in the US when war was rumbling in the distance, saying: 'Regime change begins at home.'[25]

According to Bush officials and supporters, 'regime change' had already become US policy towards Iraq with the Clinton government's Iraq Liberation Act of 1998.[26] Pro-war commentators often pointed to this in order to ward off the charge that invading Iraq was a specifically neo-conservative scheme. And now stop. Go back. In the two sentences you have just read, the Unspeak sleight of hand has already been accomplished. Because the concept of 'regime change' in Iraq was never synonymous with invading that country. In fact the specific phrase does not occur in the Iraq Liberation Act, which instead expresses the policy thus:

> It should be the policy of the United States to support efforts to remove the regime headed by Saddam Hussein from power in Iraq and to promote the emergence of a democratic government to replace that regime.[27]

The legislation says a lot about supporting the 'Iraqi democratic opposition', but nothing about invading that country. Even if you then refer to its aim with the shorthand 'regime change', that phrase still only expresses a wish as to a result – a new government – but does not name any particular means of attaining that end. Going to war was one such possible means, but there were numerous other ideas about how to get rid of Saddam Hussein. This was confirmed by none other than Paul Wolfowitz, regarded by many as one of the original architects of the war. By 2005, it was clear that the invasion had not been the quick, simple win that its propagandisers had promised, and Wolfowitz now claimed that he had preferred a different plan all along: to arm Iraqis to take back their own country, supporting them from the air if necessary.

I changed my view after 9/11 [. . .] Contrary to the myth that I
have been waiting all along for an excuse to invade Iraq, before
then I really didn't want to even think about sending in U.S.
ground forces. I had always thought the idea of occupying
Baghdad was both unnecessary and a mistake. What was
needed was to arm and train the Iraqis to do the job themselves – the way, in effect, the Afghans did, by taking
advantage of the fact that a third of the country was already liberated. I advocated supporting them with air power if
necessary. I remember congressional testimony where I think I
may have used the phrase – maybe someone else did – 'reducing Saddam to the mayor of Baghdad,' at which point he
would collapse. It was sometimes called the enclave strategy,
disparagingly, although I still don't know what was wrong
with it.'[28]

Here Wolfowitz has it pleasantly both ways. He describes
the mode of 'regime change' that he preferred before 11
September 2001, and says that after that he 'changed his view'.
Yet in what respect he changed it is not clear, because he ends
up saying that he still doesn't know what was wrong with the
old, non-invasion plan.

In any case, the idea, confirmed by Wolfowitz, that there was
at least one way to accomplish 'regime change' without actually
invading the country was suppressed in the arguments for war.
Instead, a false dichotomy was painted. Either we invade Iraq,
or we do nothing, thus encouraging Saddam in his plans. As
presented to the public, the case thus boiled down to: invade or
capitulate. Watch how Tony Blair expressed the idea: 'Now I
had a decision to make as to whether to leave Saddam there, in
breach of UN resolutions, and end up in a situation with the
international community humiliated and him emboldened, or
to remove him. I decided to remove him. [. . .] There was no
middle way, there was no fence to sit on.'[29] Blair's self-dramati-
sation as a lone decision-maker at a critical point in history was
somewhat unconvincing to those aware that he had already

secretly agreed back in 2002 to help in any US invasion.[30] And, though there was much discussion in US and UK media on the question of whether governments had lied about yellowcake uranium in Niger, or 'weapons of mass destruction' that could be fired in forty-five minutes, the controversy over these issues of detail distracted from the one really big lie. That was the false dichotomy that said the only options were war or appeasement.

No matter what

So much, then, for Third Ways. The old fallacy of positing bogus alternatives for political expediency, it seemed, was too useful to throw away permanently. It was 'Forward, not back'. It was, as George W. Bush said, 'You're either with us or against us in the fight against terror.'[31] False dichotomies propose one solution along with an obviously undesirable alternative; they deny the existence of other reasonable plans of action. Speak war, and unspeak any serious alternatives.

Before you have even engineered a special Unspeak phrase, then, you may commit an act of structural Unspeak by drawing a biased map of the terrain on which your argument will sit. Denunciations of what is 'extreme', appeals to 'moderation' or 'balance', and the exploitation of false dichotomies all help to prepare the ground in which a little verbal seed such as 'regime change', or 'anti-social behaviour', or 'war on terror' will germinate and grow into a mighty tree. Many types of Unspeak are themselves false dichotomies, too: 'pro-life' sets up a false choice between being for life and against it; 'ethnic cleansing' encourages you to think that the choice is between hygiene and filth.

Topographical metaphors that draw an arbitrary spectrum of ideas, and false dichotomies that deny the existence of real alternatives, then, are Unspeak in their very structure: Unspeak writ large. What might we call the people who indulge in such misdirection? On the basis that no one can be wrong all the time, let us consult Bill O'Reilly. 'An extremist is someone who rejects facts and holds on to opinions no matter what,' he said one night on Fox. 'Extremists have a neurosis. They really don't want to hear anything other than the conclusion they've arrived at, no matter what the evidence suggests.'[32] Well, quite. Perhaps this called for a global struggle after all.

10

Epilogue

'We cannot too earnestly recommend to our Authors the Study
of the *Abuse of Speech*.' – Martin Scriblerus, 1727[1]

A vehement heat

To trace how Unspeak is perpetrated and spread across the
world is to recognise it as fundamentally misleading. But it may
be simplistic to call it plain lying. A more melancholy possibility was recognised 250 years ago in *The Art of Political Lying*:

> Towards the End of this Chapter, he warns the Heads of Parties
> against believing their own Lies; which has proved of perni-
> cious Consequence of late, both a Wise Party and a Wise Nation
> having regulated their Affairs upon Lies of their own
> Invention. The Causes of this he supposes to be too great a
> Zeal and Intenseness in the Practice of this *Art*, and a vehement
> Heat in mutual Conversation, whereby they perswade one
> another, that what they wish, and report to be true, is really so.[2]

And so, following this scheme, it is tempting to imagine that
a 'faith community' such as the Bush administration, vehe-
mently opposed as it is to the judicious study of reality, may end
up – as Ehud Barak claimed was true of 'the Arabs' – simply
incapable of telling the difference between truth and lies at all.

Apparently, however, this does not faze their adversaries. Having witnessed the virtuoso use of Unspeak by the Bush administration, some liberals in the US desperately want to catch up in the rhetorical arms race. Studying the work on how different terms 'frame' arguments by such linguists as George Lakoff, the Democrats hit on a counter-strategy: to burnish and sharpen their own language until it became as steely and weaponised as that of the opposition. The aim was expressed thus in 2005 by Howard Dean: 'The framing of the debate determines who wins the debate.'[3] But this may end up merely as fighting Unspeak with Unspeak. One may be wearily sceptical that it will lead to any great enlightenment. The clash of Unspeaks that we saw in the Introduction between 'pro-choice' and 'pro-life' did not engender more civilised conversations about abortion. And as we saw in Chapter Two, the first fruit of the Democrats' new 'reframing' strategy – the slogan 'Prosperity. Opportunity. Community' – was just more of the same mental anaesthetic, novocaine for the soul.

Linguist Ranko Bugarski argues, by contrast: 'What is needed in replacement of "Warspeak" is not an equally crude and militant "Peacespeak", but judicious use of normal language, allowing for fine-grained selection and discrimination, for urbanity and finesse.'[4] What counts as 'normal language', of course, is already subject to ideological disagreement. But the sentiment is admirable, even if it describes an unlikely ideal. Politicians will go on trying their luck with all the rhetorical strategies in their pockets. But we should at the very least expect, and demand, that our newspapers, radio, and television refuse to replicate and spread the Unspeak virus. As BBC World presenter Kirsty Lang explains: 'It's much easier to take the language that's given to you, and the government knows that full well. So if you keep saying "coalition forces", "coalition forces", people will use it. I think people do need to be more careful. They do take phrases willy-nilly from the government without thinking, without seriously analysing what they say.'[5] The citizen's plan of action is simple. When the media do this, talk back: write and tell them. Possibly the growth of Unspeak cannot be reversed. But that doesn't mean we have to go on swallowing it.

To resist Unspeak, after all, is not just to quibble about semantics, any more than a jury deciding whether an accused person has committed 'murder' or 'manslaughter' is engaged in an arid linguistic exercise. Words have consequences in the world. To adopt the phrase 'ethnic cleansing' is to be complicit in mass killing. To talk blandly of 'abuse' turns a blind eye to the beating to death of blameless taxi drivers. It is not a coincidence that this book has largely concentrated on how Unspeak is used simultaneously to advance and disguise the claims of war and corporate interests. The masterpieces of the art are indeed 'ethnic cleansing', 'war on terror', 'repetitive administration'. Rhetorically, Unspeak is a kind of invasive procedure: it wants to bypass critical thinking and implant a foreign body of opinion directly in the soft tissue of the brain. Perhaps for this reason, it seems to have a particular affinity with projects of violence.

Unspeak itself does violence: to meaning. It seeks to annihilate distinctions – between 'anti-social' and criminal; 'resources' and human beings; 'cleansing' and killing; 'combatant' and civilian; 'abuse' and torture. Because meaning is socially constructed, the Unspeak that skews meaning for political ends can itself properly be called 'anti-social'. Unspeak finds soothing names for violence so that violence no longer surprises the deadened mind. Unspeak conjures a world where violence is the default activity, encouraging its user to think of everything in terms of violent conflict.

It was, therefore, understandable when George W. Bush, campaigning for the US presidency in September 2000, explained why he would not demolish hydroelectric dams in order to protect endangered fish. 'I know the human being and fish can coexist peacefully,' he blurted.[6] Now, the phrase *coexist peacefully* is only ever used of two groups in a warring attitude. Since when were we at war with the fish? (It is true that in two states of the US, it is legal to go fishing with an assault rifle, but let us consider this an aberration, rather than evidence for a real War on Fish.) Bush's phrasing, one might think, reflected a set of assumptions which he since made real, about the necessity for perpetual and total war.

Our distant watery cousins made a welcome return to political rhetoric three years later, when they generously furnished a symbol for the success of the war in Iraq. On Fox News, under the usual banner 'WAR ON TERROR', *At Large* host Geraldo Rivera exclaimed joyously: 'You go to the markets [in Iraq], they're thriving, big fat fish coming out of the Tigris and the Euphrates river.'[7] The invasion had thus accomplished wonders. Only a cynic would wonder how much 'depleted uranium' had ended up in these fishes' fat flesh. No, the story was a fairytale happy ending. Man's oldest and most implacable enemy, the fish, had by dint of a war become our chubby best friend, had accelerated its rate of sexual reproduction in excitement at all the bombs and missiles going off, and was now leaping happily on to the plates of grateful liberated Iraqis. If fishes were now our allies in the war on terror, maybe the tide was turning at last.

Acknowledgements

This book benefited incalculably from the surgical strikes of Schuyler W. Henderson and the reforming zeal of Daniel Fugallo, to both of whom my deepest gratitude. Valuable advice and help were also given by Zoë Waldie, Tony Rees, Gavin Rees, Robert Grant, Giles Foden, Ranko Bugarski, Philippe Sands, John Houghton, Julian Hunt, and Ted Honderich. I am grateful to editors Tim Whiting, Iain Hunt, and Brando Skyhorse, and to interviewees Harold Walker, Kirsty Lang, Stephen Whittle, Ian Mayes, and David Marsh. Thanks also to Tam Threipland and Claire Armitstead.

Others had an indirect influence on the book, though it was a long time ago and they should not be held responsible: Elizabeth MacArthur, Adrian Kilroy, Peter Holmes, Liz Marsden, and John Lennard.

Finally, special thanks to Carole Le Page, without whom I would not have got up in the mornings.

Paris, November 2005

www.unspeak.net

References

Chapter 1: Introduction

1 Confucius, *Analects*, Book XIII, in Lau, D. C. (trans.), *Confucius: The Analects* (London, 1979), p. 128.

2 Safire, William, *Safire's New Political Dictionary* (New York, 1993), p. 615; *Oxford English Dictionary (OED)*, 'pro-', 5a.

3 Skinner, Quentin, 'Some Problems in the Analysis of Political Thought and Action', in Tully, James (ed.), *Meaning and Context: Quentin Skinner and his Critics* (Cambridge, 1988), p. 111.

4 Burke, Kenneth, *Language as Symbolic Action* (Berkeley, 1966), p. 50.

5 Lakoff, George, *Moral Politics* (Chicago, 2002), p. 263.

6 Orwell, George, 'Appendix: The Principles of Newspeak', in *Nineteen Eighty-Four* (1949; New York, 1977), p. 258.

7 Whyte, Jamie, *A Load of Blair* (London, 2005), p. 18.

8 Orwell, George, 'Politics and the English Language', in Carey, John (ed.), *George Orwell: Essays* (London, 2002), pp. 954–67.

9 Klemperer, Victor, trans. Brady, Martin, *The Language of the Third Reich: LTI, Lingua Tertii Imperii: A Philologist's Notebook* (LTI Notizbuch eines Philologen, Third edition; Halle [Salle], 1957; London, 2000).

10 Interview with author, 1 March 2005.

11 Fisk, Robert, 'The Twisted Language of War that is Used to Justify the Unjustifiable', *Independent*, 7 April 2003.

12 'Defense Department Town Hall Meeting', Department of Defense (DoD), 29 June 2005.

13 Interview with Barbara Walters, *20/20, ABC News*, 14 January 2005.

14 'Secretary Rumsfeld Interview with Sir David Frost, BBC News', DoD transcript, 15 June 2005.

15 Interview with John King, *Defending America*, CNN, 18 January 2005.

16 Dao, James, and Schmitt, Eric, 'Pentagon Readies Efforts to Sway Sentiment Abroad', *New York Times (NYT)*, 18 February 2002.

17 'Secretary Rumsfeld Media Availability En Route to Chile', DoD, 18 November 2002.

18 Oborne, Peter, *The Rise of Political Lying* (London, 2004).

19 Arbuthnot, John (attrib.), Proposals for Printing A very curious Discourse, in two Volumes in *Quarto*, intitled, PSEUDOLOGIA POLITIKE: or, a Treatise of the Art of Political Lying, with An Abstract of the First Volume of the said Treatise (Edinburgh, 1746), p. 7.

20 Ibid., p. 8.

21 Bourdieu, Pierre, *Language and Symbolic Power*, ed. Thompson, John B., trans. Raymond, Gino, and Adamson, Matthew (1991; Cambridge, 2003), p. 236.

22 Cicero, 'The Treatise on Rhetorical Invention', XVII, in Yonge, C. D. (trans.), *The Orations of Marcus Tullius Cicero*, Vol. IV (London, 1913), p. 332.

23 Cicero, op. cit., XVIII, in Yonge, ibid.

24 Webb, Tom, 'Bush Regrets Glib Statements About Iraq', *St Paul Pioneer Press*, 14 January 2005.

Chapter 2: Community

1 'Anti-Social OAP Faces Jail', *BBC News*, 22 July 2003.

2 'Brothers Placed on Two Year Anti-Social Behaviour Orders', Manchester City Council, 10 March 2004.

3 Lamarra, Paul, 'Woman to Fight Underwear Asbo', *Sunday Times Scotland*, 6 March 2005.

4 Lane, Charles, 'California's "3-Strikes" Law Upheld: Supreme Court Decides Long Prison Terms Legal', *Washington Post*, 6 March 2003.

5 Crime and Disorder Bill [Lords], report of proceedings of Standing Committee B, 30 April 1998, http://www.publications.parliament.uk/pa/cm199798/cmstand/b/st980430/am/80430s01.htm

6 Crime and Disorder Act 1998 (1998, chapter 37), 1 (1) (a).

7 Public Order Act 1986 (1986, chapter 64), 5 (1).

8 *OED*, 'antisocial', 1.

9 *OED*, 'antisocial', 2.

10 Merivale, *Roman Empire* (1865), VIII. lxv. 149; cited in *OED*, 'antisocial', 2.

11 Harradine, Sally, *et al.*, 'Defining and Measuring Anti-Social Behaviour', Development and Practice Report 26, Home Office Research, Development and Statistics Directorate, 2004.

12 'Crime and Policing: Anti-Social Behaviour', http://www.homeoffice.gov.uk, August 2005

13 Anti-Social Behaviour Act 2003 (2003, Chapter 38), Part 4, Chapter 30.

14 Crime and Disorder Bill [Lords], op. cit.

15 Crime and Disorder Bill [Lords], op. cit.

16 Campbell, Siobhan, 'A Review of Anti-Social Behaviour Orders', Home Office Research Study 236, January 2002.

17 Denham, John, 'Introduction, A Guide to Anti-Social Behaviour Orders and Acceptable Behaviour Contracts', Home Office, March 2003.

18 Travis, Alan, and White, Michael, 'Liberal Law and Order Days Over, Says Blair', *Guardian*, 19 July 2004.

19 Crime and Disorder Bill [Lords], report of proceedings of Standing Committee B, 5 May 1998.

20 *Criminal Law Week*, Issue 9, 2005, p. 4.

21 Ibid.

22 Souter, J., opinion dissenting, *Lockyer, Attorney General of California v. Andrade*, 538 US 63, note 2, 5 March 2003.

23 *Criminal Law Week*, Issue 6, 2005, p. 7.

24 'Anti-Social Behaviour', The Government Reply to the Fifth Report from the Home Affairs Committee Session 2004–05 HC 80, June 2005, para 32.

25 'Asbo Attempt to Halt Woman's Suicide Bids', *Scotsman*, 25 February 2005.

26 'Bridge Ban on Suicidal Woman', *Daily Record*, 26 February 2005.

27 Walker, Duncan, 'Asbowatch V: War on a G-String', *BBC News*, 15 March 2005.

28 'ASBO on "Suicide" Woman Upheld', *BBC News*, 29 April 2005.

29 Roberts, Chris, *Cross River Traffic: A History of London's Bridges* (London, 2005), p. 33.

30 'Pakistan "Moral Laws" Spark Row', *BBC News*, 11 July 2005.

31 Wong, Edward, 'Draft Iraqi Charter Backs Islamic Law', *NYT*, 20 July 2005; 'Iraqi Leaders Struggle to Draft Consitution', Associated Press (AP), 1 August 2005; 'US "Concession" Marks Turn in Iraq Constitution', Agence France Presse (AFP), 23 August 2005.

32 Taine, Hippolyte, trans. Durand, John, *The French Revolution*, Vol. 3 (1878; Indianapolis, 2002), p. 1149.

33 'Blair Calls For Better Parenting', *BBC News*, 2 September 2005.

34 'The Crime and Disorder Act: Guidance Document: Parenting Order', Home Office, 2 June 2000.

35 Caldwell, Christopher, 'There Ought to Be a Law?', *NYT*, 22 May 2005.

36 *OED*, 'community'.

37 Golding, *De Mornay*, ii. 18, cited in *OED*, 'community', 2.

38 Blair, Tony, 'Our Politics of Hope, Not Fear', *Observer*, 28 November 2004, p. 6.

39 Quoted in 'Too Young to Die', *Economist*, 5 March 2005, p. 49.

40 Ignatieff, Michael, *Empire Lite* (London, 2003), p. 2.

41 Interview with author, 2 March 2005.

42 'Remarks by President Bush and Senator Kerry in the Third 2004 Presidential Debate, Arizona State University, Tempe, Arizona', White House, 14 October 2004.

43 Interview with author, 1 March 2005.

44 Asthana, Anushka, 'We're Not All Hardline Extremists', *Observer*, 21 August 2005.
45 Interview with author, 16 May 2005.
46 'PM's Press Conference', Downing Street, 5 August 2005.
47 Preston, Peter, 'There is No Such Thing as Community', *Guardian*, 18 July 2005.
48 'PM's Press Conference', Downing Street, 5 August 2005
49 'Inaugural Address of United States President William J. Clinton', 20 January 1993, at University of Oklahoma College of Law, Historical Documents, http://www.law.ou.edu/hist/
50 Etzioni, Amitai, 'Joining Together', *San Francisco Recorder*, 16 March 1993.
51 Quoted in Lichfield, John, 'Great Speech, Even Second Time Around', *Independent*, 3 October 1996.
52 Green, Joshua, 'It Isn't the Message, Stupid', *Atlantic*, May 2005.
53 Walker, Martin, 'Profile: Community Spirit: Amitai Etzioni', *Guardian*, 13 March 1995.
54 Phillips, Melanie, 'Father of Tony Blair's Big Idea', *Observer*, 24 July 1994.
55 Etzioni, op. cit.
56 Williams, Raymond, *Keywords* (1976; London, 1988), p. 262.
57 Quoted in Remnick, David, 'The Masochism Campaign', *New Yorker*, 2 May 2005.
58 'Economics Focus: Old Before Their Time', *Economist*, 5 March 2005, p. 85.
59 Etzioni, Amitai, 'Tony Blair: A Communitarian in the Making?', *Times*, 21 June 1997.
60 Etzioni, 'Joining Together', op. cit.
61 E.g., in Blair, Tony, 'My Vision for Britain', *Observer*, 10 November 2002.
62 House of Commons Hansard Debates for 22 June 1998, part 10.
63 Blair, op. cit.
64 Helm, Sarah, 'Plight of the Refugees: Britain Slams Door on "Economic Migrants": The second part of an investigation into refugees finds doubts over whether Britain is upholding the principles of asylum', *Independent*, 26 June 1989.
65 Shaw, David, 'Straw Out to Break Asylum Racketeers', *Evening Standard*, 22 January 1998.
66 Deans, John, 'Six Months and You're Out, Straw Tells Illegal Migrants', *Daily Mail*, 9 February 1999.
67 Johnston, Philip, 'Blunkett Defiant Over Plans for Refugee Schools', *Sunday Telegraph*, 25 April 2004.
68 'Harper's Index', *Harper's*, July 2005.
69 Cited in Cohen, Nick, *Pretty Straight Guys* (2003; London, 2004), p. 96.
70 'Steep Rise in Asbos, But Are They Working?', *Daily Mail*, 29 June 2005.
71 Holmes, Stephen, 'The Ku Klux Klan Are a Close-Knit Bunch Too', *Guardian*, 18 February 1995.

72 Ibid.

73 *Financial Times*, 10 December 1987, cited in *OED*, 'band', v., 5.

74 Editorial: 'Meeting the Homeless Crisis', *Independent*, 19 December 1990.

75 House of Commons Hansard Debates for 5 December 2001, part 8.

76 Samson, Pete, 'This is a Sh*t Job. We've No Powers ... We're Not Properly Trained ... We're Meant to Make the Public Feel Safer But it's ... Just a Fraud', *Mirror*, 11 May 2005.

77 Police Reform Act 2002 (2002, Chapter 30), Schedule 4, Section 38.

78 'President's Remarks at Faith-Based and Community Initiatives Conference', White House, 3 March 2004.

79 Keen, Judy, 'White House Staffers Gather for Bible Study', *USA Today*, 14 October 2002.

80 Interview, *Tonight with Trevor McDonald*, ITV, 4 July 2005.

81 'Remarks by President Bush and Senator Kerry in the Third 2004 Presidential Debate, Arizona State University, Tempe, Arizona', White House, 14 October 2004.

82 Interview, *Newsnight*, BBC, 6 February 2003.

83 Blair, speech 'Choice, Excellence and Equality', to Guy's and St Thomas' Hospital, London, 23 June 2004 (quoted in Whyte, Jamie, *A Load of Blair* (London, 2005), p. 60).

84 Suskind, Ron, 'Without a Doubt', *NYT*, 17 October 2004.

85 Quoted in Mishra, Panjak, 'A Cautionary Tale for Americans', *New York Review of Books*, 26 May 2005.

Chapter 3: Nature

1 Luntz, Frank, 'The Environment: A Cleaner, Safer, Healthier America' in The Luntz Research Companies: Straight Talk, memo leaked April 2003, http://www.ewg.org/briefings/luntzmemo/; cited in Burkeman, Oliver, 'Memo Exposes Bush's New Green Strategy', *Guardian*, 4 March 2003.

2 UN A/RES/43/53, 70th plenary meeting, 6 December 1988.

3 UN A/RES/44/207, 85th plenary meeting, 22 December 1989.

4 Brown, Paul, 'World Treaty on Climate Mapped Out', *Guardian*, 31 August 1990; Koopman, D., 'Aust "Joins Climate Criminals"', *Courier-Mail* (Australia), 5 November 1990; Houghton, Sir John, former director general, UK Meteorological Office, former chair, Intergovernmental Panel on Climate Change working group on scientific assessment, email to author, 16 August 2005.

5 Leggett, Jeremy, *The Carbon War* (1999; New York, 2001), p. 17.

6 Thomas, David, 'Global Warming Action Plan in Autumn', *Financial Times*, 9 June 1990; Hunt, John, 'US Stand on Global Warming Attacked; Intergovernmental Panel on Climate Change', *Financial Times*, 30 August 1990.

7 Hunt, Julian (Lord Hunt of Chesterton), professor of climate modelling, University College London, email to author, 21 July 2005.

8 Byers, Michael, 'On Thinning Ice', *London Review of Books*, 6 January 2005, p. 9.

9 Wearne, Jean, 'Letter: Global Protesters', *Independent*, 24 July 2001.

10 Leggett, op. cit., p. 16.

11 Email to author, 29 August 2005.

12 Safire, William, 'Up-Or-Down: Nominations and Global Warming', *NYT*, 15 August 2005.

13 Baede, A. P. M. (ed.), 'Appendix I: Glossary', in Houghton, J. T., Ding, Y., *et al.* (eds.), 'Climate Change 2001: The Scientific Basis. Contribution of Working Group I to the Third Assessment Report of the Intergovernmental Panel on Climate Change' (Cambridge, 2001), p. 788.

14 Ibid.

15 Walker, Joe, To: Global Climate Science Team, 'Draft Global Climate Science Communications Plan', 3 April 1998; leaked to *New York Times* and cited in Cushman, John H., Jr., 'Industrial Group Plans to Battle Climate Treaty', *NYT*, 26 April 1998.

16 Kolbert, Elizabeth, 'The Climate of Man – III', *New Yorker*, 9 May 2005.

17 McKie, Robin, 'How We Put the Heat on Nature', *Observer*, 30 January 2005.

18 Interview with author, 1 March 2005.

19 Monbiot, George, 'Climate Change', in Hubbard, Gill, and Miller, David (eds.), *Arguments Against G8* (London, 2005), p. 106.

20 Kolbert, Elizabeth, 'The Climate of Man – I', *New Yorker*, 25 April 2005.

21 E.g., Balling, Robert, 'The Increase in Global Temperature: What it Does and Does Not Tell Us', Marshall Institute Policy Outlook, September 2003; Michaels, Patrick J., Singer, S. Fred, and Douglass, David H., 'Settling Global Warming Science', *Washington Times*, 16 August 2004; Baliunas, Sallie, and Soon, Willie, 'Global Warming Speculation vs. Science: Just Ask the Experts', *Capitalism Magazine*, 22 August 2002.

22 Sherwood, Steven, Lanzante, John, and Meyer, Cathryn, 'Radiosonde Daytime Biases and Late-20th Century Warming'; Santer, Benjamin D., Wigley, Tom M. L., Mears, Carl, *et al.*, 'Amplification of Surface Temperature Trends and Variability in the Tropical Atmosphere'; Mears, Carl A., and Wentz, Frank J., 'The Effect of Diurnal Correction on Satellite-Derived Lower Tropospheric Temperature', *Science* (Science Express electronic publications), 11 August 2005.

23 'Climate Change: Myths and Realities', Remarks of Eileen Claussen, President, Pew Center on Global Climate Change, New York, 17 July 2002.

24 Oreskes, Naomi, 'The Scientific Consensus on Climate Change', *Science*, Vol. 306, Issue 5702, 1686, 3 December 2004.

25 'Experts: Global Warming Is Real', Reuters, 18 February 2005.

26 King, David, 'Global Warming: "The Imperatives for Action from the Science of Climate Change"', speech at British Embassy, Washington, DC, 13 February 2004.

27 Browne, John, 'Beyond Kyoto', *Foreign Affairs*, July/Aug 2004, p. 20ff.

28 Blair, Tony, 'A Year of Huge Challenges', *Economist*, 1 January 2005, p. 23.

29 'Climate Change, Extreme Events, and Coastal Cities', report of the Shell Center for Sustainability Conference, 9–10 February 2005.

30 Wagner, Thomas, 'G-8 Takes No Concrete Global Warming Steps', AP, 8 July 2005.

31 Lynas, Mark, 'Get Off the Fence Over Global Warming', *New Scientist*, 25 June 2005.

32 See Dawkins, Richard, *The Blind Watchmaker* (1987; New York, 1996).

33 Biever, Celeste, 'Book Thrown at Proponents of Intelligent Design', *New Scientist*, 6 October 2005

34 Discovery Institute 'Wedge Document', http://www.antievolution.org/features/wedge.html; see also Mooney, Chris, *The Republican War on Science* (New York, 2005), pp. 173–4.

35 Johnson, Phillip, 'Enlisting Science to Find the Fingerprints of a Creator', *Los Angeles Times*, 25 March 2001.

36 Dembski, William A., *Intelligent Design: The Bridge Between Science & Theology* (Downers Grove, 1999), p. 206.

37 Behe, Michael J., *Darwin's Black Box: The Biochemical Challenge to Evolution* (1996; New York, 1998).

38 *Tammy J. Kitzmiller, et al. v. Dover Area School District*, 4:04–CV–2688, Trial Day 11, Afternoon Session, Court Reporter's Record, p. 90.

39 See, e.g., Kaku, Michio, 'Hyperspace: A Scientific Odyssey', http://www.mkaku.org; Gott, Richard J., *Time Travel In Einstein's Universe* (New York, 2001).

40 Krauss, Lawrence M., 'School Boards Want to "Teach the Controversy." What Controversy?', *NYT*, 17 May 2005.

41 Allen, John L., Jr., 'Science, Theology and the Ontological Quest', *National Catholic Reporter*, Vol. 5, No. 10, 4 Nov 2005.

42 Coyne, Jerry, 'The Case Against Intelligent Design: The Faith that Dare Not Speak Its Name', *New Republic*, 22 August 2005.

43 Dembski, William A., *The Design Revolution: Answering the Toughest Questions About Intelligent Design* (Downers Grove, 2004), p. 137.

44 Behe, op. cit.

45 *Kitzmiller v. DASD*, Trial Day 12, Afternoon Session, p. 23.

46 'Standard 3: Life Science Grades 8–12', Benchmark 3, 3.d., Kansas Science Education Standards Draft 2, 12 July 2005; and also in Draft 2(d) of 9 August 2005, p. 75.

47 Emails to author, 11 August 2005.

48 Email to author, 27 August, 2005.

49 Hanna, John, 'Kansas Changes Science Learning Standards', AP, 8 November 2005.

50 'Darwin's Greatest Challenge Tackled: The Mystery of Eye Evolution', European Molecular Biology Laboratory, 28 October 2004; Arendt, D., Tessmar-Raible, K., Snyman, H., Dorresteijn, A., and Wittbrodt, J., 'Ciliary Photoreceptors with Vertebrate-type Opsins in an Invertebrate Brain', *Science*, 29 October 2004.

51 E.g., Krem, Maxwell M., and Di Cera, Enrico, 'Evolution of Enzyme Cascades From Embryonic Development to Blood Coagulation', *Trends in Biochemical Sciences*, Vol. 27, No. 2, February 2002, pp. 67–74; Jiang, Yong, and Doolittle, Russell F., 'The Evolution of Vertebrate Blood Coagulation as Viewed From a Comparison of Puffer Fish and Sea Squirt Genomes', *Proceedings of the National Academy of Sciences*, Vol. 100, No. 13, 24 June 2003, pp. 7527–32.

52 *Kitzmiller v. DASD*, Trial Day 11, Afternoon Session, pp. 38–9.

53 Orr, H. Allen, 'Devolution', *New Yorker*, 30 May 2005.

54 Dembski, William A., 'Becoming a Disciplined Science: Prospects, Pitfalls, and Reality Check for ID', 25 October 2002, http://www.design inference.com/documents/2002.10.27.Disciplined_Science.htm; and cited in Brauer, Matthew J., Forrest, Barbara and Gey, Steven G., 'Is It Science Yet? Intelligent Design, Creationism and the Constitution', *Washington University Law Quarterly*, Vol. 83, No. 1, 2005, p. 56ff.

55 Brauer, *et. al.*, op. cit., pp. 81–2.

56 'Intelligent Design', *Nightline*, ABC, 10 August 2005.

57 Ibid.

58 Mooney, op. cit., pp. 67–8.

59 Horgan, John, 'In Defense of Common Sense', *NYT*, 12 August 2005.

60 Mooney, Chris, 'Beware "Sound Science." It's Doublespeak for Trouble', *Washington Post*, 29 February 2004.

61 Chinni, Dante, 'Arsenic Flap and "Sound Science"', *Christian Science Monitor*, 14 June 2001.

62 Ibid.

63 Mooney, 'Beware Sound Science', op. cit.

64 Brainard, Jeffrey, 'How Sound Is Bush's "Sound Science"?', *Chronicle of Higher Education*, 5 March 2004.

65 Jehl, Douglas, and Revkin, Andrew C., 'Bush Reverses Vow to Curb Gas Tied to Global Warming', *NYT*, 14 March 2001.

66 'Restoring Scientific Integrity in Policymaking', statement of the Union of Concerned Scientists, http://www.ucsusa.org, 18 February 2004.

67 Revkin, Andrew C., 'Bush Aide Softened Greenhouse Gas Links to Global Warming', *NYT*, 8 June 2005.

68 Hebert, H. Josef, 'Ex-White House Official to Join Fuel Co', AP, 14 June 2005.

69 Woodward, Bob, *Plan of Attack* (London, 2004), p. 443.

70 Schwartz, Peter, and Randall, Doug, 'An Abrupt Climate Change Scenario and Its Implications for United States National Security', report commissioned for the US DoD, October 2003

71 Graham, Judith, 'Mountain Blooms Foster Warnings About Warming', *Chicago Tribune*, 17 July 2003; Campbell, Deborah, and Burkeman, Oliver, 'CIA Switches From Covert Ops to Kids' Stuff: Spy Agency's Website Puts On a Cheerful Face for Youngsters, But Contradicts the Official White House Line On Global Warming', *Guardian*, 7 April 2004.

72 *Tonight with Trevor McDonald*, ITV, 29 June 2005.

73 Hunt, Julian, 'How Can Cities Mitigate and Adapt to Climate Change?', *Building Research and Information*, Vol. 32, No. 1, January–February 2004, pp. 55–7.

74 Hunt, Julian, email to author, 21 July 2005.

75 McKinnon, John D., and Cooper, Christopher, 'Bush Will "Lead" Drive for Changes to Social Security', *Wall Street Journal*, 11 January 2005.

76 Shah, Sonia, *Crude: The Story of Oil* (New York, 2005), p. 147.

77 Billig, Michelle, 'The Venezuelan Oil Crisis: How to Secure America's Energy', *Foreign Affairs*, Sept/Oct 2004, pp. 2–5.

78 Cited in Byers, op. cit.

79 US Department of State Daily Press Briefing, 22 April 2005.

80 'National Defense Budget Estimates for FY 2005', DoD, March 2004.

81 Smith, Adam, *Inquiry into the Wealth of Nations* (1776), V. iii, cited in *OED*, 'natural', 19b.

82 Lutz, William, *The New Doublespeak: Why No One Knows What Anyone's Saying Anymore* (1996; New York, 1997), pp. 174–5.

83 Genesis 1: 26.

84 Cook, Robin, *The Point of Departure* (2003; London, 2004), p. 365.

85 ChevronTexaco advertisement, *New Yorker*, 14 and 21 February 2005, pp. 8–9.

86 'Natural Gas 1998: Issues and Trends', US Energy Information Administration, April 1999.

87 Ibid.

88 *OED*, 'human', a. (n.), 3b.

89 Klemperer, Victor, trans. Brady, Martin, *The Language of the Third Reich: LTI, Lingua Tertii Imperii: A Philologist's Notebook* (LTI Notizbuch eines Philologen, Third edition, Halle, 1957; London, 2000), pp. 148–50.

90 Hume, David, *A Treatise of Human Nature*, (1739; Oxford, 1986), III i ii, p. 474.

91 'Genetically Modified Crops: The Ethical and Social Issues', Nuffield Council on Bioethics, 1 May 1999; and cited in Cook, Guy, *Genetically Modified Language* (Abingdon, 2004), p. 99.

92 'About Us', http://www.afic.org

93 'Food Biotechnology: A Communications Guide to Improving Understanding', Asian Food Information Centre, International Service for the Acquisition of Agri-Biotech Applications, October 2001.

94 Cook, Guy, op. cit., p. 88.

95 'Communicating with Consumers on Food Biotechnology', report of the Asian Food Information Centre 2003 Qualitative Research Results, http://www.afic.org, May 2004.

96 Windsor, Charles, 'My 10 Fears for GM Food', *Daily Mail*, 1 June 1999; cited in Cook, Guy, p. 141.

97 Birkbeck Hill, George (ed.), *Boswell's Life of Johnson* (Oxford, 1897), Vol. 3, p. 105.

98 Collingwood, R. G., *The Idea of Nature* (Oxford, 1945), p. 3.

99 'Prime Minister Remembers "Inspirational" Pope John Paul II', Downing Street, 4 April 2005.

100 'President's Radio Address', White House, 9 April 2005.

101 Hume, op. cit., III ii, p. 481.

102 'Sen. Rick Santorum's Comments on Homosexuality in an AP Interview', AP, 22 April 2003.

103 See Jones, Lucien, *The Transparent Head* (Cambridge, 2005), p. 237.

104 Aristotle, trans. Jowett, Benjamin, *Politics* (Oxford, 1885), I v, 1254 a, p. 7.

105 Lukacs, John, *Democracy and Populism: Fear and Hatred* (London, 2005), p. 22.

106 Ibid, p. 23.

107 See Pinker, Steven, *The Blank Slate* (New York, 2002).

108 'Sarajevo', Human Rights Watch, 1 October 1994.

Chapter 4: Tragedy

1 Honigsbaum, Mark, 'Brazilian Did Not Wear Bulky Jacket', *Guardian*, 28 July 2005.

2 Ibid.

3 Honigsbaum, Mark and Dodd, Vikram, 'Brazilian Was Shot Eight Times, Inquest Told', *Guardian*, 26 July 2005.

4 Cowan, Rosie, *et al.*, 'Met Chief Warns More Could Be Shot', *Guardian*, 25 July 2005.

5 Thompson, Tony et al, "Man shot in terror hunt was innocent young Brazilian", *Observer*, July 24, 2005

6 'The New Face of London's Police', *Economist*, 28 July 2005.

7 'London Cops ID Two Suspects', *CBS News*, 25 July 2005.

8 Jones, George, 'Clerics Who Spit Hate Must Go, Says Major', *Daily Telegraph*, 26 July 2005.

9 Cowan, op. cit.

10 Honigsbaum, op. cit.

11 Thompson, op. cit

12 Chomsky, Noam, *Necessary Illusions* (London, 1989), p. 213.

13 Speech at UN General Assembly, 13 December 1998.

14 Okrent, Daniel, 'The Public Editor: The Hottest Button, How the Times Covers Israel and Palestine', *NYT*, 24 April 2005.

15 Kepel, Gilles, *The War for Muslim Minds: Islam and the West* (Cambridge, Mass., 2004), p. 133.

16 Nir, Ori, 'Word of the Month: Walls and Fence', Tzavta (Israel Center's Young Adults Program), February 2004.

17 Mayes, Ian, 'Addition and Long Division', *Guardian*, 9 August 2003.

18 Halliday, Fred, *100 Myths About the Middle East* (London, 2005), p. 245.

19 *Front Row*, BBC Radio 4, 3 December 2004.

20 Alpher, Yossi, 'An Israeli View: Folly', http://www.bitterlemons.org, 13 June 2005.

21 Raum, Tom, 'Bush Criticizes Israeli Fence, Tells Abbas Terror Must End', AP, 26 July 2003.

22 *Jordan Times*, 2 July 2003.

23 Mayes, op. cit.

24 Rose, Jacqueline, 'Deadly Embrace', *London Review of Books*, 4 November 2004, p. 21.

25 Izenberg, Dan, 'ACRI: ICJ Fence Ruling Correct', *Jerusalem Post*, 6 May 2005.

26 Lappin, Yaakov, 'Calls for Israel's Destruction in London', *Jerusalem Post*, 22 May 2005.

27 'Legal Consequences of the Construction of a Wall in the Occupied Palestinian Territory', International Court of Justice, General List No. 131, 9 July 2004.

28 Yoaz, Yuval, 'State to High Court: Fence Route Determined Not Only By Security Considerations', *Ha'aretz*, 4 July 2005.

29 US Department of State Daily Press Briefing, 11 July 2005.

30 Harel, Amos, '55,000 Palestinians to Be Cut Off By J'lem Fence', *Ha'aretz*, 10 July 2005.

31 'Sharon is Dividing Jerusalem', *Ha'aretz*, 13 July 2005.

32 Ibid.

33 Forman, Geremy, and Kedar, Alexandre (Sandy), 'From Arab Land to "Israel Lands": The Legal Dispossession of the Palestinians Displaced by Israel in the Wake of 1948', *Environment and Planning D: Society and Space 2004*, Vol. 22, pp. 809–30.

34 Rapoport, Meiron, 'Ces Palestiniens qui se croyaient propriétaires à Jérusalem', *Courrier International*, 27 January 2005.

35 Dor, Daniel, *Intifada Hits the Headlines* (Bloomington, 2004), pp. 45 and 144.

36 Dian Bahur-Nir and Ali Waked, '"Israel Will Eventually Disappear"', *Ynet News*, 12 July 2005.

37 Quoted in Ruthven, Malise, *Fundamentalism: The Search for Meaning* (Oxford, 2004), p. 165.

38 E.g., in Kahane, Meir, *Uncomfortable Questions for Comfortable Jews* (Secaucus, 1987), *passim*.

39 Morris, Benny, 'Camp David and After: An Exchange (1. An Interview

with Ehud Barak)', *New York Review of Books*, 13 June 2002.

40 Safire, William, 'a.k.a Abu', *NYT*, 18 May 2003.

41 Young, Michael, 'Did Mahmoud Abbas Finance the 1972 Munich Olympic Takeover?', *Slate*, 24 July 2003.

42 Cited in Stone, I. F., 'Holy War', *Les Temps Modernes*, June 1967.

43 E.g., in Garaudy, Roger, 'The Myth of a "Land Without People for a People Without Land"', *Journal of Historical Review*, Vol. 18, No. 5, p. 38.

44 Judt, Tony, 'The Road to Nowhere: An Exchange', *New York Review of Books*, 18 July 2002.

45 'History of Israeli Settlements', AP, 9 August 2005.

46 Morris, op. cit.

47 Ash, Daniel, 'Settlements: A User's Guide', Dissident Voice, 17 May 2003.

48 Ghosn, Ghassan E., personal communication.

49 UN Security Council Resolution 446, 22 March 1979.

50 'Legal Consequences of the Construction of a Wall in the Occupied Palestinian Territory', International Court of Justice, 9 July 2004.

51 King Jr., Neil, and Leggett, Karby, 'Will Bush Get Tough With Sharon?', *Wall Street Journal*, 8–10 April 2005.

52 Prusher, Elaine, 'Barak Torn Two Ways by West Bank Settlements', *Guardian*, 13 October 1999.

53 'Euphemisms for Israeli Settlements Confuse Coverage', Fairness and Accuracy in Reporting, 26 June 2002.

54 'A Performance-Based Road Map to a Permanent Two-State Solution to the Israeli-Palestinian Conflict by the Quartet (European Union, United States, the Russian Federation and the United Nations)', 30 April 2003.

55 Traubman, Tamar, *et al.*, 'Hundreds Rally in TA Against IDF Killing of 2 Palestinian Teens', *Ha'aretz*, 5 May 2005.

56 McGreal, Chris, 'Israeli Missile Attack on Hamas Leader Misses Target and Kills Passerby', *Guardian*, 27 August 2003.

57 'Syria, Iran Rebuked Over Stalled Road Map', *LA Times*, 23 July 2003.

58 Nafie, Ibrahim, 'I'm Sorry', interview with George W. Bush, *Al-Ahram*, 8 May 2004.

59 'Israel Likely to Keep 180,000 Settlers: Sharon Aide', Reuters, 4 August 2005.

60 Nir, Ori, 'Word of the Month: Connect and Disconnect', Tzavta (Israel Center's Young Adults Program), April 2004.

61 'Israeli Settler Eviction Complete', *BBC News*, 23 August 2005.

62 Morris, op. cit.

63 'Disorder Tempers Dreams of New Gaza After Israelis Go', Reuters, 21 July 2005.

64 US Department of State Briefing, 19 July 2005.

65 Halevy, Efraim, 'The Coming Pax Americana', *Ha'aretz*, 22 April 2005.

66 Shavit, Ari, 'The Big Freeze', *Ha'aretz*, 8 October 2004.

67 Brilliant, Joshua, 'Sharon's Pullback to Freeze Peace Process', United Press International, 6 October 2005.

68 Halevy, Efraim, op. cit.

69 Eldar, Akiva, 'No Oversight in Sight', *Ha'aretz*, 7 June 2005; 'Israel Sets West Bank Settlement Expansion', Reuters, 4 August 2005.

70 Keinon, Herb, 'Analysis: The Settlements Code', *Jerusalem Post*, 13 April 2005.

71 'PM Sharon's Speech to the Aipac Conference in Washington, DC', 24 May 2005.

72 Rosenblum, Mark, 'On the Road (Map) Again', Americans for Peace Now (http://www.peacenow.org), 15 April 2005.

73 Editorial: 'Ariel Sharon's Statesmanship', *NYT*, 24 August 2005.

74 'Israeli Settler Eviction Complete', *BBC News*, 23 August 2005.

75 Interview with author, 18 April 2005.

76 Quoted in Ruthven, op. cit., p. 160.

77 Quoted in Ruthven, op. cit., p. 165.

78 Cole, Juan, 'Jerusalem and Terrorism', Informed Comment (http://www.juancole.com), 11 July 2005.

79 Johnson, Paul, 'The Anti-Semitic Disease', *Commentary*, June 2005.

80 'Egyptian Foreign Minister Calls Shas Rabbi a "Racist"', *Ha'aretz*, 12 April 2001.

81 *Larry King Live*, CNN, 30 May 2005.

82 Dor, op. cit., pp. 155–7.

83 *ITV Evening News*, 9 October 2000, cited in Philo, Greg, and Berry, Mike, *Bad News from Israel* (London, 2004), p. 113.

84 Bell-Fialkoff, Andrew, *Ethnic Cleansing* (London, 1996), p. 1.

85 Cited in Novak, Viktor, *Magnum Crimen* (Zagreb, 1948), pp. 704–5; trans. Djuric, Sinisa, for The Pavelic Papers at http://www.pavelicpapers.com/documents/ndhnews/ndhn0004.html

86 Bell-Fialkoff, op. cit., p. 45.

87 *Washington Post*, 2 August 1991, cited in *OED*, 'ethnic cleansing'.

88 Cited in *OED*, 'cleanse', 2.

89 Petrovic, Drazen, 'Ethnic Cleansing – An Attempt at Methodology', *European Journal of International Law*, Vol. 5, No 3 (1994), p. 342ff.

90 'The Situation in Bosnia and Herzegovina', UN A/RES/47/121, 18 December 1992.

91 Power, Samantha, '*A Problem from Hell*': America and the Age of Genocide (New York, 2002; London, 2003), p. 288.

92 'Convention on the Prevention and Punishment of the Crime of Genocide, Approved and Proposed for Signature and Ratification or Accession by General Assembly Resolution 260 A (III) of 9 December 1948, entry into force 12 January 1951, in accordance with article XIII.'

93 Power, op. cit., pp. 53–4.

94 Gallagher, Paul, 'Srebrenica Massacre Conviction Reduced at Hague', Reuters, 19 April 2004.

95 Bugarski, Ranko, 'Language, Nationalism and War', *International Journal of the Sociology of Language*, No. 151 (2001), pp. 69–87.
96 Halliday, Fred, op. cit., p. 210.
97 Power, op. cit., p. 288.
98 Power, op. cit., p. 42.
99 Lemkin, Raphael, *Axis Rule in Occupied Europe* (1944), ix. 79, cited in *OED*, 'genocide'.
100 Power, op. cit., p. 1.
101 Cited in Power, op. cit., p. 23.
102 Matossiann, Nouritza, 'They Say "Incident". To Me It's Genocide', *Observer*, 27 February 2005, p. 23.
103 Cohen, Nick, *Pretty Straight Guys* (2003; London, 2004), pp. 86–8.
104 Stone, Norman, 'Armenia and Turkey', Letters, *Times Literary Supplement*, 15 October 2004.
105 Power, op. cit., pp. 17–19.
106 Bugarski, op. cit.
107 Power, op. cit., p. 358.
108 Ignatieff, Michael, *Empire Lite* (London, 2003), p. 70.
109 'Press Briefing on Humanitarian Crisis in Darfur, Sudan', UN, 2 April 2004.
110 'Online NewsHour: Lawmakers Decry Crisis in Sudan', PBS, 6 July 2004.
111 Straus, Scott, 'Darfur and the Genocide Debate', *Foreign Affairs*, Vol. 84, No. 1, Jan/Feb 2005, pp. 123–4.
112 Silverstein, Ken, 'Official Pariah Sudan Valuable to America's War on Terrorism', *NYT*, 29 April 2005.
113 Reeves, Eric, 'The "Two Darfurs": Redefining a Crisis for Political Purposes', http://www.sudanreeves.org, 20 May 2005.
114 Kristof, Nicholas D., 'Hypocrisy on Darfur', *International Herald Tribune*, 7 April 2005.
115 Straus, Scott, op. cit.
116 'Inaugural Address of United States President William J. Clinton', 20 January 1993.
117 'News Conference on the Former Yugoslavia', US Department of State, 10 February 1993.
118 US Department of State Archives, Vol. 4, No. 39: 27 September 1993.
119 'Leave None to Tell the Story: Genocide in Rwanda', Human Rights Watch, March 1999.
120 See, for example, Thompson, Mark, *Forging War: The Media in Serbia, Croatia, Bosnia and Hercegovina* (Second edition; Luton, 1999); Prunier, Gérard, *The Rwanda Crisis* (New York, 1995).
121 Bugarski, op. cit.
122 Empson, William, 'Missing Dates', ll 1–3, in Haffenden, John (ed), *The Complete Poems of William Empson* (London, 2004).

123 'U.S. Choices in Bosnia: Prepared Remarks of Secretary of Defense William J. Perry at the 100th Landon Lecture Series, Kansas State University, Manhattan, Kan.', DoD, 9 March 1995.

124 'Secretary William J. Perry Remarks as Prepared for Delivery, the Forrestal Lecture, United States Naval Academy Foreign Affairs Conference', DoD, 18 April 1995.

125 See Bugarski, Ranko, 'Discourses of War and Peace', *Folia Linguistica* XXXIV/3–4, 2000.

Chapter 5: Operations

1 Arkin, William N., *Code Names: Deciphering US Military Plans, Programs, and Operations in the 9/11 World* (Hanover, 2005), p. 280.

2 E.g., Chomsky, Noam, 'The Invasion of Panama', in *What Uncle Sam Really Wants* (Tucson, 1992).

3 Nunberg, Geoffrey, *Going Nucular: Language, Politics and Culture in Confrontational Times* (New York, 2004), p. 44.

4 Broder, David, 'When US Intervention Makes Sense', *Washington Post*, 14 January 1990.

5 Sieminski, Gregory C., 'The Art of Naming Operations', *Parameters* (US Army War College Quarterly), Autumn 1995, pp. 81–98.

6 Hayes, Peter, and Tannenwald, Nina, 'Nixing Nukes in Vietnam', *Bulletin of the Atomic Scientists*, Vol. 59, No. 3, May/June 2003.

7 Sieminski, op. cit.

8 Ibid.

9 Churchill, Winston, *The Second World War: Vol. V, Closing the Ring* (Boston, 1951), p. 662, cited in Sieminski.

10 Arkin, op. cit., p. 15.

11 'Press Briefing by Ari Fleischer', White House, 24 March 2003.

12 Arkin, op. cit., p. 398.

13 '"Enduring Freedom": Abuse by U.S. Forces in Afghanistan', Human Rights Watch, March 2004, Vol. 16, No. 3(C).

14 Curtis, Mark, *Unpeople: Britain's Secret Human Rights Abuses* (London, 2004), p. 297.

15 Cook, Robin, *The Point of Departure* (2003; London, 2004), p. 330.

16 'U.S.'s "Iron Hammer" Code Name 1st Used by Nazis', *San Diego Union-Tribune*, 18 November 2003.

17 Arkin, op. cit., p. 360.

18 Ibid., p. 375.

19 Ibid., p. 412.

20 Churchill, op. cit.

21 Arkin, op. cit., p. 401.

22 Ibid., p. 426.

23 American Forces Press Service, 15 July 2005.

24 *OED*, 'operation'.

25 Sorensen, T. C., *Kennedy* (1965), xxiv. 684, cited in *OED*, 'surgical', 1e.

26 *Harper's*, November 1971, cited in *OED*, 'surgical', 1e.

27 Clark, Ramsey, 'Libyan Epilogue', *The Nation*, 12 July 1986.

28 Ibid.

29 Martinot, Steve, 'Purity and Gangrene: A Meditation on the Discourse of Bombs', *Electronic Journal of Communication*, Vol. 2, No. 1, 1991.

30 Ibid.

31 'December D-Day for Fallujah', AFP, 19 September 2004.

32 'Palestinians Remove Hate Text from Web Site', Reuters, 19 May 2005.

33 Franchetti, Mark, 'Slaughter at the Bridge of Death: US Marines Fire on Civilians', *The Times*, 31 March 2003.

34 'What Is Chemotherapy and How Does It Work?', American Cancer Society, http://www.cancer.org/docroot/ETO/content/ETO_1_7X_What_Is_Chemotherapy_And_How_Does_It_Work.asp

35 Edwards, Rob, 'WHO "Suppressed" Study into Depleted Uranium Cancer Fears in Iraq', *Sunday Herald*, 22 February 2004.

36 'Uranium and Depleted Uranium', World Nuclear Association, April 2004.

37 Carr-Brown, Jonathon, 'Depleted Uranium Shells Held "Cocktail of Nuclear Waste"', *Sunday Times*, 21 January 2001.

38 'Uranium and Weapons', Uranium Medical Research Centre (http://www.umrc.net).

39 Edwards, op. cit.

40 Johnson, Larry, 'Iraqi Cancers, Birth Defects Blamed on U.S. Depleted Uranium', *Seattle Post-Intelligencer*, 12 November 2002.

41 Thompson, Mark, 'How to Squeeze a City', *Time*, 11 April 2004.

42 *OED*, 'débridement'.

43 Medline, 'debridement'.

44 'Operation Vigilant Resolve', http://www.globalsecurity.org

45 'Fallujah', http://www.globalsecurity.org

46 Barnard, Anne, 'Death Toll Near 500 in Fallujah, Baghdad', *Boston Globe*, 22 April 2004.

47 'Coalition Provisional Authority Briefing', DoD, 12 April 2004.

48 'Bush Laments "Tough Week," Bremer Vows to Rid Iraq of "Poison"', AFP, 12 April 2004.

49 Shakespeare, William, *The Tragedy of Coriolanus*, I ii 113–15, in Wells, Stanley and Taylor, Gary (eds), *The Complete Works* (Oxford, 1988).

50 Shakespeare, *The Tragedy of Coriolanus*, III i 157–8.

51 'Defense Department Briefing', 5 May 2005.

52 *OED*, 'service', I 1, 2b.

53 According to the results of full-text searches of 'provide', 'providing', 'provided' and 'provision' NEAR 'service' in the online *OED* (Second edition, 1989).

54 *OED*, 'self-service', 1.

55 'NCTE Doublespeak Award', National Council of Teachers of English, http://www.ncte.org/about/awards/council/jrnl/106868.htm

56 Safire, William, *Safire's New Political Dictionary* (New York, 1993), p. 227.

57 Ronson, Jon, *The Men Who Stare at Goats* (London, 2004), pp. 140–2, 167–8.

58 Luntz, Frank, 'The Environment: A Cleaner, Safer, Healthier America' in The Luntz Research Companies: Straight Talk, memo leaked April 2003, http://www.ewg.org/briefings/luntzmemo/; cited in Burkeman, Oliver, 'Memo Exposes Bush's New Green Strategy', *Guardian*, 4 March 2003. p. 186.

59 *OED*, 'servicing', 3, 4; 'service', v., 5a.

60 'Episode 11: Vietnam', *Cold War*, CNN, June 1996, transcript: http://www.cnn.com/SPECIALS/cold.war/episodes/11/interviews/westmoreland/

61 'Ali's Draft Conviction Upset by High Court, 8-0', AP, 28 June 1971.

62 Glossary of Military Terms and Slang from the Vietnam War, Sixties Project, University of Virginia.

63 Ibid.

64 Cook, Melvin A., 'BLU-82 Commando Vault, "Daisy Cutter"', http://www.globalsecurity.org

65 'LGM-118A Peacekeeper', http://www.globalsecurity.org; 'Intercontinental Ballistic Missiles', US Strategic Command Public Affairs, March 2004.

66 Boot, Max, 'Sparing Civilians, Buildings, and Even the Enemy', *NYT*, 30 March 2003.

67 'Turks, Saudis Ban Cruise Missile Flights', CNN, 29 March 2003.

68 Arkin, William M., 'America Cluster Bombs Iraq', *Washington Post*, 26 February 2001.

69 Ahmed, Kamal, 'Revealed: The Cluster Bombs That Litter Iraq', *Observer*, 1 June 2003.

70 Buncombe, Andrew, 'US Admits it Used Napalm Bombs in Iraq', *Independent*, 10 August 2003.

71 Quoted in Mann, Michael, *Incoherent Empire* (New York, 2003), p. 24.

72 Cited in Safire, op. cit., p. 683.

73 Ibid.

74 Bugarski, Ranko, 'Discourses of War and Peace', *Folia Linguistica* XXXIV/3–4, 2000, n.6.

75 The 9/11 Commission Report: Final Report of the National Commission on Terrorist Attacks Upon the United States (New York, 2004), p. xvi.

76 Epstein, Edward, 'Success in Afghan War Hard to Gauge', *San Francisco Chronicle*, 23 March 2002.

77 'Secretary Rumsfeld Interview with Sir David Frost, *BBC News*', US DoD transcript, 15 June 2005.

78 Buncombe, Andrew, 'Aid Worker Uncovered America's Secret Tally of Iraqi civilian Deaths', *Independent*, 20 April 2005.

79 http://www.iraqbodycount.net

80 Woodward, Bob, *Plan of Attack* (London, 2004), p. 331.

81 'Episode 11: Vietnam', *Cold War*, CNN, http://www.cnn.com/SPE-CIALS/cold.war/episodes/11/interviews/caputo/

82 Cited in Mann, op. cit., p. 138.

83 Priest, Dana, 'In War, Mud Huts and Hard Calls', *Washington Post*, 20 February 2002.

84 'R-11 / SS-1B SCUD-A, R-300 9K72 Elbrus / SS-1C SCUD-B', http://www.globalsecurity.org

85 'WMD Emphasis was "Bureaucratic"', *BBC News*, 29 May 2003.

86 'Top Bush Officials Push Case Against Saddam', CNN, 8 September 2002.

87 Cook, Robin, op. cit., p. 337.

88 'GBU-43/B "Mother of All Bombs" MOAB – Massive Ordnance Air Blast Bomb', http://www.globalsecurity.org

89 Lathem, Niles, 'The Mother of All Bombs: 21,500-lb Monster Meant to Shock Iraq into Surrender', *New York Post*, 12 March 2003.

90 Hitchens, Christopher, '"WMD" and "Inspection" – Are Saddam's Weapons Really So Unconventional?', *Slate*, 26 December 2002.

91 Cirincione, Joseph, 'The End of "WMD"', Carnegie Endowment for International Peace, July 2005.

92 Hitchens, op. cit.

93 *The Times*, 28 December 1937, cited in *OED* Online Draft Additions, 'weapon'.

94 'Cluster Bombs in Afghanistan', Human Rights Watch, October 2001.

95 'Ashcroft: Saddam's "Evil Chemistry" Justified War', AP, 26 January 2004.

96 Cirincione, op. cit.

97 'Rifle-Launched Non-Lethal Cargo Dispenser', United States Patent 6,523,478, 25 February 2003.

98 'Nuke Program Parts Unearthed in Baghdad Back Yard: U.S. Officials: Find is not smoking gun', CNN, 26 June 2003.

99 State of the Union Address, White House, 20 January 2004.

100 Syson, Neil, 'Saddam Most Deadly WMD', *Sun*, 26 April 2005.

101 Schmitt, Richard B., 'U.S. Indicts 3 Suspected Terrorist Scouts', *Los Angeles Times*, 13 April 2005.

102 *Outfoxed: Rupert Murdoch's War on Journalism* (dir. Robert Greenwald, 2004).

103 Pitt, William Rivers, 'Without Honor', http://www.truthout.org, 10 November 2003.

104 *Good Morning America*, ABC, 18 March 2003.

105 'DoD News Briefing – Secretary Rumsfeld and Gen. Pace', 20 August 2002.

Chapter 6: Terror

1 'Revised Draft Outcome Document of the High-level Plenary Meeting of the General Assembly of September 2005 Submitted by the President of the General Assembly', A/59/HLPM/CRP.1/Rev.2, US Version, 17 August 2005, leaked to Steve Clemons and posted at http:www.talking-pointsmemo.com/docs/us.comments.pdf

2 Falk, Richard, *Unlocking the Middle East: The Writings of Richard Falk*, ed. Jean Allain (Moreton-in-Marsh, 2003), pp. 136–7.

3 Cited in Rees, Phil, *Dining with Terrorists: Meetings with the World's Most Wanted Militants* (London, 2005), pp. 15–16.

4 Rees, op. cit., p. 127.

5 Collins, Lauren, 'Close Reading Dept: O.B.L.', *New Yorker*, 22 August 2005.

6 Interview on Al Jazeera, 8 July 2005, transcribed and translated in 'Special Dispatch: Jihad and Terrorism', Middle East Media Research Institute (http://www.memri.org), 12 July 2005.

7 Danner, Mark, 'Delusions in Baghdad', *New York Review of Books*, 19 November 2003.

8 Kovalev, Sergei, 'Death in Chechnya', *New York Review of Books*, 8 June 1995.

9 Kovalev, Sergei, 'Putin's War', *New York Review of Books*, 10 February 2000.

10 Falk, Richard, *The Great Terror War* (New York, 2002), p. xix.

11 *Encyclopaedia Britannica* (2005).

12 'Terrorism: What You Need to Know About U.S. Sanctions: Executive Order 13224 blocking Terrorist Property and a summary of the Terrorism Sanctions Regulations (Title 31 Part 595 of the U.S. Code of Federal Regulations), Terrorism List Governments Sanctions Regulations (Title 31 Part 596 of the U.S. Code of Federal Regulations), and Foreign Terrorist Organizations Sanctions Regulations (Title 31 Part 597 of the U.S. Code of Federal Regulations)', US Department of the Treasury publication, 15 February 2005.

13 Keegan, John, 'Necessary or Not, Dresden Remains a Topic of Anguish', *Telegraph*, 10 October 2005.

14 Oestreicher, Paul, Comment, *Guardian*, 12 February 2004.

15 McGreal, Chris, 'We're Air Force Pilots, Not Mafia. We Don't Take Revenge', *Guardian*, 3 December 2003.

16 http://www.btselem.org/english/statistics/casualties.asp

17 'Promoting Impunity: The Israel Military's Failure to Investigate Wrongdoing', Human Rights Watch, June 2005, Vol. 17, No. 7(E).

18 US Department of State Briefing with spokesperson Richard Boucher, 16 May 2005.

19 Rees, op. cit., p. 13.

20 'President Shares Thanksgiving Meal with Troops', White House news release, 21 November 2001.

21 'Remarks by the President Upon Arrival', White House news release, 16 September 2001.

22 Burke, Edmund, 'Letters on a Regicide Peace', iv, cited in *OED*.

23 Gessen, Masha, 'Chechnya: What Drives the Separatists to Commit Such Terrible Outrages?', *Slate*, 4 September 2004, http://www.slate.com/id/2106287/

24 *Outfoxed: Rupert Murdoch's War on Journalism* (dir. Robert Greenwald, 2004).

25 http://www.foxnews.com, 13 July 2005.

26 'President Pays Tribute at Pentagon Memorial', White House news release, 11 October 2001.

27 Pape, Robert A., 'Blowing Up an Assumption', *NYT*, 18 May 2005.

28 Mann, Michael, *Incoherent Empire* (New York, 2003), pp. 42–3.

29 Ibid., p. 109.

30 World Islamic Front for Jihad Against Jews and Crusaders, initial 'Fatwa' statement, originally published in *Al-Quds Al-Arabi* (London), 23 February 1998.

31 Shahak, Israel, 'Yitzhak Shamir, Then and Now', *Middle East Policy*, Vol. I, No. 1, 1992.

32 Mann, op. cit., p. 109; Shahak, op. cit.

33 'Address to a Joint Session of Congress and the American People', White House press release, 20 September 2001.

34 'President Bush Outlines Iraqi Threat', http://www.whitehouse.gov/news/releases/2002/10/20021007-8.html

35 Alleged Zarqawi audiotape released 28 May (translation: Middle East News Online).

36 Anonymous, *Imperial Hubris: Why the West is Losing the War on Terror* (Washington, DC, 2004), p. 198.

37 Interview, *This Week with George Stephanopoulos*, ABC, 1 May 2005.

38 http://www.fbi.gov/pressrel/penttbom/penttbomb.htm

39 Hanson, Victor Davis, 'The Whole World Is Watching', *National Review*, 10 September 2004.

40 Mann, op. cit., p. 164.

41 News bulletin, *Today*, BBC Radio 4, 8.30 a.m., 25 February 2005.

42 Cohen, Nick, 'Stop Castrating the Language', *Observer*, 17 July 2005.

43 Cook, Robin, *The Point of Departure* (2003; London, 2004), p. 330.

44 Langewiesche, William, 'Letter from Baghdad', *Atlantic*, Jan/Feb 2005.

45 Curtis, Mark, *Unpeople: Britain's Secret Human Rights Abuses* (London, 2004), p. 19.

46 Danner, Mark, 'Iraq: The Real Election', *New York Review of Books*, 28 April 2005.

47 Youseff, Nancy A., 'Iraqi Civilian Casualties Mounting', Knight Ridder Newspapers, 25 September 2004.

48 Condoleezza Rice, 'Remarks at the Commonwealth Club', Davies

Symphony Hall, San Francisco, State Department transcript, 27 May 2005.

49 Hitchens, Christopher, 'History and Mystery: Why does the New York Times insist on Calling Jihadists "Insurgents"?', http://www.slate.com, 16 May 2005.

50 'Briefing on Security Operations in Iraq', DoD news transcript, 21 June 2005.

51 Ignatius, David, 'What Bush Can Do to Salvage Iraq', *Washington Post*, 5 November 2004.

52 Lasseter, Tom, 'In the Face of Stubborn Insurgency, Troops Scale Back Anbar Patrols', Knight Ridder Newspapers, 20 July 2004.

53 'Secretary Rumsfeld's Speech at the National Press Club', US DoD news transcript, 10 September 2004, http://www.defenselink.mil/transcripts/2004/tr20040910-secdef1286.html

54 *BBC News*, 27 April 2005.

55 Bright, Martin, and Burke, Jason, 'Met Police Chief Demands Tighter Anti-Terror Laws', *Observer*, 17 April 2005.

56 Campbell, Duncan, *et al.*, 'Police Killer Gets 17 years for Poison Plot', *Guardian*, 14 April 2005.

57 Text of this and subsequent Acts mentioned is available in full at http://www.legislation.hmso.gov.uk/legislation/uk.htm

58 Straw, Jack, 'I'm Simply Protecting Democracy', *Guardian*, 14 December 1999.

59 Kennedy, Helena, *Just Law* (2004; London, 2005), p. 32.

60 H. CON. RES. 220, 6 May 1998.

61 H.R.3194, 'An Act Making Consolidated Appropriations for the Fiscal Year Ending September 30, 2000, and for Other Purposes', Public Law 106–113, 106th Congress, 29 November 1999: STAT. 1501A-470, 1501A-471 (pp. 112–13).

62 'Press Briefing by Ari Fleischer', White House press release, 6 December 2001.

63 'Fact Sheet: Operation Liberty Shield', White House news release, 17 March 2003.

64 'New Terrorist Screening Center Established', Office of Homeland Security news release, 16 September 2003.

65 Guidelines of the Committee of Ministers of the Council of Europe on human rights and the fight against terrorism, 11 July 2002, http://www.coe.int/T/E/Human_rights/guidelines.asp

66 Mayer, Jane, 'Outsourcing Torture', *New Yorker*, 14 and 21 February 2005.

67 Dodd, Vikram, and Cowan, Rosie, 'Police Chief Faces New Claims', *Guardian*, 19 August 2005.

68 'The Radio Factor with Bill O'Reilly', *Westwood One*, 1 March 2005.

69 *The O'Reilly Factor*, Fox News Channel, 2 June 2004.

70 McCain, Robert Stacy, 'Protecting Our Children', *Washington Times*, 11 April 2005.

71 *CNN Late Edition with Wolf Blitzer*, CNN, 9 March 2003.
72 Quoted in Rees, op. cit., p. 29.
73 Higgins, Charlotte, 'Art "terrorist" AK47 strikes again', *Guardian*, 16 June 2004.
74 Arbuthnot, op. cit., p. 18.
75 Brzezinski, Zbigniew, 'The Simple Power of Weakness', in Ahmed, Akbar, and Forst, Brian (eds.), *After Terror* (Cambridge, 2005), p. 17.
76 Interview with author, 18 April 2005.
77 *The 9/11 Commission Report: Final Report of the National Commission on Terrorist Attacks Upon the United States* (New York, 2004), p. 337.
78 'Harper's Index', *Harper's*, August 2004.
79 http://www.dhs.gov/dhspublic/display?theme=29
80 Hall, Mimi, 'Ridge Reveals Clashes on Alerts', *USA Today*, 10 May 2005.
81 *Preparing for Emergencies: What You Need to Know*, British Government leaflet, 2004.
82 'Statement by the President in His Address to the Nation', White House news release, 11 September 2001.
83 Dyer, Clare, 'Britain Accused of Creating Terror Fears', *Guardian*, 11 June 2005.
84 McGuire, Bill, *Surviving Armageddon* (Oxford, 2005), p. 53.
85 *The 9/11 Commission Report*, op. cit., p. 362.
86 Massing, Mark, 'Iraq, the Press and the Election', *New York Review of Books*, 16 December 2004, pp. 28–9.
87 'Transcript of Debate Between Bush and Kerry, With Domestic Policy the Topic', *NYT*, 13 October 2004.
88 *Newsnight*, BBC 2, 26 April 2005.
89 Interview with author, 16 May 2005.
90 'Rumsfeld Warns of "Marathon" Fight Against Terrorism', US Department of State, 20 September 2001, http://www.usinfo.org/wf-archive/2001/010920/epf404.htm
91 Blanton, Dana, 'FOX Poll: When Will War on Terrorism End? Not In My Lifetime', *Fox News*, 8 September 2005.
92 'Remarks at Westminster College Commencement Ceremony', US Department of State, 7 May 2005, http://www.state.gov/g/rls/rm/2005/45862.htm
93 Blick, Andrew, *How to Go to War* (London, 2005), p. 63.
94 *The Nation*, 7 February 1918, cited in *OED*, 'war', 2d.
95 Pound, Ezra, *The Cantos of Ezra Pound* (New York, 1972), Canto X (ll 1161–2).
96 Cited in Rees, op. cit., pp. 318–19.
97 Gaddis, John Lewis, 'Grand Strategy in the Second Term', *Foreign Affairs*, Vol. 84, No. 1, Jan/Feb 2005, p. 12.
98 Halliday, Fred, *100 Myths About the Middle East* (London, 2005), p. 246.

99 'President Unveils "Most Wanted" Terrorists', White House news release, 10 October 2001.

100 Steeves, Edna Leake (ed.), *The Art of Sinking in Poetry: Martinus Scriblerus' PERI BATHOUS* (New York, 1952), p. 59.

101 *Cape Times*, 22 October 1973, cited in *OED*, 'terrorism', 2.

102 Reboul, Olivier, *Langage et idéologie* (Paris, 1980), p. 67.

103 Rees, Phil, op. cit., p. 193.

104 'DoD Details Detainee Efforts to Senate Panel', US DoD news release, 15 June 2005.

105 Cited in Hersh, Seymour, *Chain of Command: The Road from 9/11 to Abu Ghraib* (London, 2004), p. 5.

Chapter 7: Abuse

1 Golden, Tim, 'Army Faltered in Investigating Detainee Abuse', *NYT*, 22 May 2005.

2 *OED*, 'abuse', 2.

3 'Defense Department Operational Update Briefing', 4 May 2004.

4 Bybee, Jay S., 'Memorandum for Alberto R. Gonzales', 1 August 2002, in Danner, Mark, *Torture and Truth* (London, 2004), p. 115.

5 Sands, Philippe, *Lawless World* (London, 2005), p. 212.

6 Yoo, John C., Letter to Alberto R. Gonzales, 1 August 2002, in Danner, op. cit., pp. 108–14.

7 Bybee, Jay S., 'Memorandum for Alberto R. Gonzales', 1 August 2002, in Danner, op. cit., p. 138.

8 'Memo: LTC Jerald Phifer to MG Michael Dunlavey', 11 October 2002, in Danner, op. cit., p. 167.

9 'Memo: William J. Haynes II to Donald Rumsfeld', 27 November 2002, in Danner, op. cit., p. 182.

10 Hochschild, Adam, 'What's in a Word? Torture', *NYT*, 23 May 2004.

11 Hettena, Seth, 'Iraqi Died While Hung From Wrists', AP, 17 February 2005.

12 Hu, Benjamin, 'Nightmares from the North', *Washington Times*, 30 April 2004.

13 'Email from REDACTED to M. C. Briese, Gary Bald, T. J. Harrington, Frankie Battle and other redacted parties Re Request for Guidance regarding OGC EC dated 5/19/04, signed [REDACTED], "On scene Commander—Baghdad",' released to American Civil Liberties Union on 15 December 2004.

14 Field Manual No. 34-52, 'Intelligence Interrogation', Headquarters, Department of Army, Washington, DC, 28 September 1992, 1–8.

15 'Memo: LTC Jerald Phifer to MG Michael Dunlavey', 11 October 2002, in Danner, op. cit., p. 168.

16 Cited in 'Guantánamo and Beyond: The Continuing Pursuit of Unchecked Executive Power', Amnesty International, 13 May 2005, pp. 111–13.

17 Risen, James, Johnston, David and Lewis, Neil A., 'Harsh C.I.A. Methods Cited in Top Qaeda Interrogations', *NYT*, 13 May 2004.

18 'Legal Brief: LTC Diane E. Beaver', 11 October 2002, in Danner, op. cit., pp. 176–7.

19 Neumeister, Larry, 'Army Destroyed Mock Execution Pictures', AP, 18 February 2005.

20 'Second Abu Ghraib Abuse Trial Opens', AP, 12 May 2005.

21 Bybee, Jay S., 'Memorandum for Alberto R. Gonzales', 1 August 2002, in Danner, op. cit., pp. 115–20.

22 'Break Them Down: Systematic Use of Psychological Torture by US Forces', Physicians for Human Rights, May 2005, p. 6.

23 Ibid., p. 52.

24 Cited by Durbin, Senator Richard J., Floor Statement on Guantánamo Bay, 14 June 2005.

25 'Email from REDACTED to M. C. Briese', op. cit.

26 FM 34-52, 1–7.

27 'Email from REDACTED to M. C. Briese', op. cit.

28 Editorial: 'Amnesty's "Gulag"', *Wall Street Journal*, 28 May 2005.

29 'Email from REDACTED to Gary Bald, Frankie Battle, Arthur Cummings, Fwd: Impersonating FBI at GMTO, dated December 5, 2003', released to ACLU.

30 'Bush Defends Detainees Policy', AP, 7 November 2005

31 'Iraq Abuse "Ordered From the Top"', *BBC News*, 15 June 2004.

32 Interview with Lt. Gen. James Conway, *Frontline*, http://www.pbs.org, 9 October 2003.

33 'Transcript: Bush Holds Post-G-8 Summit', *Washington Post*, 10 June 2004.

34 Gonzales, Alberto R., 'Memorandum for the President', 25 January 2002, in Danner, op. cit., p. 85.

35 Ashcroft, John, letter to President, 1 February 2002, in Danner, op. cit., p. 92.

36 542 U.S. 03-334 and 03-343 (2004).

37 'Military Order of November 13, 2001: Detention, Treatment, and Trials of Certain Non-Citizens in the War Against Terrorism', in Danner, op. cit., p. 79.

38 Bybee, Jay S., 'Memorandum for Alberto R. Gonzales', 1 August 2002, in Danner, op. cit., pp. 145–6.

39 Hibbits, Bernard, 'Law Deans Assail Torture Memos as Gonzales Hearing Concludes', http://www.jurist.law.pitt.edu, 6 January 2005.

40 Bush, George W., 'Memorandum: Humane Treatment of al Qaeda and Taliban Detainees', February 7, 2002, in Danner, op. cit., p. 106.

41 Bush, George W., Memorandum on 'Humane Treatment of al Qaeda and Taliban Detainees', 7 February 2002, in Danner, op. cit., pp. 105–6.

42 Bybee, Jay S., 'Memorandum for Alberto R. Gonzales', 1 August 2002, in Danner, op. cit., p. 163.

43 CNN, 11 December 2003.

44 Geneva Convention IV Art. 5.

45 'Bush Sets Case as "War President"', *BBC News*, 8 February 2004.

46 Hitchens, Christopher, 'Confessions of a Dangerous Mind', *Slate*, 13 June 2005.

47 'Article 15-6 Investigation of the 800th Military Police Brigade [The Taguba Report]', in Danner, op. cit., p. 284.

48 'Final Report of the Independent Panel to Review DoD Detention Operations [The Schlesinger Report]', in Danner, op. cit., p. 323.

49 Taguba Report, in Danner, op. cit., p. 280.

50 'Roundtable Interview of the President by Foreign Print Media', White House transcript, 5 May 2005.

51 'Secretary Rumsfeld Interview with David Kelso, KOKC-AM/KRXO-FM, Oklahoma City, Okla', DoD transcript, 21 June 2005.

52 White House Daily Briefing, 8 June 2005.

53 *Fox News Sunday*, Fox News Channel, 29 May 2005.

54 Syal, Rajeev, 'I Had a Good Time at Guantánamo, Says Inmate', *Sunday Telegraph*, 8 February 2004.

55 'Guantánamo and Beyond: The Continuing Pursuit of Unchecked Executive Power', Amnesty International, 13 May 2005, pp. 60–1.

56 Hitchens, op. cit.

57 Zagorin, Adam, and Duffy, Michael, 'Inside the Interrogation of Detainee 063', *Time*, 20 June 2005.

58 Luvaas, Jay, *Napoleon on the Art of War* (New York, 1999), p. 11.

59 FM 34-52, 1–7.

60 Applebaum, Anne, 'The Torture Myth', *Washington Post*, 12 January 2005.

61 'Email from REDACTED to Gary Bald, Frankie Battle, Arthur Cummings', op. cit.

62 'President Hosts United States-European Union Summit', White House news release, 20 June 2005.

63 'Bush: "The War On Terrorism Goes On"', AP, 7 July 2005.

64 Mayer, Jane, 'Outsourcing Torture', *New Yorker*, 14 and 21 February 2005.

65 'Meat Rendering Plants', at http://www.epa.gov/ttn/chief/ap42/ch09/final/c9s05-3.pdf

66 Jackson, Derrick Z., 'Rumsfeld's "Fungible" Facts', *Boston Globe*, 21 April 2004.

67 White, Josh, 'Army, CIA Agreed on "Ghost" Prisoners', *Washington Post*, 11 March 2005.

68 Hettena, op. cit.

69 Cited in 'In Re: Guantánamo Detainee Cases, Civil Action No. 02-299, etc.', Memorandum Opinion by Judge Joyce H. Green, United States District Court for the District of Columbia, 31 January 2005.

70 'In Re: Guantánamo Detainee Cases', op. cit.
71 Lewis, Neil A., 'Interrogators Cite Doctors' Aid at Guantánamo', *NYT*, 24 June 2005.
72 Bloche, M. Gregg, M.D., J.D., and Marks, Jonathan H., M.A., B.C.L., 'When Doctors Go to War', *New England Journal of Medicine*, Vol. 352: 3–6, 6 January 2005, No. 1.
73 Bloche and Marks, op. cit.
74 Mayer, Jane, 'The Experiment', *New Yorker*, 11 and 18 July 2005.
75 Carroll, Lewis, *Through the Looking Glass*, Chapter VI.
76 Danner, op. cit., p. 16.
77 Lewis, Neil A., 'Red Cross Finds Detainee Abuse at Guantánamo', *International Herald Tribune*, 1 Dec 2004.
78 'Cheney: Iraq Will Be "Enormous Success Story"', http://www.cnn.com, 24 June 2005.
79 Bush, George, *BBC News 24*, 7 July 2005.

Chapter 8: Freedom

1 'President Commemorates Memorial Day at Arlington National Cemetery', White House transcript, 30 May 2005.
2 Russell, Bertrand, 'Freedom in Society', in *Sceptical Essays* (1928; London, 2004), p. 144.
3 Goodwin, Barbara, *Using Political Ideas*, Second edition (London, 1987).
4 Locke, John, *Two Treatises of Government* (1689; London, 1764), Ch. 6 §57, p. 242.
5 Ignatieff, Michael, 'Lesser Evils', *NYT Magazine*, 2 May 2004.
6 Cited in *OED*, 'march', 2b and 2c.
7 'President Bush Sworn-In to Second Term', White House transcript, 20 January 2005.
8 Condoleezza Rice, 'Remarks at the Commonwealth Club', Davies Symphony Hall, San Francisco, State Department transcript, 27 May 2005.
9 'President Bush Speaks to United Nations', White House, 10 November 2001.
10 'President Addresses Nation, Discusses Iraq, War on Terror', White House transcript, 28 June 2005.
11 Woodward, Bob, *Plan of Attack* (London, 2004), p. 421.
12 State of the Union Address, 27 January 1987.
13 Clinton, William J., 'American Foreign Policy and the Democratic Ideal,' campaign speech, Pabst Theater, Milwaukee, WI, 1 October 1992; cited in Mearsheimer, John J., *The Tragedy of Great Power Politics* (New York, 2001).
14 Rice, op. cit.
15 Milmo, Cahal, 'The Proof: Marketplace Deaths Were Caused By a US Missile', *Independent*, 2 April 2003.

16 Condoleezza Rice interview, National Public Radio, State Department transcript, 26 May 2005.

17 Russell, Bertrand, ' The Need for Political Scepticism', in *Sceptical Essays* (1928; London, 2004), p. 115.

18 Naess, Arne, with Christophersen, Jens A., and Kvalø, Kjell, *Democracy, Ideology and Objectivity: Studies in the Semantics and Cognitive Analysis of Ideological Controversy* (Oslo, 1956), pp. 137–8.

19 Naess, *et al.*, op. cit., p. 137.

20 Kepel, Gilles, *The War for Muslim Minds: Islam and the West* (Cambridge, Mass., 2004), p. 293.

21 *BBC News*, 13 June 2005.

22 Lippmann, Walter, *Public Opinion* (London, 1922), p. 281.

23 Naess, op. cit., p. 131.

24 Hayek, F. A., *The Confusion of Language in Political Thought* (London, 1968), pp. 35–6.

25 Young, Michael, 'Down with Meritocracy', *Guardian*, 29 June 2001.

26 Interview with author, 18 April 2005.

27 Barber, Benjamin R., *Strong Democracy* (1984; California, 2004), *passim*.

28 Green, Philip, 'New Texts for Government', *The Nation*, 4 February 1978.

29 Amin, Samir, 'The American Ideology', *Al-Ahram Weekly*, 15 May 2003.

30 Naess, op. cit., p. 137.

31 'Bush: Iraq Elections Won't End U.S. Mission', CNN, 29 January 2005.

32 Hersh, Seymour, 'Get Out the Vote', *New Yorker*, 25 July 2005.

33 Ibid.

34 Quoted in Hider, James, and Beeston, Richard, 'Democracy, Bush's Biggest Export, Faces its First Reality Check in Iraq', *The Times*, 22 January 2005.

35 'Transcript of Bush Interview', http://www.washingtonpost.com, 16 January 2005.

36 'Negroponte, Casey Call Iraqi Vote "Heroic" and "Humbling"', US Department of State, 14 February 2005.

37 Cited in Meyer, Karl E., 'Forty Years in the Sand', *Harper's*, June 2005.

38 Page, Susan, 'Confronting Iraq', *USA Today*, 1 April 2003.

39 Morganstein, Jonathan, 'A Reality Check from Iraq', Center for American Progress, 13 July 2005.

40 Bowden, Mark, 'Wolfowitz: The Exit Interviews', *Atlantic*, July/August 2005.

41 Baker, Peter, 'History is Likely to Link Bush to Mideast Elections', *Washington Post*, 9 January 2005.

42 'Transcript: Bush and Putin's News Conference', *NYT* (http://www.nytimes.com), 24 February 2005.

43 Marshall, Tyler, 'Bush's Foreign Policy Shifting', *Los Angeles Times*, 5 June 2005.

44 Falk, Richard, 'Democracy Died at the Gulf', *Vietnam Generation Journal*, Vol. 3, No. 4, January 1992.

45 Condoleezza Rice, 'Remarks at the Commonwealth Club', op. cit.

46 US Department of State Daily Press Briefing, 22 April 2005.

47 Dickie, Mure, 'Don't Mention Democracy, Microsoft Tells China Web Users,' *Financial Times*, 11 June 2005.

48 Cited in Cook, Robin, *The Point of Departure* (2003; London, 2004), p. 55.

49 Mulkern, Anne C., 'When Advocates Become Regulators', *Denver Post*, 24 May 2004.

50 Skinner, Quentin, 'Some Problems in the Analysis of Political Thought and Action', in Tully, James (ed.), *Meaning and Context: Quentin Skinner and his Critics* (Cambridge, 1988), p. 113.

51 Skinner, Quentin, 'Language as Social Change', in Tully, op. cit., pp. 126–7.

52 Ibid., p. 127.

53 Ibid., p. 128.

54 *OED*, 'economy'.

55 Hayek, op. cit., p. 30.

56 *OED*, 'corporation'.

57 *OED*, 'executive'.

58 'Leaders at Conference Tackle Strategies Against Terrorism', DoD press release, 20 July 2005.

59 'President Bush Closes the White House Economic Conference', White House, 16 December 2004.

60 'PM's Speech in Reply to the Speech from the Throne (SFT)', 5 October 2004, Canadian Parliament transcript.

61 Sanger, David E., 'There's Democracy, and There's an Oil Pipeline', *NYT*, 29 May 2005.

62 'Full text: State of the Union Address', *BBC News*, 30 January 2002.

63 'President Bush Closes the White House Economic Conference', White House, 16 December 2004.

64 Stevenson, Richard W., *NYT*, 17 December 2004.

65 Beckett, Margaret, 'Towards Full Market Access', *Financial Times*, 10 July 1997, cited in Curtis, Mark, 'Britain and the G8', in Hubbard, Gill, and Miller, David (eds.), *Arguments Against G8* (London, 2005), p. 46.

66 Condoleezza Rice, 'Remarks at the Commonwealth Club', op. cit.

67 'Speech by Chancellor of the Exchequer Gordon Brown to the Federal Reserve Bank, New York', HM Treasury transcript, 16 November 2001, http://www.hm-treasury.gov.uk/newsroom_and_speeches/press/2001/press_126_01.cfm

68 See George, Susan, 'Trade', in Hubbard, Gill, and Miller, David (eds.), op. cit., pp. 112–13.

69 Hilary, John, 'Profiting from Poverty', War on Want/PCS report, June 2005.

70 Hilary, op. cit.

71 Mann, Michael, *Incoherent Empire* (New York, 2003), p. 70.

72 Sands, Philippe, *Lawless World* (London, 2005), p. 120.

73 Thornton, Philip, and Gumbel, Andrew, 'America Puts Iraq Up For Sale', *Independent*, 22 September 2003.

74 Walker, Andrew, 'Iraq Oil Assets "Up for Sale"', *BBC News*, 23 September 2003.

75 Barboza, David, ' Chinese Company Ends Unocal Bid, Citing Political Hurdles', *NYT*, 2 August 2005.

76 'U.S.-Iraq Economic Commission Seeks Iraq's Economic Revival', US Department of State, 11 July 2005.

77 UN Security Council Resolution 1483.

78 See Harriman, Ed, 'Where Has All the Money Gone?', *London Review of Books*, 7 July 2005.

79 Waxman, Rep. Henry A., Letter to Subcommittee Chairman Shays, 20 June 2005.

80 'Halliburton's Questioned and Unsupported Costs In Iraq Exceed $1.4 Billion', report of the House Committee on Government Reform, 27 June 2005.

81 Executive Order 13303, 22 May 2003.

82 'President Bush Discusses Early Transfer of Iraqi Sovereignty', White House, 28 June 2004.

83 Lukacs, John, *Democracy and Populism: Fear and Hatred* (London, 2005), pp. 217–18.

84 Paine, Thomas, *Rights of Man: Being An Answer to Mr. Burke's Attack on the French Revolution* (London, 1791).

85 Cook, Robin, 'Morally, This is Indefensible. Politically, it's Plain Stupid', *Guardian*, 4 March 2005, p. 28.

86 Schneider, Gregory L. (ed.), *Conservatism in America Since 1930* (New York, 2003).

87 Lukacs, John, op. cit., p. 218.

88 Chomsky, Noam, *Necessary Illusions* (London, 1989), p. 349.

89 Blair, Tony, 'Seven Pillars of a Decent Society', speech in Southampton, 16 April 1997.

90 Halliday, Fred, *100 Myths About the Middle East* (London, 2005), p. 58.

91 Heilbroner, Robert L., 'Military America', *New York Review of Books*, 23 July 1970.

92 Gumbel, Andrew, 'How the War Machine is Driving the US Economy', *Independent*, 6 January 2004.

93 'National Defense Budget Estimates for FY 2005', DoD, March 2004.

94 Pound, Ezra, *The Cantos of Ezra Pound* (New York, 1972), Canto LXXIV (ll 12688–90).

95 See Hambling, David, *Weapons Grade* (London, 2005).

96 Hamilton, Alexander, 'Concerning Dangers from War between States', Federalist Paper No. 6, in Hamilton, Alexander, Jay, John, and Madison, James, ed. Carey, George W., and McClellan, James, *The Federalist* (Indianapolis, 2001), p. 23.

Chapter 9: Extremism

1 Schmitt, Eric, and Shanker, Thom, 'U.S. Officials Retool Slogan for Terror War', *NYT*, 26 July 2005.
2 Proletary, No. 22, 24 October (11), 1905; Marxists Internet Archive.
3 *OED*, 'struggle', n. 3.
4 Schmitt and Shanker, op. cit.
5 *OED*, 'extreme'.
6 Lakoff, George, '"War on Terror", Rest in Peace', http://www.alternet.org, 1 August 2005.
7 'NRA Urges Voters to Protect Sportsmen's Rights', NRA, 29 March 2005.
8 Heehs, Peter, 'Terrorism in India During the Freedom Struggle', *Historian*, Spring 1993.
9 Ibid.
10 Johnson, Larry, 'He What on Terrorism?', TPM Café, 2 August 2005.
11 'President Discusses Second Term Accomplishments and Priorities', White House, 3 August 2005.
12 'Rumsfeld Says Free Nations Cannot Wait for Terrorist Attacks', US Department of State news release, 5 August 2005.
13 Student Movement Coordination Committee for Democracy in Iran, 'Public Letter for the Attention of G-8 Summit in Scotland', 30 June 2005.
14 Symonds, William C., 'Who's the Real Howard Dean?', *Business Week*, 11 August 2003.
15 'Powell to Quit Bush cabinet', *BBC News*, 15 November 2004.
16 'Loyal and Experienced: Cheney a Washington Insider With a Long Political Resume', *Democracy in America*, CNN Special, 2000.
17 'That Was Then: Edgar Griffin', *BBC News*, 29 August 2002.
18 Email to author, 27 April 2005.
19 Rutenberg, Jim, and Carter, Bill, 'A Nation Challenged: The Media; Network Coverage a Target Of Fire From Conservatives', *NYT*, 7 November 2001.
20 Roig-Franzia, Manuel, and Hsu, Spencer, 'Many Evacuated, but Thousands Still Waiting', *Washington Post*, 4 September 2005.
21 Kirkpatrick, David D., and Hulse, Carl, 'On Social Security, Lieberman the Centrist Ruffles Democratic Feathers on the Left', *NYT*, 7 March 2005.
22 Ibid.
23 Hakim, Danny, 'CALIFORNIA/MOTOR CITY; Pollution Fight Turns From Smog to Global Warming', *NYT*, 22 October 2003.
24 Froomkin, Dan, 'Rove Questions Liberals' Sympathies', *Washington Post*, 23 June 2005.
25 Henderson, Schuyler W., M.D., email to author.
26 E.g., Christopher Hitchens, interview on *The Daily Show with Jon Stewart*, Comedy Central, 26 August 2005.

27 Iraq Liberation Act of 1998, 112 Stat. 3178, Public Law 105-338, 31 October 1998.

28 Bowden, Mark, 'Wolfowitz: The Exit Interviews', *Atlantic*, July/August 2005.

29 *Newsnight*, BBC, 20 April 2005.

30 Woodward, Bob, *Plan of Attack* (London, 2004), p. 178.

31 'You Are Either With Us Or Against Us', CNN, 6 November 2001.

32 'Talking Points Memo: Are You An Extremist?', Fox News, 25 August 2005

Chapter 10: Epilogue

1 Steeves, Edna Leake (ed.), *The Art of Sinking in Poetry: Martinus Scriblerus' PERI BATHOUS* (New York, 1952), pp. 43–4.

2 Arbuthnot, John (attrib.), Proposals for Printing A very curious Discourse, in two Volumes in *Quarto*, intitled, PSEUDOLOGIA POLITIKE: or, a Treatise of the Art of Political Lying, with An Abstract of the First Volume of the said Treatise (Edinburgh, 1746), p. 17.

3 Graff, Christopher, 'Dean Says Democrats Must Take Offensive', AP, 9 August 2005.

4 Bugarski, Ranko, 'Discourse of War and Peace', *Folia Linguistica* XXXIV/3-4, 2000.

5 Interview with author, 3 March 2005.

6 'Notes and Quotes from the 2000 Campaign', AP, 29 September 2000.

7 *Outfoxed: Rupert Murdoch's War on Journalism* (dir. Robert Greenwald, 2004).

Index